MADNESS, ART, AND SOCIETY

How is madness experienced, treated, and represented? How might art think around – and beyond – psychiatric definitions of illness and well-being?

Madness, Art, and Society engages with artistic practices, from theatre and live art to graphic fiction, charting a multiplicity of ways of thinking critically *with*, rather than *about*, non-normative psychological experience. It is organised into two parts:

- 'Structures: Psychiatrists, Institutions, Treatments' illuminates the environments, figures, and primary models of psychiatric care, reconsidering their history and contemporary manifestations through case studies including David Edgar's *Mary Barnes* and Miloš Forman's *One Flew Over the Cuckoo's Nest*.
- 'Experiences: Realities, Bodies, Moods' problematises diagnostic categories and proposes more radically open models of thinking in relation to experiences of madness, touching upon works such as Richard Kelly's *Donnie Darko* and Duncan Macmillan's *People, Places, and Things*.

Reading its case studies as a counter-discourse to orthodox psychiatry, *Madness, Art, and Society* seeks a more nuanced understanding of the plurality of madness in society and, in so doing, offers an outstanding resource for students and scholars alike.

Anna Harpin is Associate Professor of Theatre and Performance at the University of Warwick, and Co-Artistic Director of the theatre company Idiot Child, with whom she works as a writer and director.

MADNESS, ART, AND SOCIETY

Beyond Illness

Anna Harpin

Routledge
Taylor & Francis Group

LONDON AND NEW YORK

First published 2018
by Routledge
2 Park Square, Milton Park, Abingdon, Oxon, OX14 4RN

and by Routledge
711 Third Avenue, New York, NY 10017

Routledge is an imprint of the Taylor & Francis Group, an informa business
© 2018 Anna Harpin

The right of Anna Harpin to be identified as author of this work has been asserted by her in accordance with sections 77 and 78 of the Copyright, Designs and Patents Act 1988.

British Library Cataloguing-in-Publication Data
A catalogue record for this book is available from the British Library

Library of Congress Cataloging-in-Publication Data
Names: Harpin, Anna, author.
Title: Madness, art, and society: beyond illness / Anna Harpin.
Description: Milton Park, Abingdon, Oxon; New York: Routledge, 2017.
Identifiers: LCCN 2017031431 | ISBN 9781138784277 (hardback) |
ISBN 9781138784284 (pbk.) | ISBN 9781315149257 (ebook)
Subjects: LCSH: Mental illness in literature. | Mental illness in motion
pictures. | Psychiatry in literature. | Psychiatry in motion pictures. |
Mental illness–Social aspects. | Psychiatry–Social aspects.
Classification: LCC PN56.M45 H37 2017 | DDC 809/.933561–dc23
LC record available at https://lccn.loc.gov/2017031431

ISBN: 9781138784277 (hbk)
ISBN: 9781138784284 (pbk)
ISBN: 9781315149257 (ebk)

Typeset in Bembo
by Deanta Global Publishing Services, Chennai, India

For Tom, who exists …

CONTENTS

FIGURES

ACKNOWLEDGEMENTS

This project has been brewing for a number of years and thus has had the enormous benefit of varied and rich support and input from a wide range of people, places, and things. I have had the opportunity to share early drafts and ideas in a variety of settings and thus would very much like to thank the following folks and forums: Lisette M. Lovett and the Association for Medical Humanities Annual Conference, hosted by the University of Keele; Zoë Mendelson and the Live Art Development Agency for their one-day interdisciplinary event, *Spectacular Medicine: Theatres of the Observed Mind*; Shane Boyle and Bridget Escolme at Queen Mary University of London for the opportunity to present work as part of their innovative MSc in Creative Arts and Mental Health; Amanda Stuart-Fisher and James Thompson and the *Performing Care* symposium held at the Royal Central School of Speech and Drama; Nadine Holdsworth and the University of Warwick Theatre Research Seminar; Broderick Chow, Bryce Lease, and Louise Owen for the chance to discuss ideas at the London Theatre Seminar; and Ana Antic, Joanna Bourke and Louise Hide for the *Cultures of Harm* conference at Birkbeck, University of London. An earlier draft of a section of Chapter 4 appears in Trish Reid's *The Theatre of Anthony Neilson* (London: Methuen, 2017), and thus I had the benefit of Trish's expertise in the development of this chapter.

In addition to these moments of sharing, the book has been hugely supported by institutions including the University of Warwick, the University of Exeter, the Victoria and Albert Museum, the BFI Archive, and the Oregon State Hospital Museum, and in particular Dennie Brooks. I am particularly grateful to the University of Warwick for a period of research leave in which to complete the manuscript. I would also like to thank the students at the University of Exeter and the University of Warwick whose imaginative, creative, and astute contributions to my modules 'Madness and Cultural Representation' and 'Mad, Bad, Sad' respectively significantly enriched and challenged my thinking.

The book has also benefitted from generous conversations with people including Rachel Clements, Simon Cross, Patrick Duggan, Juliet Foster, Hilary Marland, Aoife Monks, and Mischa Twitchin. Many others have given their time and support to the book in varied manners. I am immensely grateful to Peter Barham for his perceptive remarks about R. D. Laing and insightful commentary on the first draft of Chapter 1. Kate Dorney was an intrepid and generous reader of the full manuscript and offered acute and helpful comments. Thank you for letting me occupy too many train journeys and lending me your brain for a bit. James Leadbitter has been a key figure in the book project, and I have benefitted enormously from his ideas, generosity, and creative practice. His work has not only been inspiring, but he has offered his time and energy in immensely generous ways. His mind has enriched this book. I am also, of course, indebted and grateful to the team at Routledge: Talia Rodgers, Ben Piggott, and Kate Edwards who have commissioned and steered this project with generosity, skill, and grace. I would also like to thank the anonymous peer reviewers at both proposal and manuscript stage for their invaluable feedback, which has significantly improved the quality of the final book in plural manners. The remaining flaws, mistakes, and quirks remain entirely my own.

A number of personal relationships have helped this book appear. Amy Logan, Angela LeComber, and my therapist Peter have just been there when it mattered. My very dear friend, Bryce Lease, deserves special mention. His perceptive comments on early drafts of the work have sharpened my thinking, and his ever-insightful questions in conferences and symposiums have productively kept my brain always on the hop. Not only this, but he has offered love, encouragement, fitness workouts, and holiday escapes, as well as well-timed and *very firm* instructions to 'work!'. Jane Harpin must also be thanked for sharing my enthusiasm for Darian Leader and being apparently happy to get his books for every birthday and Christmas for a number of years now just so that we can discuss his ideas. Her professional expertise in mental health care has also made her an invaluable and sage sounding board for my thoughts. Moreover, as 'the mother' she has kept a more generally beady eye on me throughout. Thanks, Mam. Tim Harpin and Heather Flint have been unstinting supporters and provided much-needed cheerleading. And fizz. They know how immensely important they are and that nothing ever gets done without the team. I hope you're chuffed and not gutted. Lewis Harpin: thanks for putting up with me and occasionally sitting through 'weird' plays and pretending to be interested. My final and most fulsome thanks go to Tom Cornford. Thank you for reading every single word and making them better words; for fennel, ferns, and the whole night sky; for making this book and life heaps better. If there was ever one … it's you. Thank you.

INTRODUCTION

Beyond Illness

It is April 2007, and I have told my brother to go and see a new play called The Wonderful World of Dissocia. *It's brilliant, I tell him. He rings me after the show to say that he loved it too. But he also says it will change how he treats the patients on his ward. He says he will remember to be more gentle, less functional – that it's easy to forget to be gentle some days. He says he will remember that he is at work but they are, amongst other things, in pain. I am doing my PhD, and this moment is encouraging for what it says about art and humans.*

It is August 2014, and I have just seen a play at the Edinburgh Fringe Festival called The Eradication of Schizophrenia in Western Lapland, *by Ridiculusmus. I do some background research about the play's content and I start telling a psychiatrist I know about the development of Open Dialogue therapy in Western Lapland and the startling improvement in both rates of diagnosis and in outcomes for those living under the description of schizophrenia. I am relating how the Finnish model has apparently contradicted the received wisdom that long-term use of neuroleptics for treating schizophrenia is indispensable: 'If it really worked, we'd have heard of it', she replied. I discuss the power of the pharmaceutical companies to author and disseminate research that will be profitable and bury that which won't: 'If it really worked, we'd have heard about it.' I stare at the wall and instead we talk about what to have for our tea.*

It is November 2015 and I am suicidal. I ring someone close to me who is a psychiatric nurse to ask for advice: 'Ring the GP now. That's your depressed brain talking. You just need some drugs.' I resisted: 'OK, fine, well just put it in one of your plays then.' I rang the GP and got a prescription in a consultation that lasted less than five minutes. This was the fourth time I had been prescribed psychiatric medication in the past four years. This time, as with all the others, I do not take the drugs. I do not kill myself. I do make a piece of art. I continue to experience things that are, at times, paralysing — hallucinations, nightmares, panic attacks, obsessive thoughts, despair. I start seeing a therapist. And I talk. And I am listened to. And it is a bit easier some of the time.

These vignettes point to several concerns that inform *Beyond Illness*. Namely, they are the overuse of psychiatric medication; the uncritical acceptance of a biomedical model of mental illness; the emphasis on surface symptoms as opposed to depth of experience; the erasure of agency in medical care; the systematic and systemic manipulation of evidence by pharmaceutical companies; the tenacity of a drug-focussed disease model as *the* response to distress; and the failure of listening and dialogue in certain current care practices. This book, then, departs from a keen sense that our current understandings of, and responses to, madness are not only flawed but are, paradoxically, making us sicker. I propose that artistic practice has a vital intervention to make in this field and this is the case that this volume sets out to make. I want to make plain before we begin that the spirit of the book is not to establish an antagonism between psychiatry and art. I recognise and appreciate the tireless, and often humanistic, work being done across the psy-disciplines. In this sense, my primary critique is of the broad structures of thinking and practice that shape and govern orthodox psychiatry, as opposed to the individuals working hard to support those in distress. Moreover, I am alive to the value many find in drugs and other practices that I critique in the course of these pages. The book is offered, then, as a bold contribution to a dialogue between art and psychiatric care. My aim is to provide ground for collaboration rather than division in the reimaging of madness and its treatment. *Beyond Illness* argues that there is an urgent need to reassess how we articulate, conceive of, and treat madness. Art also offers a set of practices that, I propose, may have clinical value in the care of those in need of help. Furthermore, artistic practices offer a means of resisting what I argue are toxic elements in the current cultures of psychiatry and pharmacology. I will argue that art allows us to apprehend the dimensional, relational, embodied nature of madness in important ways. I will also argue that art illuminates the generative capacity of madness and helps us to understand its manifestations as acts of political expression. In short, the book proposes that there is profound value, meaning, and insight in madness that can teach us how to live better with ourselves, and each other, if only we would take the time to properly listen and to care.

Madness, as opposed to mental illness, is the operative language of this book. While accepting its limitations as a necessarily homogenising term and recognising its pejorative connotations for some, I embrace it readily for many reasons. Firstly, the term mental illness is burdened with a number of problematic assumptions. The term presumes a neat bifurcation between health and illness, which is at best misleading and at worst detrimental to so-called health. The term also implies a stable and agreed-upon understanding of the nature and course of such mental illnesses. However, as countless critics and meta-analyses of psychiatric literature and research conclude, no such stability and consensus exists. James Davies neatly surmises: 'there are still no discovered bio-markers for nearly all mental disorders.'[1] Joanna Moncrieff likewise reminds us: 'there is *no established* specific physical basis to psychiatric disorders.'[2] Furthermore, 'illness' affords no positive or generative capacity to the experiences categorised under its umbrella. While a great deal of such mental experiences are marked by profound suffering, in fact, exquisite and joyful experiences likewise labour under the rubric 'mental illness'. Madness, to my mind, is a more accommodating language in this regard (in part owing to its literary and historical associations, including insight, inspiration, and creativity): it is hospitable to the generative and hopeful aspects of this diverse range of felt and cognitive experiences. Secondly, madness wears its contentious uncertainty on its sleeve. Indeed, it invites dialogue by virtue of its troubled status as an unacceptable term. In jutting out awkwardly from the hegemonic contemporary discourse of 'well-being', the word reminds its audience that this debate is, in fact, far from complete. Moreover, in signalling its own uncertainty, 'madness' foregrounds the subjective and interpretive qualities of this field. This is radically important as a counter to the categorical imperative at the core of key psychiatric tools, such as the *International Classification of Diseases* (ICD) and the *Diagnostic and Statistical Manual of Mental Disorders* (DSM). Madness, unlike mental illness, resists the chimera of scientific objectivity beneath which psychiatry (in the guise of the *DSM*) masquerades. Finally, I employ madness as a means to emblazon the politics of this subject matter on these pages. I here position myself alongside the growing field of mad studies that seeks to forge new modes of understanding that cannot be articulated within existing, official structures of thought and feeling about mental illness. Madness is offered, thus, as a language that sets itself deliberately against illness, deficit, and the neoliberal agenda of mental hygiene and well-being. In its place I argue for a radically open, relational, experience-led model that disturbs old certainties and makes room for the positive, generative, and political capacities of those people and phenomena we call 'ill'.

Art is the optic through which this subject is apprehended. Moreover, I have selected a range of artistic practices including theatre, cinema, live art, graphic fiction and more to house this book's discussions. The diversity of examples is not at the expense of attention to form but instead permits a different kind of debate from single-form studies. Here distinct creative practices collide in the pursuit of common concerns. While far from exhaustive, the aim of this methodological decision is that the breadth witnessed allows us to glance towards the sheer wealth of material in this field and, moreover, sharpens our attention to the precise nature of how different forms seek to intervene in this particular subject matter. I here dispense with any special claims that one form may stake for being exemplary or articulating madness 'correctly'. This helps to un-anchor distracting questions about the 'authenticity' or 'truth' of any particular representation from this discussion. In this regard, the book is not concerned with defining what madness *really is* via art. Instead, I am preoccupied with how madness is made (conceptually), experienced (individually, collectively), and treated (in both clinical and non-clinical contexts). Art offers fruitful occasions for such an endeavour. The book, in this sense, will chart how art thinks in contradistinction to how psychiatry thinks. Rather than pursuing a binary opposition between art and psychiatry or claiming that art *knows better*, I am concerned with what is all too often left out of social, political, and medical debates about madness, care, and psychiatry. Key figures such as Darian Leader take care to emphasise the place of art in critical thinking around mental distress and its care. Leader recalls: 'It [...] occurred to me that perhaps the scientific literature on mourning that I had been searching for was simply *all literature*.'[3] However, creative practices are all too often marginalised as the soft distraction from hard science, overlooked as of anecdotal interest but of no real clinical value, or simply jettisoned entirely from the debating chamber. Indeed, even progressive voices in the field such as Nikolas Rose do not accord the arts a speaking role in the fray. For example, in *Inventing Ourselves: Psychology, Power, and Personhood*, he charts the range of figures who help fashion personhood: from lawyers, economists, accountants, sociologists, anthropologists, to political scientists and so on.[4] The artist simply does not figure. This book seeks to establish art and artists' place at the feast and make plain their contribution to clinical and non-clinical care.

Art thinks in interesting ways. Moreover, it thinks in particularly interesting ways for considering alternatives to current modes of care practice and cultural thinking in relation to madness and psychiatry. While I do not wish to collapse psychiatry and the *DSM* into the same, the *DSM* does offer one key example of the guiding structures of thought that govern psychiatric practices. In the global north, the *DSM* and *ICD* are the primary diagnostic tools, and they are increasingly in accord with one another: 'ICD and DSM categories have increasingly converged, and by all accounts the next edition of ICD, the eleventh, will see an even closer rapprochement between the two systems.'[5] The *DSM* is corpulent, now listing over 300 specific disorders and running to nearly 1,000 pages. However, Christopher Bollas has remarked that in fact: 'This [the volume of "illnesses"] says more about America's phobia regarding anyone outside the boundaries of what is considered normal than it does about what is actually wrong with people and why.'[6] The *DSM* is subjective despite its adoption of a categorical, disease-model of thinking. As Mick Power summarises: 'the approach taken with DSM is atheoretical and relies instead on expert consensus.'[7] Davies concurs: 'In the absence of any guiding neurobiological research, and in the face of mostly contradictory and incomplete clinical data, diagnostic committees largely relied on subjective processes of committee consensus, often attained by way of a vote.'[8] However, as Andrew Scull notes the ambition for the latest *DSM* (V) was to try to move towards a more dimensional mode of thinking. This ambition failed: 'Having thrashed about in pursuit of this chimera [moving away from a symptom-based model], those running the project were ultimately forced to concede defeat, and by 2009 they were back to tinkering with the descriptive approach.'[9] The *DSM*, then, pursues objectivity via processes that are subjective. Moreover, its members are far from diverse in terms of race, nationality, profession, class, gender and so on (less than a fifth of the Task Force were women, for example). And, given the influence of pharmaceutical companies on psychiatry in general and *DSM* specifically, it is increasingly difficult to see how its processes and personnel can be immune to corruption. As Davies reports, over two-thirds of the *DSM* Task Force had previously 'received honoraria, consultancy fees or funding from pharmaceutical companies, including the Chair of the *DSM-5* Task Force, David Kupfer, and the Vice Chair, Darrel Regier.'[10] It is clear then that it is a flawed model. To summarise: one of the dominant structures of thinking in contemporary psychiatry as made manifest in *DSM* is categorical, fixed, and authored by a homogenous, privileged group. In highly problematic ways, then, its systemic and notational performance of objectivity serves to obscure the implicit and explicit influences on these 'objective', 'stable' criteria, criteria that profoundly impact the life-paths of millions of people.

Art is an altogether more vague and diverse set of practices. Where the *DSM* is (or seeks to be) categorical, objective, static, certain, neutral, and concerned with surface behaviours, art is dimensional, relational, dynamic, uncertain, affective, and occupied with depth of experience. I propose six general artistic qualities that have both clinical implications and also wider ramifications for cultural attitudes towards madness and care. Firstly, art is, I argue, necessarily a dimensional practice. Both in the internal landscapes of form and content and in the broader ecology of art as a discipline of making, it is situated within the contested, dimensional realms of history, relationships, subjectivity, intertextuality, frames of reference and so forth. In these ways, it invites a dialogue that is not closed but rather wilfully attends to depths and breadths of experience. This is important insofar as it exposes the mismatch between criterion-thinking and the felt dimensionality of human experience. Secondly, art is by its nature relational. Of course, psychiatric practice is too, insofar as it involves inter-subjective encounters. However, a fixed system of categorisation and evaluation inevitably conditions the terms of exchange along already pre-established terms. Art, I propose, is engaged with a more radical sense of relationality that is alive to the precariousness and transience of such inter-subjective encounters. This is not to disavow the power structures, codes and languages that are also at play in art as an institution; rather it is to value its general willingness and capacity to confront the politics of relationality. It is also to acknowledge the extent to which art is always already concerned with the structures of relationality, of how one is positioned in relation to the art object. It is, in this sense, keenly alive to the nature of the aesthetic and political invitation it makes. There is opportunity for critical dialogue here between art and psychiatry in thinking through the implications of diverse, and supposedly 'minor', concerns – from the location of the nurses' station in the design of a ward, to the positioning of chairs in a therapeutic encounter, to the choice of posters on noticeboards in waiting rooms to the language of assessments, and so on. In this sense, one can consider the dramaturgy of the clinic and the clinical encounter. Art offers valuable ways into reconsidering the performative, aesthetic, and political implications of how therapeutic encounters and experiences are structured. Thirdly, it is engaged with ideas of change. If perception is a dynamic experience, then art has a particular capacity to remind us of the possibility of change through the embedded promise of futurity and alterity. This runs counter to the fixity of diagnostic, identity-based thinking. Indeed, if perception is dynamic, then a vital possibility of hope enters the frame. The opportunity here for care practices is to move away from a model that implies this is what you *are* and towards a model that explores what you are currently *experiencing*. Moreover, this dynamic quality encourages a thinking *with* as opposed to *about* by reminding us of meaning-making as an active process. In this way, one puts aside myths of cure and instead enables a dialogue with an individual about how to live with and through their felt and experienced coordinates. Fourthly, art is incomplete. As Fred D'Aguiar has reminded us, there can be no such thing as the last essay about slavery, rather each generation must have the story nuanced their way.[11] Likewise, art is unfinished business. In holding a space for ambiguity, uncertainty, and flux, artistic practices are productively at ease with ontological and epistemic uncertainty. Moreover, art criticism is similarly engaged with the partiality and temporality of its knowledge. There is value in psychiatry becoming an altogether more uncertain practice owing to the power and agency that this would confer to its subjects. A hospitable embrace of uncertainty makes room for patients as active, expert makers of meaning and understanding of their own experiences and care needs. Fifthly, art is a feeling encounter and thus perpetually creates new languages for expressing that which resists or defies ready articulation. As Darian Leader has suggested:

> If melancholia means that the passage from things to words is blocked, would the aim be to reverse this? Or, taking the idea of impossibility seriously, to try less to access so-called thing representations than to allow the person to find words to index the impossibility ... to find words to say how words fail. And isn't that one of the functions of poetry?[12]

Art is, then, a communicative act that is less concerned with making experience and articulation synonymous, and more concerned with unfolding feeling gestures of living. Art offers proximate encounters with experiences without recourse to the false promise of totalised understanding. In making languages anew with audiences, readers, and viewers, art thus reminds us how to listen and underscores the urgency to listen attentively with each new encounter. The clinical implication here is to consider the question as to the particular manners in which you are being invited to listen by someone, in any given moment: to consider closely what the particular conditions are for this moment of listening. And further, to listen consciously to the language proffered, rather than simply translating it back into the words you expect to find and think you already understand. Finally, and perhaps most simply, art (amongst other things) chronicles human experience. Moreover, it invites you to inhabit an Other's coordinates temporarily. The simple lesson here is to reconsider the role and value of representation and narrative in acts of care. A patient is a person and thus exists within histories (personal, social, cultural, medical and so forth). Narrative forms a vital sense-making practice in this regard. To abolish a symptom thus may be to abolish a narrative of self or world that was important, even life-saving. It is vital then to understand the place of narrative when working with people in order to better establish how to live as they see best and what makes life worthwhile (and by contrast, unbearable). Art, I propose through my chosen examples, offers rich ways of thinking that may be hard to implement. This does not diminish the urgency of the endeavour.

We, in the global north, are living in pharmacological times. James Davies describes this epidemic:

> in 2015 there were over 61 million prescriptions of antidepressants dispensed in England alone, constituting a 170% increase since 2000, while even larger increases have occurred in the United States, with now over 314 million anti-depressant prescriptions being dispensed last year [2016] ... approximately 15% of the British and 20% of the US adult population is psychiatrically medicated at any given time.[13]

A disease-centred model of psychiatry argues that such drugs act in specific ways on neurobiological illnesses that these drugs help to 'correct'. Indeed, their very labelling promises just such a thing: *anti*-depressants, *anti*-psychotics. Theorems, such as the chemical imbalance in the brain notion, suggest, as Moncrieff argues, 'that psychiatric disorders or their symptoms are caused by abnormalities in the chemicals in the brains that are involved in the transmission of nerve signals, known as neurotransmitters [dopamine, serotonin, adrenalin etc.].'[14] A 2007 Healthcare Commission Survey of psychiatric hospitals 'found that 98–100% of inpatients were prescribed drugs and that most take several different ones at the same time ... Outside hospitals over 90% of patients in contact with psychiatric services are prescribed medication.'[15] The near-universal use of pharmacological treatments implies not only a psychiatric but a socio-cultural consensus regarding the efficacy of such interventions. However, as David Healy and others have consistently reported, such accord in the house of psychiatry is, in fact, resting on sand. Darian Leader and David Corfield illuminate:

> They [the pharmaceutical companies] now fund about two thirds of clinical studies, and medical journals have increasingly become marketing devices for new products and diagnoses ... After thirteen years editing the *British Medical Journal*, Richard Smith concluded that the studies funded by industry are subtly manipulated to give positive results. The same research will be published again and again in different journals, with minor variations, to give the impression of a unanimous acceptance and weight of evidence. Studies funded by industry, he observed, are four times more likely to have positive results than those funded by other sources.[16]

This is all the more problematic given that 'positive' does not even ensure efficacy. As Healy has demonstrated:

> "two positive studies" doesn't mean the drug works for depression in two studies. It means there are two studies in which the drug can be shown to have an effect in depression – can be shown to do *something* ... In other words, these trials do not offer evidence the drug works in the sense that most people mean by the word "works" – that is, it clears the problem up.[17]

This is not to say drugs do not *work* for many people. Indeed, there is much evidence that argues for the valuable placebo effect in anti-depressants or that suggests, for example, that short-term use of neuroleptics can assist in managing psychosis. However, I wish to reiterate Moncrieff and others' call to re-view psychotropic medication more honestly as mind-altering as opposed to mind-fixing. The primary reason for this shift is that it fundamentally changes the prescribing conversation and simultaneously invites a profound reconsideration of how we understand the nature, course, and value of madness:

> Unless someone's behaviour is seriously antisocial or criminal, they should be allowed to decide for themselves whether the effects of the drugs or the mental disorder are more intolerable. By promulgating the disease-centred model of drug action, the idea that drugs are correcting a biological defect, we deny patients this possibility.[18]

In changing the conversation around drugs in this way, we move beyond a sense of madness as something to be fixed, banished, or corrected and instead create space for a more complex dialogue about how and why people get 'ill'.[19]

Pharmaceutical companies are, of course, not the whole story. They simply use their capital to amplify their voices in global debates about the treatment of madness, resulting in exponentially increasing sales of their products:

> Abilify (an anti-psychotic manufactured by Bristol-Myers Squibb) is selling at a rate of $6 billion per year. Cymbalta (an anti-depressant and anti-anxiety pill for Eli-Lilly) has projected worldwide sales of $5.2 billion. Zoloft, Effexor, Seroquel, Zyprexa and Risperdal, all drugs used to treat depression or schizophrenia, had sales between $2.3 billion and $3.1 billion in 2005 … In 2010 global sales of antipsychotic drugs totalled $22 billion; anti-depressants, $20 billion; anti-anxiety drugs, $11 billion.[20]

However, as William Davies has detailed, there is also an interlocking set of 'wellness' industries that sell us snake oil happiness: 'In the early twenty-first century, there is a growing body of experts in "resilience" training, mindfulness and cognitive behavioural therapy.'[21] Davies argues that such industries focus on individuals managing their difficult experiences as opposed to encouraging any examination of systemic or social inequity or conflict. This illness model of individual responsibility represents a further facet of the move under neoliberal governmentality of, in Wendy Brown's words, 'rendering human beings as human capital.'[22] It creates comfortable conditions for governments and businesses insofar as it means that, as Peter Kinderman has argued, 'we don't have to harbour uncomfortable thoughts about the human cost of war, domestic abuse, rape, the sexual abuse of children, unemployment, poverty, loneliness, and failure.'[23] It would be invidious to suggest that there is no biological component to madness, or that society simply makes us ill, or to advance an argument for a social constructivist model of understanding.

I am not a relativist nor would I claim there is no such thing as madness or that we ought to just all be 'positive' about mental diversity. Instead, I am arguing that the current way that we conceive of and treat madness is not working in any meaningful sense. Indeed, neither the drugs nor the well-being industries are making us 'better' as the exponential growth in prescriptions, heavy use of Community Treatment Orders (CTO), increasing rates of diagnosis, rising numbers of disability claims, increased rates of morbidity, and the common occurrence of drug non-compliance collectively reveal. I would argue that the answer to the question of who actually benefits from our current diagnostic and treatment practices is all too rarely the patient. Indeed, it seems increasingly plain that a neoliberal model of mental health care serves to proliferate the very distress it purports to treat. Moreover, it does so in manners that render the patient not the treatment the source of failure. As Healy notes: 'Psychoanalysts blamed their patients' underlying neurosis for their failure to get better. Psychiatrists blamed patients' underlying schizophrenia for anti-psychotic tardive-dyskinesia. Everyone blames the patients' personality or her illness, rather than the agent she was being treated with.'[24] This book seeks alternatives to a hyper-individualised disease model of mental illness. In so doing, it seeks to help forge a set of understandings and practices that are altogether more tender.

One recurrent complaint from psychiatric patients is not feeling listened to or having any agency in either the authorship of their experiences or in their treatment options. As Christina Katsakou *et al.* recently reported following research into patients' views on hospitalisation: 'Various experiences, including not receiving sufficient information, not being involved in treatment decisions, perceiving professionals as having power over patients, and experiencing coercive measures contributed to the patients feeling out of control during their hospitalisation.'[25] Moreover, as Bollas argues, hospitalisation for certain patients can actually serve to replicate the disembodied and alienating experiences of psychosis: 'The tragic irony of this approach [drugs and detention] is that the patient is then met with a process parallel to schizophrenia itself: radical incarceration, mind-altering actions, dehumanization, isolation.'[26] Some researchers have argued for the efficacy of Community Treatment Officers (CTOs) as more humane than hospitalisation.[27] Yet, as Delphine Coyle *et al.* have discovered:

> The evidence of benefits from CTOs is at best limited: two randomised controlled trials (RCTs) of CTOs in the USA showed no overall difference between those on a CTO and those not in terms of readmission and clinical and social outcomes.[28]

This inconclusive support for their efficacy has to be considered alongside the hidden violence of CTOs under whose terms one is always vulnerable to compulsory readmission. Thus, via surveillance, one is never really *out* of hospital. It is here that I propose art has a contribution to make to the conversation through its attentiveness to questions of empathy, agency, narrative, power, and so forth. Art does not have 'the solution' with respect to institutional issues in psychiatry. It does not *know* whether inpatient or outpatient experiences are, on balance, *better*. Rather, I argue that artistic practice is well placed to rethink the nature of the offer of psychiatry along more intimate and tender lines. If psychiatry can be experienced as brutal or brutalising for a sizeable group, then artistic practice may yield valuable insights for both care and personhood.

In its most basic form, this book is an argument for tenderness. It is an argument to be tender and to tend to one another in more radically open and uncertain manners. To tend, as a verb, first emerges in the fourteenth century and means 'to turn one's ear, give auditory attention, listen, hearken.'[29] Later developments of the term include the adjective tender, meaning 'soft, delicate, easily broken, divided, compressed, or injured'; to grow tender, meaning to become soft or be moved with pity or compassion; to tender, meaning to offer for acceptance (often goods, service, or a plea); or, as a noun, a tender is one who tends or waits upon another. Etymologically, one can trace connections to both the French, 'tendre' – to hold out, offer, and to the Latin 'tendere' – to stretch, hold forth. This striking configuration of resonances is apposite for the subject of madness and the arguments advanced in this book. The temporal dynamic of waiting invests tenderness with a quality of patience. The recurrent understanding of tenderness as involving an offer, a stretch, a holding-forth reminds us that tenderness is an intersubjective dialogue. Moreover, it is not a certain gesture. To be tender or to tender is to make an offer without assurance of its reception. Moreover, it dispenses with the associations of transaction that sometimes haunt 'care-giving' in contemporary discourse and practice. Tenderness, in this sense, cannot simply be *done to you*, rather it must happen *with* your consent. In this sense tenderness is vulnerable. It risks rejection. Thus, tenderness, as word, feeling, and action, does not swagger with certainty. It does not know it is right in the moment it makes its offer. Indeed, the tentativeness written into its conceptual shape renders tenderness a gesture of not quite knowing, not yet knowing. In this sense, it is perhaps distinct from the more bogus promises of empathy that lay claim to *knowing* and identification. To be tender with you is to admit the thresholds of our difference and to persist in the offer none the same. Tenderness is, therefore, a relation. It calls for an interlocutor. Moreover, it runs counter to resilience. It privileges the human condition of being 'easily broken or divided' over the false universal of invulnerability. Indeed, tenderness is ordinary, insofar as it can also connote day-to-day pain that is to be borne, carried, or held. Furthermore, tenderness emphasises sensation and tactility. It is, in this sense, an embodied phenomenon. I argue, then, that all of the examples studied in this book evidence the dire need for tenderness in how we think of and respond to madness. Furthermore, the means of achieving such tenderness is found in their varied practices that cumulatively make plain the urgency of fleshy listening: of listening that extends beyond the ears and is dispersed throughout the body in acts of radically generous relational exchange. In this spirit, I do not deploy tenderness as an overarching theory *done to* the book's contents, a theory that will unlock the book's secrets or stitch up its gaps. Instead, I offer tenderness as a conceptual gesture towards my subject. I hope that such a stretching forth may enable you generously to hold the different stories I am calling upon you to hear.

Wendy Brown critiques political categories of identity that are founded on states of injury, woundedness, or vulnerability. Building upon Nietzsche's idea of 'ressentiment' – 'the moralising revenge of the powerless, the triumph of the weak as weak' – she exposes how far any challenge to power from a position of injury ultimately 'reiterates impotence … reinscribes incapacity and powerlessness.'[30] Brown interrogates such 'reactive' identities arguing that they necessarily remain tethered to the violent history that produced them:

> In its emergence as a protest against marginalization or subordination, politicised identity thus becomes attached to its own exclusion both because it is premised on this exclusion for its very existence as identity and because the formation of identity at the site of exclusion, as exclusion augments or "alters the direction of the suffering" entailed in subordination or marginalization by finding a site of blame for it.[31]

In troubling pain as a foundational political claim, Brown argues for a movement away from identity (I am) and towards desire (I want). She claims that such a shift enacts a dynamic departure from an identity fixed and grounded in a wounded past and propels us politically towards a more open, alternative political future. In arguing for the value of tenderness I am not arguing for 'mad' as a fixed political category of *woundedness*. Indeed, I advocate a shift from the fixity of identity to a fluidity experience as a model of thinking, and from deficit to capacity as a way of understanding the politics of such experiences: from 'I *am* schizophrenic' to 'I hear voices'; from 'I *am* bipolar' to 'I sometimes experience joyful cosmic connections that other people do not'. Echoing Brown, then, I am less concerned with what madness *is* than with what it *wants* and what it *needs*. In listening tenderly, I argue that one returns vital dynamics of futurity, agency, and power to those of us called mad. Furthermore, I share Ann Cvetkovich's understanding that attending to the politically generative capacities of experiences such as depression is not to engage in panglossian thinking. She writes that depression is not 'thereby converted into a positive experience; it retains its associations with inertia and despair, but these feelings, moods, and sensibilities become sites of publicity and community formation.'[32] She suggests that we ought to understand depression as hidden knowledge that is making a bid for communication.[33] In this sense, she shares my argument that many experiences that might be termed 'mad' might also usefully be understood as protest against, or resistance to, the norms, values, and roles we are expected to adhere to and adopt. In understanding madness as acts of personal and political communication, then, we may make room to hear what it actually wants and needs, and thereby hold its presence more tenderly.

It follows from this decision to move from a fixed model of identity to a fluid notion of experience, that I structure this book in two parts. The first, 'Psychiatrists, Institutions, Treatments', is perhaps more familiar terrain in the field. It analyses examples from theatre, film, and photography in order to illuminate the rich critiques of orthodox models of psychiatric care that are at stake in these diverse works. Chapter 1 examines the figure of the psychiatrist in general and R. D. Laing in particular in order to re-evaluate his profound contribution to the politics of psychiatric care. In particular, I examine Ken Loach's *Family Life*, David Edgar's *Mary Barnes*, and Luke Fowler's *All Divided Selves*. Chapter 2 explores three primary sites of madness – the asylum, the hospital, the community – in order to engage with the felt experiences of environments of care. In this regard, I analyse Frederick Wiseman's *Titicut Follies*, Joe Penhall's *Blue/Orange*, and the live art practices of the vacuum cleaner. Chapter 3 interrogates the history of psychiatric treatments and their contemporary manifestations as a way to understand the thinking that undergirded such practices, but also their lived experience by patients. The three case studies in this chapter are Miloš Forman's *One Flew Over the Cuckoo's Nest,* Terry Johnson's *Hysteria*, and Brian Yorkey and Tom Kitt's *next to normal*. These more familiar 'mad' materials create the conditions for understanding the bolder interventions of Part 2.

The second part, 'Realities, Bodies, Moods', decisively rejects a diagnostic structure. In lingering with how theatre-makers, filmmakers, and graphic novelists have attempted to capture and communicate non-normative psychological experiences, I aim to illuminate both the value of such experiences but also to underscore their commonality. I argue that these artists and examples make plain some creative and humane alternatives to conceiving of, and responding to, our diverse encounters with self, world, and feeling. Chapter 4 considers experiences of unusual perceptual phenomena and considers how reality is made, fathomed, and managed. The case studies here are Richard Kelly's *Donnie Darko*, Anthony Neilson's *Realism*, and debbie tucker green's *nut*. Chapter 5 is concerned to explore women's experiences of their own pathologised bodies, particularly with respect to issues of class, race, and addiction. My examples are Mike Leigh's *Life Is Sweet*, Lee Daniels' *Precious*, and Duncan Macmillan's *People, Places, and Things*. The final chapter lingers with experiences of profound feeling-states and considers how moods think and communicate. The case studies that comprise this chapter are Marsha Norman's *'night, Mother*, Ellen Forney's *Marbles*, and Lodge Kerrigan's *Clean, Shaven*. All these examples are offered not as exemplars of *the right way to do madness* but instead have been selected owing to their diverse, and at times contradictory, attitudes to, and articulations of, madness and the role of art within its landscapes. The periodisation of the book is loosely organised around the rise of the second wave of biological psychiatry, as most acutely symbolised in the publication of *DSM III* in 1980.

In its organisation, then, the book embeds its political methodology. In liberating the reader from biomedical frames of reference and understanding, the book is able to offer new insights into madness and its meanings. The book is also methodologically underpinned by a keen sense of the place of performativity in tangling with questions of madness, art, and society. If performance is acutely alive to the given coordinates and enactments of power in plural situations, then it offers an astute lens for dissecting the field of madness and psychiatry. Moreover, performance as a methodology is always *with* and thus resonates with a key intervention of this volume regarding the centrality of looking *with* not *at* madness. This methodological 'withness', while not collapsing particularity, is marked by gestures of commonality rather than exception. Such gestures are starkly political in the context of madness. Performativity, witnessed via my attention to notions including spatial dramaturgy, dramatic atmospheres, embodiment, co-presence, and so on, permits a perspicuous attentiveness to the organisation, animation, and execution of knowledge, authority, and power. Given that a central intention is to contribute to a wider reimagining of the very basis of how we conceive of madness and care, this appears an apt mode of approach. *Beyond Illness* is an argument for new ways of thinking about madness and its care and treatment through careful engagements with artistic practices. The primary aim of this book is to generate new political atmospheres of understanding in order to begin thinking not *about* but *with* madness. I tender these thoughts, then, not in a spirit of knowing, but rather in a hopeful gesture, stretching towards a more generous embrace of distress and alterity.

Notes

1 James Davies, 'Introduction' in James Davies (ed.), *The Sedated Society: The Causes and Harms of Our Psychiatric Drug Epidemic* (London: Palgrave, 2017), pp. 5–6.
2 Joanna Moncrieff, *The Myth of the Chemical Cure: A Critique of Psychiatric Drug Treatment* (London: Palgrave, 2009), p. 23, emphasis mine.
3 Darian Leader, *The New Black: Mourning, Melancholia, and Depression* (London: Penguin, 2009), p. 6, emphasis original.
4 Nikolas Rose, *Inventing Ourselves: Psychology, Power, and Personhood* (Cambridge: Cambridge University Press, 1998), p. 11.
5 Andrew Scull, *Madness in Civilisation: A Cultural History of Insanity from the Bible to Freud, from the Madhouse to Modern Medicine* (London: Thames & Hudson, 2015), p. 389.
6 Christopher Bollas, *When the Sun Bursts: The Enigma of Schizophrenia* (New Haven, CT & London: Yale University Press, 2015), p. 34.
7 Mick Power, *Madness Cracked* (Oxford University Press, 2015), p. 33.
8 Davies, p. 6.
9 Scull, p. 407.
10 Davies, p. 6.
11 Fred D'Aguiar, 'The Last Essay About Slavery' in Sarah Dunant and Roy Porter (eds), *The Age of Anxiety* (London: Virago, 1996), pp. 125–47.
12 Leader, pp. 190–1.
13 Davies, pp. 1–2.
14 Moncrieff, p. 9.
15 Ibid., pp. 2–3.
16 Darian Leader and David Corfield, *Why Do People Get Ill?* (London: Hamish Hamilton, 2007), p. 10.
17 David Healy, *Let Them Eat Prozac* (Toronto: James Lorimer & Company Ltd, 2003), p. 86, emphasis original.
18 Moncrieff, p. 115.
19 I am here borrowing my turn of phrase from Leader and Corfield.
20 Scull, p. 402.
21 William Davies, *The Happiness Industry: How the Government and Big Business Sold Us Well-Being* (London: Verso, 2015), p. 35.
22 Wendy Brown, *Undoing the Demos: Neoliberalism's Stealth Revolution* (New York, Zone Books: 2015), p. 37.
23 Peter Kinderman, *A Prescription for Psychiatry: Why We Need a Whole New Approach to Mental Health and Wellbeing* (London: Palgrave, 2014), p. 4.
24 Healy, p. 324.
25 Christina Katsakou *et al.*, 'Psychiatric Patients' Views on Why Their Involuntary Hospitalisation Was Right or Wrong' in *Social Psychiatry and Psychiatric Epidemiology*, 2011, 47:427, pp. 1169–79, p. 1169.

26 Bollas, p. 9.
27 See, for example, Julie Wood *et al.*, 'Community Treatment Orders: Implications of the Drafting of the Mental Health Act 2007 for Emergency Detention of Community Patients' in *Medicine, Science, Law*, Jan 2015, 55:1, pp. 2–5.
28 Delphine Coyle *et al.*, 'Compulsion in the Community: Mental Health Professionals' Views and Experiences of CTOs' in *The Psychiatrist*, October 2013, 37:10, pp. 315–21, p. 315.
29 www.oed.com (last accessed 24 June 2017).
30 Wendy Brown, *States of Injury: Power and Freedom in Late Modernity* (Princeton, New Jersey: Princeton University Press, 1995), p. 66, p. 69.
31 Ibid., pp. 73–4.
32 Ann Cvetkovich, *Depression: A Public Feeling* (Durham & London: Yale University Press, 2012), p. 2.
33 Ibid., p. 146.

PART 1

Structures: Psychiatrists, Institutions, Treatments

1

'I AM NO MORE MAD THAN YOU ARE; MAKE THE TRIAL OF IT IN ANY CONSTANT QUESTION'[1]

R. D. Laing and the Figure of the Psychiatrist

In the opening act of Joe Penhall's 2000 play *Blue/Orange*, two psychiatrists, Bruce and Robert, are debating the most appropriate response to, and treatment of, their patient, Christopher:

Robert: The human species is the only species which is innately insane. 'Sanity is a conditioned response to environmental …

Bruce: I don't believe you're saying this …

Robert: … stimulae.' Maybe – just maybe it's true.

Bruce: Maybe it's *utter horseshit* (*Beat*). I'm sorry. Doctor Smith. But. Which, which existential novelist said that? I mean, um, you'll be quoting R. D. Laing next.

Robert: That was R. D. Laing.

Bruce: R. D. Laing was a *madman*. They don't come any fruitier.

Robert: I think there's something in it … [2]

Bruce continues, with incredulity, noting that this is not what he was taught at medical school, and soon they will be donning tights and speculating about Hamlet's various diagnoses if they persist with this line of thinking. Theatre is here tacitly cast as the frivolous emotional side-show in the real arena of hard, empirical science. There is also an implied swipe at psychoanalysis in general, and Freud in particular, owing to his (and others) engagement with canonical literature as creative case studies. The anti-intellectualism of Bruce's voice here superciliously hums with the false bifurcation of the humanities and the sciences that will become a recurrent note of contention throughout this book. However, several ideas for this chapter are nested within this 'fruity' moment of Penhall's perspicacious play: firstly, the ancient debate as to the origins and thresholds of the kingdom of madness; secondly, the long-standing joke that psychiatrists are often madder than their patients; thirdly, that R. D. Laing is a 'crackpot' relic of a bygone period in psychiatric history, best left to the arts students and their many tights. Penhall's theatrical study of contemporary psychiatric discourses and practices also, in the course of its unfolding, raises the question as to precisely what a psychiatrist is and does. It is telling then that the play twice glances back to the twentieth century's most controversial psychiatrist, Ronald D. Laing. Indeed, later an audience hears Bruce describe Robert's work as 'R. D. Laing in a gorilla suit.'[3]

Psychiatrists have long been objects of admiration and derision. They are simultaneously the guardians of the soul and peddlers of mesmeric claptrap, men of science and trick cyclists, carers and quacks. As Glen and Krin Gabbard write: 'Their perceived omniscience is envied and feared, so mental health professionals must be continually ridiculed and put in their place to neutralise these negative feelings.'[4] Nikolas Rose expounds upon such figures further, observing how notions of freedom and autonomy have become organising principles for the forging of modern personhood. Therapies thus offer strategies to help us become better at being ourselves: 'Freedom, that is to say, is enacted only at the price of relying upon experts of the soul.'[5] Frank Furedi likewise charts the 'phenomenal expansion of psychological labels and therapeutic terms' whose 'main legacy so far is the cultivation of a unique sense of vulnerability.'[6] Furedi here critiques notions including self-fulfilment and self-actualisation as forms of therapeutic governance, arguing that such a 'therapy culture' 'posits the self in distinctly fragile and feeble form and insists that the management of life requires the continuous intervention of therapeutic expertise.'[7] In these ways, some of our fundamental anxieties about what it means to be a worthwhile human huddle – needy but hopeful – around the compromised figure of the mind doctor. Think, for example, of the oft-encountered anxious jokes that abound when an individual discloses to a group that they are a psychiatrist or a psychologist. Feelings of admiration and suspicion mingle with dynamics of exposure and concealment. A medical Eye of Providence is thus apparently conferred to such figures (though notably not to their nursing counterparts, even though these actors in psy contexts very often *see* a great deal more and in different ways than the authoritative eyes). The mind doctor (in his plural guises) is thus a figure, culturally, of desire and dread.[8] What might be at stake, then, in our cultural remembrances of Laing? If the psychiatrist is a fiercely contested social, medical, political, and cultural figure at the best of times, what might we glean about ourselves and our attitudes to madness from examining a deeply divisive figure like Laing? This chapter will examine key artistic works about the late R. D. Laing in order to consider what they illuminate about his ideas and legacies. The chapter advances from a keen sense that we still have much to learn from this psychiatric 'maverick', for good and ill, and that close engagement with artistic practice offers a particularly apt strategy for this endeavour.

Knots

Adrian Laing describes the polarising nature of his father: 'There tends to be very few neutral [opinions].'[9] Indeed, for every declaration that 'He was probably the most unethical person I have ever met,'[10] one also uncovers unabashed adoration:

a booking form from 1978 for his lecture at the Roundhouse bellows from the archive: 'THE MAN HIMSELF IN PERSON!'[11] Alongside this are the innumerable accounts by patients like Mary Barnes whose lifelong tune became a song of praise for 'Ronnie'.[12] Moreover, Laing himself was a mesh of paradox and contradiction. As Daniel Burston narrates in his astute biography of Laing: 'There is surely no one else in the history of ideas who has embodied the sceptical and the visionary modes of thought with equal zeal.'[13] Certainly manifold tensions abound in the vast materials by and about Laing with respect to his theories versus his practices. Further, here is a man who both courts and abhors power, a man who clamours for professional respect and yet razes such structures of legitimacy to the ground. Yet, while he is a man fretted with flaws, he is also a radical and important voice in the field of madness and psychiatry. Burston proposes that 'Freud and Jung continue to hold a firm place in posterity ... Laing's contribution to psychology and psychiatry – though different, of course, and distinctively his own – is possibly of the same order of magnitude as theirs.'[14] I here concur with Burston and offer this chapter as a contribution to the burgeoning reassessment of Laing as a pivotal voice in twentieth-century psychiatry and mad politics.

Laing's enduring legitimacy is somehow, however, less secure than the great grandfathers of psychoanalysis. This is perhaps in part owing to the obscuring impact of his lively personal biography as well as his later moves towards mysticism and intrauterine experience. Indeed, the personal lives of psychiatrists are often subject to marked scrutiny: and in seeking paragons of virtue, we don't necessarily frequently find either gods or monsters. Laing's precariousness as an important figure is also, without question, in part owing to the juggernaut second wave of biological psychiatry that throttles such alternative voices by force of its din. As we will see in later chapters, after *DSM III* (though not straightforwardly *because* of it) in 1980, the biomedical model of psychiatry and its ally psychopharmacology bulldoze the landscape of non-normative psychological experiences. Throughout the 1980s, 1990s, and 2000s in both Britain and North America, brain chemistry, drugs, and faulty cognition wholesale displace the 'soft' practices of talking, occupation, and community. This bio-domination is celebrated by figures such as Edward Shorter who proclaim that: 'If there is one central intellectual reality at the end of the twentieth century, it is that the biological approach to psychiatry ... has been a smashing success.'[15] Indeed, Shorter lambasts 'zealot researchers' who have 'seized the history of psychiatry to illustrate how their pet bugaboos – be they capitalism, patriarchy, or psychiatry itself – have converted protest into illness.'[16] However, as Allan Beveridge has noted there has been a resurgence of interest in Laing in recent years after a period in the wilderness. He writes:

> For a period in the 1960s Ronald Laing was the most famous psychiatrist in the world ... Laing's reputation subsequently went into serious decline, but in recent years there has been a renewed interest in him and a number of biographies and books have been published. This interest has been fuelled by disenchantment with the claims of the neurosciences and an unease about

biotechnology. Laing's existential approach of treating the patient as a person rather than a malfunctioning mechanism has new-found appeal.[17]

Furthermore, as Beveridge notes, key questions Laing was asking about the nature of psychosis, its comprehensibility, and the interrelationships between madness and society, are yet to be fully or satisfactorily answered. Thus, while such questions remain pregnant and urgent, perhaps it is valuable to re-examine some of Laing's answers anew. This chapter thus explores three key thematic areas in order to unpick the artistic and clinical legacies of R. D. Laing for our times: empathy, communication, and gaze. How does one practice empathy – both therapeutically and artistically – without falling into the trap of explaining another's experience through the prism of one's own emotional, intellectual, political (and so on) coordinates? If a common complaint of patients is not feeling properly *heard*, then how can we change the structures of listening to afford more dynamic, relational acts of communication? How can artistic work offer new kinds of listening for clinical encounters? Finally, what does observation *feel* like? And how can one look at another without only perceiving what one expects to discover? In this sense, the chapter, like the volume, will tease out the threads that might enable a creative reunification of art and science in order to reimagine the practice of caring for, and about, madness.

Reasonable madness

Malvolio, in this chapter's title quotation, offers up reason and logic as the essential instruments for unmasking madness wheresoever it may lurk. Reason promises to cut an uncompromising line through the fog of minds that have forgotten themselves and thereby illuminate the truly sane. Anticipating Enlightenment thinking and the privileging of rational scientific understandings of human experience, Malvolio here also assures himself and us that madness is a definite *thing*; and, moreover, it is a thing that one either *is* or *is not*. Laing, in many ways, embodies the antithesis of this view. For him, reason (read: psychiatric science) is a blunt instrument that all too frequently wilfully obscures better understandings of the human condition. Moreover, for Laing, madness is a constellation of diverse experiences that defy reductive, positivistic scientific categorisation. He is, of course, not the first or last to propose such ideas. Furthermore, it is a common misunderstanding that Laing was anti-psychiatry and all its treatment methods.[18] However, he was certainly concerned to advocate a more inter-disciplinary approach to caring for people in distress. Art, as opposed to 'reason', thus was a key preoccupation of Laing's throughout his life. Examining Laing's library, which bears witness to his rapacious intellect, Beveridge observes, 'It is interesting to note what subjects did *not* interest Laing. There are comparatively few books on science compared with those on the arts.'[19] Owing to this, alongside this book's firm sense that artistic practices offer acute insights about the nature of madness that have clinical, social, political, and creative implications, this chapter will consider three artistic works that explore Laingian ideas and histories. Ken Loach's 1972 film, *Family Life*, will be examined followed by David Edgar's 1978 play, *Mary Barnes*. I am particularly preoccupied here with the legibility of the 'mad' woman's body and how it is being represented and read within these works. Thirdly, Luke Fowler's Turner Prize nominated work, *All Divided Selves*, will be discussed. Here I consider the chronicling and historicising of Laing's life and work and note how the mode of artistic address in this example revivifies the kinds of alternative ways of seeing, thinking, and listening that Laing sponsored. However, throughout the chapter I seek to continually knit together the relationships between some of Laing's thinking and their re-imagination through aesthetic practices. In this vein, I draw regularly from Dominic Harris's work of photographic history, *The Residents: Stories of Kingsley Hall, East London, 1965–1970 and the Experimental Community of RD Laing*, which is a collage of voices and images looking back on the period. Through these strategies, I aim to meet Laing's cease-less demand for active listening to other voices. The chapter will show that, if one puts the distracting biography aside temporarily, one can hear a clarion call for humane treatment for those of us who find ourselves divided.[20]

Will the real R. D. Laing please stand up?

I am not concerned with the degree to which the selected works 'accurately' depict Laing; nor is my aim hagiography or even a detailed appraisal of Laing's writings and clinical practice. The object of study is how his ideas (and to a much lesser degree he himself) have been portrayed in artistic works in the hope that this might yield food for thought regarding our contemporary attitudes to both madness and the figure of the psychiatrist. Indeed, it is notable that in almost all the art works 'about' Laing, he is never actually portrayed.[21] There is frequently a Laingian figure but none are explicitly 'the man himself'. We capture his image askew; he is, in this way, like Holbein's skull, only visible via sideways glances. This marks an interesting contrast to, say, Freud who is almost always a fully realised character in comparative artistic examples about his career and ideas. Freud's image has, in some ways, calcified into a familiar, slightly perverted, avuncular bearded figure, forever aesthetically and intel-lectually suspended in popular imagination. With a cigar.[22] Laing, I propose, cuts an altogether less certain, and more destabilising, cultural figure. I wish, here, to linger in long shadows of his thinking. Owing to this approach, a brief biographical sketch will offer a partial but (nearly) sufficient introduction for our purposes.[23]

Laing was born in Glasgow in 1927 and died in 1989. He trained as a psychia-trist in Glasgow and then as a psychoanalyst at the Tavistock. While it is accurate to describe him as both psychiatrist and analyst, these were titles that he wrestled feverishly beneath and attempted to refashion throughout his life. During his pro-lific career, he wrote a series of best-selling books that reached global audiences in the millions, including: *The Divided Self* (1960), *Self and Others* (1961), *Sanity, Madness, and the Family* (with Aaron Esterson, 1964), and *The Politics of Experience and The Bird of Paradise* (1967). His writings advance along existential phenomeno-logical terms and draw heavily on figures including Sartre, Kierkegaard, Nietzsche, and Heidegger. Laing was, therefore, preoccupied with interpersonal engagements and environments and was accordingly concerned with ideas of self and authenticity. Indeed, as Beveridge describes, 'There are hardly any books on politics [in Laing's library], though there is a biography of Trotsky and a book by Lenin. Given the Left's adoption of Laing in the 1960s this might seem surprising, but he was actually more interested in change from within than without.'[24] This library, now housed at Glasgow University, reveals a lifelong fascination with artists including Blake, Beckett, Kafka, and Dostoyevsky.[25] Alongside these outputs he became well known for experimenting with the nature, structure, and terms of therapeutic environments and communities; from his early work in hospitals and his 'Rumpus Room' experiments to, perhaps most famously, the establishment of Kingsley Hall. His later career becomes increasingly preoccupied with religious and mystical experience along with his explorations of natal life and memory.

In the course of the 1960s, Laing became an icon of the counter-culture and attained a guru-like status with international reach and appeal. He is perhaps most commonly associated (apart from being the 'fruity' psychiatrist we hear of in *Blue/ Orange*) with the notions that madness is comprehensible, that it is society that is mad and that so-called madness is in fact a sane response to an insane environment, and that 'schizophrenia' is a consequence of disturbed family communication. These popular impressions are a diminution of his thinking and this sketch necessarily, in part, replicates this reduction. However, while such apprehensions of his work have been much discussed elsewhere, I am concerned to draw attention to his steadfast understanding of notions of empathy, co-presence, and communication that persistently resonate throughout his uneven career. It is striking, if unsurprising given Laing's literary mind, that these notions shimmer in their similarity to certain tenets of humanities scholarship. For example, Laing's keen sense of the value of co-presence (an attentive being and listening together in space and time) for therapeutic dialogue strikes one as essentially theatrical in its sensibility. Similarly, one hears throughout Laing's writings a keen sense of the necessity of an empathetic holding of an Other's story in the therapeutic encounter. This chimes with Derek Attridge's sense of the act of reading of a literary text as an 'active engagement and a letting-go, a hospitable embrace of the other.'[26] Laing, like the literary critic, was alive to the dialogic relationship between self and other and their co-constitution of reality, experience, meaning, and truth. Let us then turn to the three works under discussion to uncover what truths and realities they may offer about Laing, madness, and psychiatry.[27]

'You're my daughter and I know exactly what you want'[28]

Ken Loach's 1972 film, *Family Life*, is a realist study of a young woman's journey from suburbia to the bin.[29] The film chronicles Janice's transformation into a career mental patient at the hands of others. Based on David Mercer's and Loach's Wednesday Play, *In Two Minds*, *Family Life* was a film that, in the words of Graham Fuller, was both 'a superb feature … about Laingian solutions to family-induced schizophrenia' and 'a commercial failure'.[30] Moreover, Norman Silverstein reveals that the Paris premiere was delayed for a week owing to anxieties about its distressing nature. It was eventually shown but with warnings in the foyer that the film may be 'disturb-ing to some moviegoers'.[31] This concern perhaps reflects a sense that madness is, at this moment, a still somewhat taboo topic for the realist screen. An audience is introduced to Janice, a woman struggling to confidently find her place and path in the world. Raised in a working-class community and reared on traditional family values, Janice is a somewhat timid woman, dominated by her formidable mother. After falling pregnant to her 'student' boyfriend, she is coerced into an abortion which functions as a narrative catalyst for the escalation of her despair. Increasingly Janice describes a profound sense of dissociation from her own body and experi-ences: 'When it comes to making a decision … it doesn't feel real. I don't feel there's a me I can choose for.'[32] The family is unambiguously framed as schizophrenogenic (that is to say one that causes schizophrenia owing to damaging and defective communication patterns and structures). Furthermore, during the course of her mounting distress, she is repeatedly buffeted between the family, the institution, and the counterculture, with each bastion offering a different approach to, and set of knowledges about, her present condition. The film embodies Laing's thinking (and by extension Gregory Bateson's notion of the double bind within disturbed family communication) and comes out firmly in favour of less restrictive and more com-municative approaches to treating mental distress.[33] Indeed, the Laingian figure, Dr Donaldson, is probably the film's most astute, if ultimately powerless, voice (as is so often the case in Loach's canon). The film concludes with Janice taking comfort in orthodox psychiatry's sedative denuding of her feelings: 'At least I don't feel unreal. I don't feel anything.'[34] She next appears on-screen as a mute archetypal case history presented, specimen-like, to a lecture theatre of uninterested trainee psychiatrists. The film encapsulates, then, fierce debates about the nature of the family, the power of psychiatry, and the place of the radical left within society. Moreover, it directs our attention productively to questions of gaze and the politics of looking.

The purpose of this chapter is not Laing-spotting. His writings are not deployed here as a Rosetta Stone to 'decode' the art objects. While an exercise in mapping his texts on to various artistic works would be viable and possibly fruitful, it is not the nettle I am seeking to grasp. Rather I aim to make audible the vibrations between some of Laing's thinking and the form and aesthetics of these pieces in order to consider the political legacies and futures of his thinking for madness, care, and psychiatry. It is my contention, with respect to *Family Life*, that the moments of collision between the Laingian theory and the filmic practice yield clinical and social insights. What follows, then, is an analytic account of gaze and metaphor that exposes both the promise and flaws of Laing's vision of madness and treatment.

See me

Laing's most famous book *The Divided Self* begins with a consideration of, amongst other things, the visible. A black and white image, which is simultaneously a sketch of two faces in profile and a picture of a white vase, is offered as a visual example of the ambiguity of perception (Figure 1.1). Laing writes:

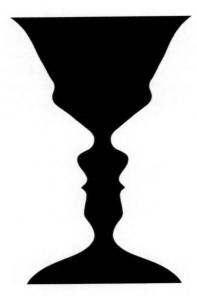

FIGURE 1.1 Two Faces optical illusion

the same thing, seen from different points of view, gives rise to two entirely different descriptions, and the descriptions give rise to two entirely different theories, and the theories result in two entirely different sets of actions. The initial way we see a thing determines all our subsequent dealings with it.[35]

If one replaces the word 'thing' with 'patient' here one has a shrewd account of the interpretative framework that underpins much contemporary psychiatric diagnostic practice in the name of scientific objectivity. However, it also chimes with what has long been understood in the humanities – that one's geopolitical, social subjective position informs one's 'reading' of a given text or scenario. An art object, like a life, is always in progress and unfinished; its final meaning never fully possessed. Moreover, the risk of deterministically reading a patient is a perennial problem in any form of therapy. Laing was acutely alive to such psychic determinism and thus was critical of aspects of Freudian theory: 'first, its mechanistic model of mind; second, its contention that all mental life and behaviour are meaningful; thirdly, its lack of an ethical dimension; and fourthly, its neglect of the interpersonal and social context.'[36] The point of significance here is the shared ambiguity with respect to perception and interpretation that snakes through both *The Divided Self* and *Family Life*.

Tony Garnett notes, with regret, the polarised responses to the earlier version of *Family Life*, *In Two Minds*:

> The letters divided, fifty per cent saying "oh the poor parents, with a girl like that, what a terrible time they had". The other half said, "the poor girl, with parents like that, no wonder she went mad". Both of which were failures from our point of view, because if you make those kind of moral judgements when [sic] you're ceasing to understand the predicament.[37]

One way in which this issue was addressed in the feature film version (apart from a more sophisticated and nuanced script) was the casting of Grace Cave as Janice's mother. Loach here used a non-actor from Walthamstow Conservative Association who, being of a shared world-view to the character, would not cast judgement on Mrs Baildon: 'In her mind [Grace's] the mother was being as good a parent as she could be under the circumstances.'[38] The spirit of the casting here is the pursuit of integrity. The hope is that such realist authenticity will necessarily produce cinematic complexity and thereby circumnavigate didactic moral verdicts. The film also cast an actual progressive psychiatrist to play Dr Donaldson and used several real people from Laingian therapeutic communities in the group therapy scenes. Indeed, Loach has described *Family Life* as 'almost a documentary about the people in the film.'[39] Whether finally Loach achieved this desired-for critical ambiguity is another question. However, what these casting choices here do underscore (apart from reflecting Loach's usual practices) is the notion expressed both by Laing and Loach that perception is a pivotal but contested notion in the politics of madness. The final scene of the film perhaps offers the most incisive image of *Family Life* in this respect: it captures how far Loach understood the prescriptive horizons of thinking in psychiatry and how he sought to expose gaze as an inherited behaviour.

Doctor, doctor

Two psychiatrists are juxtaposed in *Family Life*; Laingian Dr Donaldson and traditional Mr Carswell (who bears more than a passing resemblance to real-life psychiatrist Dr G. Morris Carstairs with whom Laing had numerous debates).[40] Broadly representative of unorthodox and orthodox psychiatry respectively, the pair proffer divergent treatments (and cures in the case of Carswell) for Janice's mental state. As noted, the film affords much more generosity to Donaldson's approach. Scenes of lively group therapy and tender one-to-one talking therapy are contrasted with later shots, under Carswell's regime, of Janice and anonymous others lined up in beds in post-ECT catatonia (Figure 1.2).

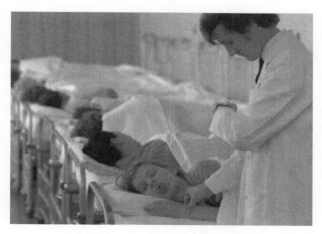

FIGURE 1.2   Post-ECT, *Family Life*

Here the composition of the shot recalls the film's opening black and white scenes of rows of identical houses and later images of factory production lines. The cinematic framing serves to equate the human with the object within the interlocking power structures of capitalism and psychiatry. As student (read: left wing) Tim explains to Janice:

> Early to bed, early to rise, out to work. That's your mam and dad. Do as they're told and that's what they're gonna do to you. And that's normal … But is it sane? … Punctual, passive, in their place. So they can go out there to one of those factories and do a day's work. [41]

This moment is swiftly followed with Janice and Tim quite literally putting their colourful mark on suburbia as they spray-paint the garden. And herein lies a seductive visual conflation of art, freedom, rebellion, 'true' sanity, and social revolution captured in the image of a bright blue garden gnome. It is also, however, at this point that the contest for Janice's best interest begins in earnest. Nevertheless, it is Carswell's approach, backed by the family, that 'wins'. Carswell expels Donaldson from the hospital, sanctions physical treatments against Janice's will, and returns her to the deeply damaging familial home. While Tim attempts to 'save' Janice from this destiny, the film suggests that her fate was already sealed owing to the imbalance of power heavily weighted in mainstream psychiatry's favour. The situation is deliberately hopeless. As Loach explains in response to the suggestion that the film suffers from pessimistic funnel vision:

> The idea that there can be any optimism gleaned from within the way we treat mentally ill people now, would be false. To say, "The whole system is terrible, but hang on folks, there's a chink here". It would be as false as saying, "Couldn't Billy Kes be gotten a job in a zoo". It's not on. [42]

What is particularly striking though in these later scenes is how far Janice has become a problem to be solved, a contest to be won. Her best intentions are claimed by all – from Mr Carswell to her sister to Tim – and she thus becomes a symbolic object being traded in the wide fray of (predominantly male) politicised debates. It is perhaps questionable as to how far, via his conflation of varied political discourses of power and freedom in the film, Loach is similarly culpable of ultimately rendering Janice a generalised emblem or metaphor for injustice and thereby robbing her of the particular coordinates of her political situation. Indeed, as the final scene makes plain she comes to embody the 'logical expectation' of her case history. [43]

Loach has suggested that no splinter of hope is offered for Janice. If one does exist, however, it occurs in the film's final line: 'Now, any questions?' [44] Janice's final scene opens with a shot from the very back of the lecture theatre within which she is being presented as an exemplary case to trainee doctors. Our position as viewers is most obviously aligned with that of the students observing the mute woman before us. However, the echoing sound of Mr Carswell's voice that reverberates just a little too loudly in our ears invites us, momentarily, to experience Janice's perspective: 'How are you this morning?'[45] Janice's sense of unreality and fractured sense of self are fleetingly captured in the hollow sound of the audio track and in the long-range shot of her body. For a moment, we look and listen with, not at, Janice. We perceive Janice as she perceives herself; far away. While this is a fleeting moment in an otherwise bleak, realist picture, it effects a crucial political skewing of our perception. Namely, that in the moment of her most brutal exposure as a pathological specimen an audience is reminded not only of the ideological work at stake in our own act of looking but we find themselves caught, fly-like, in the sticky proximity of Janice's felt experience. The heightened visual frame, when coupled with the amplified audio, snags our presence into the diagnostic gaze momentarily. It is, then, a highly textured cinematic moment that enfolds an audience's sense of bearing witness to an on-screen act of looking with the feeling of oneself being in the frame, imaginatively observed.

The focus of the scene, however, is predominantly on the gaze of the students. As Carswell describes her background, 'happy childhood', and symptoms, 'thought blocking, over-inclusion, emotional apathy, over-obedience', the camera pans between the student's somewhat bored faces.[46] Moreover, Janice is expressly framed as an unambiguous clinical picture. As Carswell describes her as a 'good example of extreme mutism' the camera cuts to place Janice in the centre of the frame with all eyes, including our own, fixed downwards upon her body. This scene makes luminous the training of medical gaze. The students are inheriting certain ways of seeing that categorically obscure the picture of the patient's experience. In a decisive shift from the original TV play, *In Two Minds*, the psychiatrist in *Family Life* rules out the possibility of environmental factors being of any influence. Moreover, where the original ending had the students interrogating the dominant framing of Janice as a chronic schizophrenic, here the invitation for further questions is left expectant, unanswered. Loach tacitly asks us to reflect upon whether *we* have any questions about such systems of training for care. Indeed, Carswell is off-screen at this point and thus his quasi-omniscient voice rings in our ears and thus implicates us as the co-addressee. In this way, Loach places the burden of hope for this situation with the spectators.

The closing scene also recalls one of the most famous passages from *The Divided Self*. Laing quotes Emil Kraepelin's (a key architect of the first wave of biological psychiatry) description of his patient's responses when they were presented to a lecture-room of students. Kraepelin describes the voice of his patient as incomprehensible and inarticulate: sound and fury signifying nothing. Kraepelin is concerned only with the structure as opposed to content. Laing counters Kraepelin's reading of the scene by attempting to decipher the patient's apparently illogical monologue. Kraepelin heard gabble babble. Laing heard an exasperated, but audible, plea. The patient's voice is narrated by Kraepelin in the text but I have expressed it here as script for ease of reading:

Patient: I tell you who is being measured and is measured and shall be meas-
                 ured. I know all that, and could tell you, but I do not want to.
Kraepelin: When asked his name, he screams, "What is your name?"

For Laing, unlike for Kraepelin, the patient's dialogue is crystalline: 'He is object-
ing to being measured and tested. He wants to be heard.'[47] Laing here returns us to
the two faces optical illusion and its implications for clinical diagnosis: 'One may
see his behaviour as "signs" or a "disease"; one may see his behaviour as expressive
of his existence.'[48] Similarly, Carswell introduces Janice's profile before she enters
the room and thereby ineluctably shapes his student's mode of viewing. In this
way, she is a pathology exhibit, a living cadaver to be visually dissected, and not
a person. The question of perspective is, of course, doubled in the cinema. Our
engagement with Loach's film (and indeed your perception of this chapter) will
be shaped by a set of values and experiences that condition the gaze. The point at
stake here is not whether Kraepelin or Laing is 'right' about the patient or even
whether Loach's left-wing bias predetermines the horizons of his filmic thinking
about mental health care; rather, what is of value from both Laing and Loach is their
critical engagement with naturalised ways of seeing in clinical contexts. Loach's
framing of Janice makes plain the psychiatric legibility of her body and behaviour.
Reading Janice as two-dimensional dead text to be deciphered via positivist symptoms (whether as psychiatrist or cinemagoer) flattens out available meaning and is
studiously blind to interiority, life history, feeling, and patient experience. Loach
here brings Laing's understanding of the value of true patient dialogue (as opposed
to a series of questions to check against a set of diagnostic assumptions) to light. In
so doing, Loach replenishes our understanding of the fraught politics of looking at,
and listening to others.

'Home is where I want to be, pick me up and turn me round'[49]

Between 2014 and 2019 artist and political activist the vacuum cleaner, aka James
Leadbitter, is leading an innovative project called *Madlove*. This interdisciplinary
initiative draws a range of individuals together in a series of workshops and aims to
collaboratively design a creative asylum and a 'safe place to go mad' because 'a lot of
psychiatric hospitals are more punishment than love.'[50] The project calls on plural
voices but places experts-by-experience of the UK mental health system at the
heart of this development. The culmination of the workshops will be the opening,
in 2019, of a mental health day unit inspired by the process. In the 1960s, a collective of psychiatrists and psychologists came together with the hope to create an
asylum, in the root sense of the word, that would provide a safe, creative space for
people to go mad and avoid the mental hospital: Kingsley Hall. The group behind
this were the Philadelphia Association and the figure at their helm, R. D. Laing.[51]
The point here, of course, is not to suggest that Leadbitter is the heir apparent to
Laing; rather more basically I suggest that we are still in dire need of more creative

and humane environments within which to care for and support people in crisis. We return to this artist and these questions of space and care at length in Chapter 2 but their ongoing relevance is a necessary ghost for the following discussion of Kingsley Hall and its most famous inhabitant, Mary Barnes. That is to say that in an interval of 50 years between Kinglsey Hall and *Madlove* the needs for alternative models of mutual, humane care in psychological breakdown have not been adequately met.

Continuing the discussion of gaze and legibility, we turn now to David Edgar's 1978 play, *Mary Barnes*, which is based on her 1971 co-authored illness memoir (with psychiatrist Joe Berke), *Mary Barnes: Two Accounts of a Journey Through Madness*. Here again, in Edgar's play, we encounter a mad woman as metaphor and case study. However, Mary Barnes's story diverges significantly from Janice's insofar as this is what Arthur W. Frank terms a restitution narrative.[52] If *Family Life* resisted spectacular madness and epiphanic recovery, the story of Mary Barnes turns on such moments. Indeed, Mary Barnes in life, in memoir, and in the play, embodies the 'triumph' of Laing's approach to treating psychosis.[53] However, what I wish to trouble in this section is the manner in which we look backwards and read Mary, Kingsley Hall, and *Mary Barnes*. It is my contention that plural narratives composed by and about Mary cumulatively reveal the male gaze through which she is constructed and reconstructed. *Mary Barnes*, I suggest, becomes a problematic exercise in spectacle and conservative nostalgia. While many at the time of the original production noted its empathetic engagement with madness and the progressive ideas of Laing, on closer inspection one can also discern a problematic disavowal of radical psychiatry, an investment in a narrative of scientific progress, and a failure to ever really look beyond the surface expressions of Mary Barnes.

Mary Barnes was Kingsley Hall's most famous resident during its Laingian years, 1965–70 (the building itself has a long history of famous guests including Gandhi and his goat). She notoriously went to Kingsley Hall in order to 'go down' and regressed to infancy in order to 'come up again' and reassemble herself anew.[54] She is an infamous figure owing to her activities such as being bottle fed by her psychiatrist, Joe Berke, and painting with her own shit. She is famous for her later art works with paints and charcoals. However, she is significant for our concerns insofar as she functions as a personification of Laing's theory of psychosis and recovery. Mary herself embraced this role with fervour and pride throughout her life. However, some have questioned the veracity of Mary's recovery. Elaine Showalter observes:

> Mary's madness becomes the myth of Kingsley Hall; she is its heroine and its symbolic ideal. On the opening night of the play [Edgar's *Mary Barnes*], however, the impact of Laing's theories was significantly undermined, for those who could look away from the image to the reality, by the presence of the real Mary Barnes, a lisping, bouncing, and giggling fifty-five-year-old woman … who admitted to a reporter from *The Guardian* that she was still wrestling with acute attacks of depression and withdrawal.[55]

Aside from the continued infantilisation and essentialising of Mary at work here, Showalter also partly misses the point about Mary's state of mind. Firstly, the recurrence of depression is taken as evidence of the *failure* of Laing's work in ways that presuppose that recovery means cure, a total and permanent eradication of such experiences. Secondly, Showalter marginalises Mary's own perspective by omitting Mary's voice from the very *Guardian* article she is referring to in the quotation above. In this article, Mary remarks, in contradistinction to Showalter's problematic sense that Mary *admits* to ongoing distress, that:

> I don't think of myself as cured because I know I still need support, caring and therapy at times. If I were to tell myself I was cured I would have to stop looking for help and my whole process of growth would stop.[56]

The new narrative and identity that Mary has co-created at Kingsley Hall has provided her with a way to live. One may wish to critique the self-perpetuating dependency that Mary appears to have adopted but again this is to miss the point. The self that was forged in the crucible of Kingsley Hall became the means by which Mary could live with her psychosis and melancholy rather than being forever frightfully embattled with them. I wish to pause, therefore, over the consequences of Edgar's ideological appropriation of her complex tale.

Mary, Mary, quite contrary

Mary Barnes was first performed at the Birmingham Repertory Theatre on 31 August 1978 and transferred to the Royal Court in January 1979. The three-act play is set inside Kingsley Hall and employed split-level staging with Mary's room suspended above the main playing area. It faithfully stages the memoir and thus charts Mary's arrival, descent, and recovery. Only Mary retains her actual name: all other Kingsley Hall figures are given pseudonyms. For example, Joe Berke becomes Eddie, Laing is Hugo, John Latham is Zimmerman, and so forth. Owing to the blending of imagined dialogue with the truth claims made by this kind of theatrical work, Edgar offers a nominal gauze between the person and the representation. Indeed, in a letter to the Press Officer at the Royal Court, Harriet Cruickshank, Edgar suggests: 'There is no way we can stop people guessing which character "is" R. D. Laing but I think it's best if we don't assist with such speculation.'[57] While Laing is actually a relatively minor character in the play, it is nonetheless quite clearly a piece about Laingian ideas.

The play opened to mixed notices. Hans Keller attacked the 'aesthetic sanctification of infantilism' and concluded that it was 'the most boring and predictable play I have ever seen.'[58] J. C. Trewin concurred lamenting the works' 'excremental realism' and 'clumsily contrived' dramaturgy.[59] Michael Billington, on the other hand, found it 'refreshing' in its lack of 'shibboleths' or 'facile answers', praising it as a 'well-documented account of one treatment that worked.'[60] Nicholas de Jongh too felt it to be a 'powerful and moving affirmation of the value of alternative psychiatry.'[61]

The reviews are, however, almost unanimous in their admiration of Patti Love's committed portrayal of Mary, which the real Mary Barnes also endorsed: 'Watching her it was like watching me.'[62] Mary's life, as the title would suggest, plays front and centre. However, it is important to also critique the autonomy this may appear to confer to Mary's voice. In fact, this play is quadruple refracted through authoritative male voices. Firstly, Mary functions as a symbolic embodiment of Laing's theories and community: she *is* Kingsley Hall and her body is the text upon which Laing's thinking is inscribed. Secondly, the original source text is co-authored with her male psychiatrist. Thirdly, her life is adapted for the stage by Edgar. Finally, it is realised by the director, Peter Farago. It is valuable, therefore, to treat the alleged *authenticity* of the play with a degree of criticality. Furthermore, to over-emphasise Mary's story is to miss the drama of the group that is also taking place on stage. It is a play then that stages the unusual life of an individual but in the context of a radical therapeutic community.

Janelle Reinelt and Gerry Hewitt's study of Edgar's canon notes the playwright's tireless pursuit of hope in the wreckages of failed projects. They argue that 'Theatre attends to the amendment of existing arrangements by exploring and pursuing what is intimated in them' and praise Edgar's 'commitment to retrieval, to finding the shard, fragment, or remnant from even the most disappointing and discouraging outcome, that can be taken forward to begin again.'[63] In the context of *Mary Barnes* this can, perhaps, be most clearly heard in the voice of Brenda who, in the play's penultimate scene, remarks: 'We didn't build the future. But we are no longer, other, to ourselves.'[64] Further, Tim Shields suggests that the play is 'balanced between an optimistic view of recovery (for Mary) and a pessimistic view for those still caught within "the system."'[65] And Edgar certainly captures the hope offered by Mary's case: 'She's better than she was. And she's better without shocks or drugs or anything. That's all.'[66] Moreover, Mary, as Showalter intimated, is *the* image of Kingsley Hall. In the play, as in life, she thus came to both embody its values – no 'hierarchies, chains of authority, unspoken rules' – but also to bring these values to crisis point:

> If you want Mary, take her, live with her, and have your house covered in her paintings and her shit and have her scream at you, assault you, and that's fine. Or give her rules and keep her in control, and keep her here, and that too is all fine. But she is taking over.[67]

She is then the experiment itself, the limit case, and in many ways, encapsulates what the Laingian character Hugo calls, 'the vertigo of freedom'.[68] This sense of Mary as both person and emblem finds echo in the recurrent use of her name throughout the play and her repeated references to herself in the third person:

Eddie   Knock, who's there –
Mary   It's Mary –
Eddie   Mary who
Mary   IT'S MARY BARNES![69]

On the one hand, this is simply an accurate account of Mary's dual role in the history of Laing and Kingsley Hall. On the other hand, it underscores the problematic concentration on surface behaviour at the expense of interiority that characterises the play. She is afforded scant depth. In Act One Scene Four, we listen to Hugo ventriloquising Mary's history as she sits mute *'clutching her teddy'* in a spotlight: 'The agony inside her. Like a bomb. The tearing pain.'[70] In this way, Edgar replicates, rather than complicates, the *use* of Mary's story in male discourses around madness. Moreover, Farago's direction further underscores the vision of Mary as both passive child and wild woman. In literalising the male gaze in props and lighting here, Farago betrays the problematic and repeated use of Mary as spectacular evidence in men's stories about women's madness.

'And till my ghastly tale is told / This heart within me burns'[71]

Speaking in 2012, Morton Schatzman – one of the therapists at Kingsley Hall – describes how 'The Mary Barnes story is, in a sense, the paradigm case.'[72] Adrian Laing similarly notes that Mary represented 'the sort of madness my father wanted to write about, with a very identifiable beginning, middle, and end, a sort of journey through it, enlightened and so on as a painter, and so people started to emulate that kind of madness.'[73] Notably, Laing himself was very quiet throughout his career on the 'topic' of Mary Barnes and consistently sought to create distance between himself and her case:

> Mary Barnes and I could have gone around the world as a double act propagating Mary Barnes' trip. I never wrote, I never asked, I never wanted to write an introduction or a preface, or a review or anything of Mary Barnes' number … I've never used her as an example or a paradigm case or set her up in anything I've written or in lectures I've given.[74]

Contrarily, Thomas Szasz, one of Laing's fiercest critics, was concerned to expose the embedded power structures and flaws within Laing *et al.*'s strategies in relation to individuals like Mary:

> The psychiatrist cures and calls it diagnosis, and the patient, especially if he believes it, duly deteriorates. The antipsychiatrist blesses it and calls it discovering genius, and the patient, especially if he believes it, reverently recovers. But how many geniuses can one produce by the method?[75]

Former resident James Greene also recollects that, to his mind, 'Mary Barnes was actually the only person, of the people who were really disturbed, who seemed to benefit from being there.'[76] This tissue of quotations not only affirms the notion of Mary as symbolic ideal, but it also reminds us that she became a show piece for radical psychiatry and, by extension, radical madness. Indeed, Jutta Laing (Laing's second wife) has explained:

> I remember when this, what's his name, Edgar David somebody, wrote a play about Mary Barnes and people said, have you been to see the play? I said gosh, I don't need to go to the theatre, I have the play in my living room.[77]

Edgar's dramaturgical decision to locate Mary's story within a traditional three-act structure serves to maintain the restitution narrative. Furthermore, his decision to locate the scene of Mary appearing like a 'creature from the black lagoon' covered in her own shit in the middle of the drama allows this moment to operate as a narrative climax on which the action turns.[78] One may suggest that Edgar is simply 'telling it how it was'. However, such a reading underestimates the capacity of the playwright to complicate 'history' and neatly sidesteps the political ramifications of such choices. Mary's madness is made neat — a thing to be observed — and spectacular in Edgar's dramatic frame in manners that encourage an audience to look on in pity. Indeed, even in the only scene in the piece in which Mary is afforded monologic freedom, Hugo gazes on:

Hugo Petrifying.
　　　　Pause.
　　　　'Mean, so bloody thin.
　　　　Just on the edge.
　　　　Pause. **Hugo** *goes to* **Mary**.
　　　　Oh Mary, must you suffer so.[79]

While Mary resists Hugo's pronouncements, she remains suspended in his (and Edgar's) exhibition. Again, at another point we hear Douglas and Hugo debate Mary's behaviours:

Douglas Of course she thinks she's a foetus.
Hugo No. She *is* a foetus. That's what she's experiencing.[80]

Moreover, the dramatic faithfulness to the memoir repeats the tale of 'successful' Mary in some uncritical manners. Notably, the recovery story stands in stark contrast to Janice's downward narrative arc in *Family Life*. In both examples, however, the women's lives become the 'inevitable outcomes' of narratives authored by powerful men.

　　The above interpretations may smack some readers as marred by presentism. The primary reservations offered in relation to this play are its unproblematic framing of female madness as sensational, its uncomplicated engagement with the restitution narrative of the memoir, and the manners in which it sustains Mary as the symbolic ideal of 'progressive' male power. The play as a whole, though formally conservative, is nonetheless a valuable and thoughtful piece about this moment in psychiatric history. However, the criticisms advanced above actually find echo in the archive. On BBC Radio 3's *Critics Forum* in 1979, Anthony Thwaite found the play to be partly a spectacle and one that invited a diagnostic gaze:

> I must admit that quite early on I began to have the feeling that er ... I was like one of my ancestors going to Bedlam on a Sunday to see the lunatics ... and one was observing 'acting out' as if one were oneself an involved therapist.[81]

David Harsent, meanwhile, discerned a vaudeville quality to the on-stage madness because such 'bizarre' behaviours 'tend to get laughs; indeed they invariably *did* get laughs.'[82] Clancy Sigal (who wrote a scathing roman-à-clef about Laing, *Zone of the Interior*) also struggled with how paradoxically anodyne the play rendered madness: 'The questions that remain in my mind are is it very true to the err ... to the experience of schizophrenia ... It really doesn't talk about what the majority of schizophrenics are like.'[83] Moreover, Beverly Brown found the portrait of illness merely a 'succession of stage effects' and that, paradoxically, 'allowing the emotional life full play has the opposite effect – to make it private, obscure, and mysterious.'[84] Nevertheless, while surrendering the playing space to Mary for the majority of the piece, Edgar does offer a quiet critique of her infamy through the character of Laurence, whose less spectacular tale is intimated through a sequence of small stage images. For example, a scene that captures an ebullient Mary following an exhibition of her work concludes with Laurence, quite literally stuck in a groove, mute, and lost in the fray of Kingsley Hall. In a recurrent image, we watch him play his records: '*The* **OTHERS** *look at* **Laurence**. *He goes and puts the record player back on.*'[85] Laurence's narrative concludes thus: '**Laurence** *sits in front of the record player* ... **Laurence** *turns the music louder* ... **Laurence** *turns the music even louder* ... **Laurence** *turns the music even louder. BLACKOUT* ... *smashing metal and wood, followed by the broken record-player being thrown on the floor.*'[86]

In addition to the issue that, as an audience, we only ever look *at* and never *with* Mary, one might broaden the aperture to consider Edgar's retrospective gaze on the counter-culture and radical psychiatry more generally. Edgar, I suggest, is culpable of using Mary as a vehicle or protest metaphor to make glib, generalised points about the failures of the radical left and the counter-culture in the course of the play. However, a perhaps more complex issue is the assumption of failure that undergirds the play's attitude to radical psychiatry before curtain up. The nostalgic framing of the period via popular music scoring key scenes and transitions, the references to LBJ, Bob Dylan puns, and the satirising of counter-culture discourse during the dinner scenes converge to create a joss-stick image of an already dead party: 'I have just been to a committee meeting of an organization of radical therapists entitled Shrinks for Socialism ... the first step is to take over the world on strict Marxist-Jungian lines.'[87] While there can be few who would describe Kingsley Hall as an unmitigated triumph, to seal its fate as a kooky mausoleum of forgotten failures is a reductive disservice that fundamentally misses its radicalism (and the continued urgency of its ambition). Moreover, if one returns to Mary, the ostensible hero of the drama, a cavalier attitude to her life is exposed as she too is inevitably cast as an exotic souvenir of a failed male enterprise.

The play's final scene occurs some years after the departure of the Philadelphia Association and takes place on a set festooned in dust sheets. Angie, who unsuccessfully aped Mary's journey, returns to Kingsley Hall in a state of post-ECT amnesia that lets her 'forget the things that hurt'.[88] She gazes upon a painting of Mary: '*She doesn't remember. With a shrug.*'[89] Placing Mary in a frame, in effect, under a metaphorical dust sheet, prematurely arrests her as (already forgotten) history. Perhaps the lesson here, if one can be salvaged, as with Loach, is that the responsibility lies with us; in this case, the responsibility is to not forget. However, this feels like rather slim political pickings. In *Mary Barnes* Kingsley Hall is already, less than a decade after its closure, largely reduced to a museum relic that, if it did anything at all, helped one woman. Indeed, its optimism is stridently individualised in Edgar's overall reckoning. However, for Zimmerman the best of Kingsley Hall was its ability to allow a group of individuals to be together in their 'lumpy nakedness' and 'messy majesty'.[90] Yet even here, this framing of the place as a collection of odd socks tacitly endorses a narrative of psychiatric progress. Edgar here is culpable of diluting the radicalism of the experiment to a bumper-sticker slogan of 'far out' personal freedom. The cynicism of *Mary Barnes*, I propose, exposes the shallowness of Edgar's engagement with madness and the politics of its discontents. To put it bluntly, he utilises madness and Mary primarily as vehicles to stage a creaking and predictable account of the failure of radical leftist politics. Indeed, madness and Mary are infantilised and serve as emblems of epistemic naivety.

Speaking in January 1979, around the opening of the play at the Royal Court, Edgar responded to the suggestion that Barnes's original memoir is indulgent and fallacious thus: 'Yes, quite. But you've got to remember that in the sixties people believed in things and causes in an intense and uncompromising way … Now we have found that in fact there is a chemical which helps schizophrenia.'[91] This is an opinion he reiterated in 1981: 'Laing has been undermined, since it is now much clearer that there is a chemical causative effect to schizophrenia.'[92] Reinelt and Hewitt, writing almost 25 years later, account for Laing's decline along similar lines: 'He lost most of his influence, however, in the 1980s because significant scientific research had since shown that schizophrenia can be treated, at least in part, through new pharmacology and psycho-surgical techniques.'[93] As Joanna Moncrieff explains, however, 'Decades of research have failed to produce clear and independent evidence of a dopamine abnormality in people with psychosis and schizophrenia that cannot be attributed to some other cause.'[94] Moreover, use of neuroleptic drugs shortens life and is associated with a host of drug effects including tardive dyskinesia (which mimics Parkinson's disease) and 'spontaneous movement, difficulty initiating movement, slowness of movements, reduced facial expression, apathy, reduced emotional responsiveness, and slowness of thinking.'[95] It is perhaps time, then, to reconsider the narrative of Kingsley Hall as a hippy casualty on the road to biological success. Might it be time to have the courage to 'blast open the continuum of [psychiatric] history' and instead reflect politically upon why, 47 years after it closed in 1970, we are still looking for a safe place to be, and go, mad?[96]

'there is something the matter with him'[97]

The final example of this chapter is Luke Fowler's art film *All Divided Selves*. This is the third work of Fowler's that takes Laing as its central subject.[98] Nominated for the Turner Prize in 2012, it is a visually riddling and expansive piece that both captures the complexity of Laing in his own times and yet sutures this with contemporary images that invite us to reflect upon his legacies. However, far from fastening a taut line from there to here, then to now, Fowler invokes a deliberately bifurcating, entangled aesthetic. One might equally describe it is as a schizophrenic aesthetic insofar as it embraces formally disordered patterns of thought and image structures. Indeed, as Laing's voice-over describes the root meaning of the word schizophrenia as a fractured heart or soul, we see ecological images of multiplicity (Figure 1.3). In the course of the film, we see footage of Laing that is clearly time-marked through its technology and production quality and other shots of Laing on a TV monitor in an archive that doubly frames him as historical object (as well as foregrounding Fowler's own act of retrieval and composition). However, such images are contrasted with the voice-overs that speak to us as if in the here-and-now and serve to amplify both the vitality and anachronisms of his prolific voice. The disturbing of tenses in this way renders Laing both past and present. Moreover, the film is consciously engaged with matter, all that is, the tangible. Its visual choreography of nature, machines, materiality, and bodies seeks, like Laing, to tease out the light from between reality and unreality and in so doing disturbs their mutual conviction. Indeed, the film is a communion with vital uncertainty.

FIGURE 1.3 'Broken heart', *All Divided Selves*

It is a bold film that encompasses many of the concerns that one witnesses in both *Family Life* and *Mary Barnes*. Fowler attends to the politics of poverty, community, class, and wealth in relation to madness, treatment, and care. He allows us to glimpse into familial and social worlds, peeking at the manners, conformity, and rituals that codify such spaces. A short sequence with a patient, his mother, and a psychiatrist is strikingly similar to *Family Life* insofar as it captures the young man's numb distance from his own experience and the mother's abhorrence at the generational decline with respects to manners and language: 'it [his way of speaking] appals me. His friends all speak the same. It's not as I want him to speak I suppose.'[99] One also witnesses the promise and fracture of the counterculture alongside the rise of capitalism, Big Pharma, and the second wave of biological psychiatry. Moreover, there is a sustained engagement with questions of audibility, legibility, and the professional deciphering of the mad. There are, for example, recurrent scenes of (predominantly male) psychiatrists decoding and translating patient's (predominantly female) words and behaviours (Figure 1.4). However, Laing is not crudely contrasted as hero to villainous orthodox psychiatry. While we encounter the violent consequences of decarceration as patients are 'restored to the community', we also encounter David – a long-term figure on the Philadelphia Association scene, who appears in several films including *Family Life* and Peter Robinson's documentary *Asylum* (from which Fowler draws in his films).[100] David does not fulfil the Mary Barnes restitution narrative and occupies a complex figure in this history insofar as he *remains*. The film allows the question to emerge as to how far Laing is culpable of abandoning those who do not conform to his narratives of madness and recovery. Indeed, this is the particular strength of the film; its capacity to hold complexity and thereby artistically realise Laing's ideal of empathetic listening to other ways of thinking. Far from sitting on a fence, however, Fowler listens attentively to the roar of this history and in it discerns the notes of humanity that we might compose anew. In this way, he helps us to look backwards carefully in order to look forwards creatively.

FIGURE 1.4 'Training gaze', *All Divided Selves*

'Just nod if you can hear me'[101]

Speaking at the University of Exeter in September 2014, sociologist Arthur W. Frank posed the question, in relation to illness memoirs: what kind of listener does this story call upon me to be? He argued for the need for focussed and sustained attention to a person's story, not for its generalisability but for the value of listening properly. Moreover, he articulated the value of lingering with a story rather than seeking its conclusion. In this vein, Frank noted the difference between chronicle and history observing that the latter presupposes an arc and invites expectations of causality. The chronicle, however, places events side by side without firmly establishing their interrelationships. The chronicle, for Frank, somewhat loosens the interpretive frame in this way. Frank offers the graphic memoir as a form that is particularly apt for the synthesis of chronicle and history, in its capacity for simultaneity, juxtaposition, and multiple focuses of attention. Moreover, he notes that the clinical value of such an approach to understanding illness and patient history is that it diminishes narrative expectations and self-fulfilling clinical prospects. Moreover, as we will explore in Chapter 6, the particular possibilities for instability that are afforded by the graphic form also make more room for the unfinished and multiple nature of stories. One's sickness narrative not only shifts in relation to the listener but morphs over time as one lives in, and with, one's unfolding experience of illness. For Frank, the graphic memoir is well placed to accommodate such erratic momentum.[102] The resonances with respect to listening and being responsible with an Other's story (however told) that one can hear in relation to Laing's writings are clearly audible. Indeed, one is put in mind of moments from Laing's therapeutic career when he sat in silence with a mute patient communicating through hospitable and active presence until she was able to talk verbally, or his stripping off to sit with a patient who refused to wear clothes. Laing here embodies Frank's call to be the type of listener that a story invites one to be and, what is more, to listen in fully embodied manners. Moreover, one can readily perceive the relevance of Frank's insights for Fowler's film. In his resistance to linearity, his visual accommodation of contrasting imagery via intercutting, jump-cuts, layering and use of stills, his disturbance of time signatures, and his acute attention to tangibility, he disrupts ordinary ways of seeing, listening, and thinking. Here then, Fowler, like Frank, aims to disrupt clinical narratives and thereby resists the imposition of pathological expectations. In short, Fowler offers a creative, optimistic articulation of Laing's (never consistently realised) radical aim of listening properly to others.

Fowler's film, in its preoccupation with acts and modes of communicating and understanding, then, might recall a figure like Bakhtin. Fowler's texturing and layering of image and inclusion of silence, natural and mechanical sound, distorted noise, and polarised voices certainly has a heteroglossic quality that could be characterised as Bakhtinian. Moreover, the film, in its footage of human touch, community gatherings, and social conditions is visually ablaze with tender feelings of textures, layers, and connectivity. Meaning accrues through a dialogic encounter between bodies, matter, and systems. Fowler makes a moving case in the film's closing sequence for human relations and communication as the source of recovery. He seeks, like Laing, to rehabilitate the notion of the family. Laing explains, 'What I hoped I was doing then and still hope that I can be perceived as having done, and still trying, is to make a contribution towards the survival of the family.'[103] The film concludes with an elegiac but hopeful, Scottish song, *The Hidden Sin*, that cantillates: 'In the underworld of feeling, divided selves will all be healed.'[104] The point of significance here is that Fowler not only conjures Laingian thinking in all its complexity but extends it. If Laing was, at times, culpable of holding power while decrying it, the form and structure of Fowler's film invite a deliberate diffusion of authority and shatter singularity. If Laing argued incisively for proper listening but began to supply some brittle narratives of illness and recovery, then Fowler asks his audience to decentre their mode of viewing and listening in manners that seek to hospitably hold alterity and frustrate ambitions for fixity of experience. In these ways, Fowler replenishes the vitality of the offers to remake care for those in mental distress.

Fowler also offers a filmic, living sculpture of contemporary radical therapy: Open Dialogue. This therapy, pioneered in Western Lapland, has led to a profound decline in schizophrenia in the region and is based on a collaborative, dialogue-led system of care for psychosis.[105] As Robert Whitaker explains, this needs-adapted treatment programme has led to an 80 per cent recovery rate at the five-year check with low uses of neuroleptics. This intervention runs counter to the accepted wisdom that drugs are efficacious in schizophrenia. As Moncrieff reminds us: 'It is often claimed that neuroleptic drugs have improved the outcome of schizophrenia but it is actually quite difficult to find evidence to support this position.'[106] Moreover, as James Davies reports, a World Health Organisation study into long-term use of neuroleptics covering ten countries found that 'the best symptomatic and functional outcomes were not found in the developed countries where 90% of patients were taking antipsychotics, but in countries such as Nigeria, Columbia, and India where, on average, only about 15% of the patients were taking antipsychotics.'[107] This, of course, indicates the centrality of socio-cultural factors in recovery, but it also upsets the case for drugs as a necessary intervention: 'Further, since the Finnish implementation of Open Dialogue Therapy, 'only two or three new cases of schizophrenia appear each year in Western Lapland, a 90 per cent drop since the early 1980s.'[108] It is important here to acknowledge not only its clear heritage in 1960s radical psychiatry, of which Laing was a world-leading proponent, but also its synergy with *All Divided Selves*. The practice is, in part, informed by continental poststructuralist philosophy, and organised around three principles, 'tolerance of uncertainty', 'dialogism', and 'polyphony'. As Jaakko Seikkula and Mary E. Olsen explain:

> there is no conception of truth or reality that can be known as separate from and outside of human expression. The therapeutic ingredient comes from the effect of dialogism on a social network as new words and stories enter the common discourse. To accomplish this, the language practices

of the treatment meeting have the double purpose of holding people long enough (tolerance of uncertainty) so that the inexpressible can be given voice (dialogism) with the help of important others in the network (polyphony).[109]

While not collapsing the distinction between clinical and artistic practice, their reciprocity is luminous. Furthermore, Fowler offers a creative articulation of the new possibilities for how we look, hear, and understand others. The synthesis of philosophy, psychiatry, and art witnessed in Open Dialogue and *All Divided Selves* carry forward Laing's radical hope for healing fractured souls. As Seikkula and Olsen suggest, 'As we face the current crisis, perhaps it is useful to recall the "road not taken" and to take seriously the promise of the open dialogue approach.'[110] Laing too is a road not taken. I argue that it is time to take him seriously again.

The listening project

In 1969 Laing reflected on Kingsley Hall:

> One of the problems of recounting this story of Kingsley Hall is that the linear form of a verbal narrative is unadapted to the reality of the events, which are a set of patterns that undergo transformations, involving many people. And it is I think essentially impossible to translate without fundamental distortions the nature of those transformations into a narrative, which by its very nature requires you to put one word after the other.[111]

One might be tempted to similarly suggest that Laing too resists linearity and thus any account is subject to necessary distortions. The aim of this chapter is to re-view Laing through the lens of creative practice, and thus arguably I offer a double distortion as we move farther from 'the man himself'. However, his legacies in artistic practices allow us to consider the continued and developing value of his thinking and practice for reshaping clinical approaches to madness, psychiatry, and the figure of the psychiatrist. The threads that unite the three primary works are empathy, communication, and gaze. And here, as they variously grapple with the legibility and knowability of madness, they allow us to reconsider the valuable questions that Laing asked but that have yet to be answered. Moreover, while all markedly distinct in their forms and approaches, they share a common concern to make more room for alterity and thus recuperate madness from outside to within the ordinary spectrum of common human experience. Furthermore, all three works expose the manifest power structures of family life, psychiatry, and social communities. Indeed, in all three works the central characters are cast within multiple, interlocking social and medical structures. Moreover, the works expose their interdependence in the regulation of ordinary and 'normal' behaviours, both for individuals and communities. In so doing *Family Life, Mary Barnes*, and *All Divided Selves* examine alternatives to psychiatric expertise in the lives of patients. Here again they reignite our perception of the urgency of Laing's (and others') challenges to orthodox systems of thought and conduct. Finally, all three cast curious light on the capacity of artistic practice as a methodology for understanding and responding to mental distress. In so doing they pose a challenge to clinical practice by inviting a reconsideration of the terms of engagement in psychiatric assessment. At root, the three works consider how we speak, how we listen, and how we look at others. For example, rather than seeking to put one word after the other in patterns we already know, these three works reconfigure the very possibilities of language. Similarly, in engaging us in varied, distorted acts of listening, they return us to the limits and capacities of our ears for hearing. Likewise, through their exposure of psychiatric gaze we, as audiences, are reminded of the ideological labour at stake within all acts of spectatorship and looking in everyday life. Collectively, then, they invite us to consider if such alternative ways of speaking, listening, and seeing advanced by Laing and others ought not to be obsolete. In short, they offer that if we undertake the serious project of listening attentively to history, to Laing, to others, we might just hear the chords for a different future for psychiatric care.

Notes

1 William Shakespeare, *Twelfth Night* in *The Norton Shakespeare*, Stephen Greenblatt *et al.* (eds), (London and New York: W. W. Norton & Company, 1997), IV: ii, line 42–3, p. 1810.
2 Joe Penhall, *Blue/Orange* (London: Methuen, 2001), I, p. 28, emphasis original.
3 Penhall, III, p. 86.
4 Glen O. Gabbard and Krin Gabbard, *Psychiatry and the Cinema*, 2nd edn (Washington: American Psychiatric Press, 1999), p. 185. It is notable that of the works that study depictions of psychiatry on-screen, stage and in literature, a significant proportion are written by psychiatrists and other psych professionals.
5 Nikolas Rose, *Inventing Our Selves: Psychology, Power, and Personhood* (Cambridge: Cambridge University Press, 1998), p. 17.
6 Frank Furedi, *Therapy Culture: Cultivating Vulnerability in an Uncertain Age* (London: Routledge, 2004), p. 2, p. 21.
7 Ibid., p. 21.
8 I chose 'he' here deliberately. I am not an accidental misogynist; rather I am using it to reflect that historical (and still contemporary) fact that this is a profession dominated and led largely by men.
9 Adrian Laing interviewed in Dominic Harris, *The Residents: Stories of Kingsley Hall, East London, 1965–1970 and the Experimental Community of RD Laing*, self-published PDF and hardback, available only at www.dominicharris.co.uk (last accessed 24 September 2014), p. 61.
10 James Greene interviewed in *The Residents*, p. 61.
11 Miscellaneous document from The Round House relating to R. D. Laing lecture on 22 January 1978 in V&A archive; reference THM/271/2/2/149. (Accessed 2 September 2014), emphasis original.
12 See, for example, Mary Barnes and Joseph Berke, *Mary Barnes: Two Accounts of a Journey Through Madness* (London: Penguin, 1973).
13 Daniel Burston, *The Wings of Madness: The Life and Work of R. D. Laing* (Cambridge, MA: Harvard University Press, 1996), p. 233.
14 Ibid., p. 8.
15 Edward Shorter, *A History of Psychiatry: From the Era of the Asylum to the Age of Prozac* (Oxford: John Wiley & Sons, 1997), p. vii.
16 Ibid., p. viii.

17 Allan Beveridge, *Portrait of the Psychiatrist as a Young Man: The Early Writing and Work of R. D. Laing, 1927–1960* (Oxford: Oxford University Press, 2011), p. xiii.
18 While Laing is regularly framed as the figurehead of the so-called 'anti-psychiatry' movement, he did not coin the term (his colleague David Cooper did) and he firmly rejected this label throughout his career.
19 Beveridge, p. 48, emphasis original.
20 There are, of course, other ways one could approach Laing's legacies. There are numerous other artistic works about Laing that could be explored. There are innumerable documentaries and biographies about his life and writings. Moreover, this is to say nothing of Laing's own project of self-representation through his own poetry, song, film work, autobiography, and prose. However, the focus and examples have been selected owing to their particular imaginative engagement with his enduring notions of empathy and communication. As such this chapter is far from exhaustive. Readers, therefore, may wish to also explore the following: Noel Cobb's *Der Huset* (called *The House* in the UK), Erica Jong's *Fear of Flying*, Doris Lessing's *In the Four Gated City* and *Briefing for a Descent into Hell*, Mike Maran's *Did You Used to be RD Laing?* Anne McManus's *I Was a Mate of Ronnie Laing*, David Reed's *Anna*, Karel Reisz's *Morgan!* (called *A Suitable Case for Treatment* in the UK), Peter Robinson's *Asylum*, Clancy Sigal's *The Zone of the Interior*.
21 Notably a new play about R. D. Laing by Pamela Carter is currently in development with the National Theatre of Scotland and a film biopic, *Mad to Be Normal*, directed by Robert Mullan, was released by Gizmo Films just as this book manuscript was submitted (hence its omission) in February 2017.
22 See, for example, Richard Appignanesi and Sława Harasymowicz's *The Wolf Man*, Hugh Brody and Michal Ignatieff's *Nineteen Nineteen,* Christopher Hampton's *The Talking Cure* (and the film adaptation *A Dangerous Method*), John Huston's *Freud*, Terry Johnson's *Hysteria*, Mark St Germain's *Freud's Last Session*. While these works vary considerably in their style and framing of Freud, they share keen concern with biography and case histories in their approach. Important historical works like Adam Phillip's *Becoming Freud: The Making of a Psychoanalyst* are, however, revivifying Freud's contemporary relevance through the biographical frame.
23 There are a number of excellent biographies of Laing (some that also encompass critical thinking on his books). Four are of particular note: Adrian Laing's *R. D. Laing: A Life*, Daniel Burston's *Wings of Madness* and *The Crucible of Experience: R. D. Laing and the Crisis of Psychotherapy*, and Allan Beveridge's *Portrait of the Psychiatrist as a Young Man*. Laing's own autobiographical works are also of note: *Self and Others* (1961) and *Wisdom, Madness, and Folly: The Making of a Psychiatrist* (1985).
24 Beveridge, p. 48.
25 See Beveridge for a detailed discussion of his literary influences, pp. 158–81.
26 Derek Attridge, *The Singularity of Literature* (Abingdon: Routledge, 2004), p. 130.
27 The synergies between therapeutic and literary encounters are, of course, not new to observe; nor are gestures of feeling such as empathy solely the preserve of Laing. However, in the context of the rise of the second biological psychiatry in which the patient's experience is all too often marginalised, it is nonetheless worth re-exploring for our times. Laing had a firm sense that clinicians could learn from artists and his arguments for genuine interdisciplinary practice in psychiatry are yet to be properly realised and thus beg our attention.
28 *Family Life*, dir. by Ken Loach (EMI, 1972) [on DVD]. Hereafter *FL*, 14:16.
29 'Bin' is a British colloquialism for mental hospital or 'looney bin'.
30 Graham Fuller (ed.), *Loach on Loach* (London: Faber & Faber, 1998), p. 32.
31 Norman Silverstein, 'Two R. D. Laing Movies: *Wednesday's Child* and *Asylum*, in *Film Quarterly*, 26:4, Summer 73, pp. 2–9, p. 2. *FL* was titled *Wednesday's Child* outside the UK.
32 *FL*, 25:40.
33 In an interview for *Jump Cut* magazine, the film's producer Tony Garnett explains the direct influence of Laing's writings on the film. See 'Interview with Tony Garnett and Ken Loach: *Family Life* in the Making' in *Jump Cut*, no. 10–11, 1976, pp. 43–5.

34 *FL*, 01:37:06.
35 R. D. Laing, *The Divided Self* (London: Penguin, 1960), p. 20.
36 Beveridge, p. 71.
37 Tony Garnett, *Jump Cut*, p. 45.
38 Ken Loach in *Loach on Loach*, p. 45.
39 Loach in Jacob Leigh, *The Cinema of Ken Loach: Art in the Service of the People* (London: Wallflower, 2002), p. 119.
40 See, for example, 'Will the Real Ronnie Laing Stand Up?', dir. by Ken Craig, episode 124 of *Something to Say*, first aired 30 October 1972.
41 *FL*, 58:46.
42 Loach in *Jump Cut*, p. 45.
43 *FL*, 01:42:32.
44 *FL*, 01:42:42.
45 *FL*, 01:42:12.
46 *FL*, 01:41:13.
47 Laing, *The Divided Self*, p. 31.
48 Ibid.
49 Talking Heads, *This Must Be the Place (Naïve Melody)* (Sire, 1983) [on vinyl].
50 the vacuum cleaner, www.thevacuumcleaner.co.uk/madloveasylum (last accessed 1 October 2016)
51 Laing is not the sole pioneer of this kind of initiative. Related activities were happening in North America such as Maxwell Jones' Belmont Hospital.
52 See Arthur W. Frank, *The Wounded Storyteller: When Bodies Need Voices* (Chicago: Chicago University Press, 1995).
53 I recognise that *Mary Barnes*, unlike *Family Life*, is based on memoir and, therefore, is drawn from Mary's lived experiences which, by all accounts, were dramatic. However, what I wish to pay close attention to here is a broader sense of narrative(s) that surrounds Mary's life, artistic representation, and self-representation.
54 Mary Barnes, in Mary Barnes and Joe Berke, *Mary Barnes: Two Accounts of a Journey Through Madness* (London: Penguin, 1973), p. 109.
55 Elaine Showalter, *The Female Malady: Women, Madness, and English Culture, 1830–1980* (London: Virago, 1987), p. 236.
56 Mary Barnes, Interview with Angela Neustatter in *The Guardian*, 5 January 1979.
57 David Edgar, 'Letter to Harriet Cruickshank', in V&A Theatre Archives. Catalogue reference: THM/273/712/474.
58 Hans Keller, *Spectator*, 20 January 1979.
59 J. C. Trewin, *The Illustrated London News*, March 1979.
60 Michael Billington, *The Guardian*, 2 September 1978.
61 Nicholas de Jongh, *The Guardian*, 12 January 1979.
62 Mary Barnes, Interview with Angela Neustatter in *The Guardian*, 5 January 1979.
63 Janelle Reinelt and Gerry Hewitt, *The Political Theatre of David Edgar* (Cambridge: Cambridge University Press, 2011), p. 10, p. 268.
64 David Edgar, 'Mary Barnes' in *Plays: One* (London: Methuen, 1987), III:8, p. 164. Hereafter *MB*.
65 Tim Shields, 'Theatricality & Madness: Minding the Mind-Doctors' in Daniel Meyer Dinkgräfe (ed.), *The Professions in Contemporary Drama* (Bristol: Intellect Books, 2003), pp. 37–45, p. 41.
66 Edgar, *MB*, III: 8, p. 163.
67 Ibid., II: 4, p. 134.
68 Ibid., I: 10, p. 120.
69 Ibid., III: 3, p. 162.
70 Ibid., I: 4, p. 105.
71 Samuel Taylor Coleridge, 'The Rime of the Ancient Mariner', *The Complete Poems*, W. Keach (ed.), (London: Penguin, 1997), p. 158.
72 Morton Schatzman interviewed in *The Residents*, p. 46.

73 Adrian Laing interviewed in *The Residents*, p. 20.
74 See, for example, an interview with Laing on the subject of Kingsley Hall in Robert Mullan's *Mad to Be Normal* (London: Free Association Books, 1995), pp. 172–93, p. 185.
75 Thomas Szasz, quoted in *Spectator*, 20 January 1979.
76 James Greene, interviewed in *The Residents*, p. 46.
77 Jutta Laing, interviewed in *The Residents*, p. 44.
78 Joe Berke, in *Mary Barnes: Two Accounts of a Journey Through Madness*, p. 268.
79 Edgar, *MB*, II: 8, p. 142.
80 Ibid., I: 5, p. 105.
81 Anthony Thwaite, *Critics Forum*, BBC Radio 3, broadcast on 13 January 1979.
82 David Harsent, *New Statesman*, 19 January 1979.
83 Clancy Sigal, *Critics Forum*.
84 Beverly Brown, *Morning Star*, 30 January 1979.
85 Edgar, *MB*, III: 5, p. 156.
86 Ibid., III: 7, p. 161.
87 Ibid., II: 3, pp. 127–8.
88 Ibid., III: 9, p. 165.
89 Ibid., III: 9, p. 166.
90 Ibid., III: 8, p. 164.
91 Edgar, *Time Out*, 12 January 1979.
92 Edgar, Interviewed in Simon Trussler (ed.), *New Theatre Voices of the Seventies* (London: Methuen, 1981), p. 163.
93 Reinelt and Hewitt, p. 177.
94 Joanna Moncrieff, *The Myth of the Chemical Cure: A Critique of Psychiatric Drug Treatment*, rev'd edn (London: Palgrave, 2009), p. 95.
95 Ibid., p. 101.
96 Walter Benjamin, 'Theses on the Philosophy of History, XVI' in *Illuminations*, trans. by Harry Zorn (London: Pimlico, 1999), p. 254.
97 R. D. Laing, 'I', *Knots* (London: Penguin, 1970), p. 5.
98 The other two are *What You See Is Where You're At* (2001) and *Bogman Palmjaguar* (2007).
99 Quotation taken from therapeutic meeting in Fowler, *All Divided Selves*, LUX Distribution, 2011, 40:11.
100 Quotation taken from a news report in Luke Fowler's *All Divided Selves*, 01:13:03.
101 Pink Floyd, 'Comfortably Numb', Harvest/Columbia, 1979.
102 One may wish to extend Frank's assessment to other visual forms that demand multiple focusses of attention and allow for simultaneity, juxtaposition, discontinuity such as theatre practice. However, this is not the moment for this discussion.
103 Laing, interview footage in *All Divided Selves*, 01:29:44.
104 Alasdair Roberts, 'Hidden Sin', in *All Divided Selves*, 01:32:55.
105 A play from 2014 by Ridiculusmus, *The Eradication of Schizophrenia in Western Lapland*, explores this practice in detail. Notably, the piece makes explicit reference to Laing's writings.
106 Moncrieff, p. 99.
107 James Davies, *The Sedated Society: The Causes and Harms of our Psychiatric Drug Epidemic* (London: Palgrave, 2017), p. 4.
108 Robert Whitaker, *Mad in America: Bad Science, Bad Medicine, and the Enduring Mistreatment of the Mentally Ill*, rev'd edn (Philadelphia: Basic Books, 2010), p. 303.
109 Jaakko Seikkula and Mary E. Olsen, 'The Open Dialogue Approach to Acute Psychosis: Its Poetics and Micropolitics', in *Family Process*, 42:3, 2003, pp. 403–18, pp. 410–11.
110 Ibid., p. 416.
111 Laing, quoted in *The Residents*, p. 2.

2

'I GUESS THAT THIS MUST BE THE PLACE'[1]

Sites of Madness

Upon his committal to Bethlem Asylum, it is (infamously) reported that the Restoration dramatist Nathaniel Lee remarked, 'They called me mad, and I called them mad, and damn them, they outvoted me.'[2] Aside from its wit, the retort conveys several themes that cling, limpet-like, onto the institutional history of psychiatry: the collective, faceless power of the professional 'they'; the role of language in the social and medical execution of difference; the quivering thresholds of normalcy. If Chapter 1 considered the figure of the psychiatrist and argued for the centrality of empathetic, attentive listening in any act of psychiatric care, then this chapter turns to consider the spaces in which those dialogues have been staged. I am concerned to examine how artists have figured the asylum, the hospital, and the community in order to understand the human and aesthetic meanings of space in mental care contexts and practices. How do environments, bodies, and behaviours collide and thereby mutually produce the feelings and realities of a given place and time? It is not new to suggest that space is an active constituent of social meaning and values. Nor is it bold to contend that spaces do not have static, singular, or spontaneous meanings, but rather it is through the interactions of people, things, and the material space that lived experience is forged. However, in the context of the history of madness and its sanctioned civic places, space has a particularly pockmarked history. This is witnessed not least in the segregative spirit that has characterised much of the past two hundred years or so of psychiatric practice, but also more casually in the metaphors of madness that dust our everyday speech: one is round the twist, in a dark place, gone doolally, out of your tree.[3] Moreover, research with survivors, service-users, and those with a mental illness diagnosis also reveals that space and journeying are dominant modes of narrating our experiences of pain, despair, joy and anguish.[4] However, while institutional spaces have played front and centre in the big narratives of psychiatric history, less room overall has been given to both patients' experiences of sites and also the inter-relations between these places and their wider social and political milieus.[5] This chapter picks up, though, a third dropped stitch in the knit of this story:

culture. How have artists captured and communicated psychiatric spaces? And what *kinds* of evidence can we gather from their work to help forge more creative and humane alternatives to current practices? It is the contention of this chapter that the three artists examined collectively seek to redistribute the terms and structures of knowledge and power in relation to the psychiatric treatment spaces. They thereby take vital steps towards making sure that we all have a place, and a safe place to be.

Frederick Wiseman's 1967 documentary *Titicut Follies*, Joe Penhall's 2000 play *Blue/Orange*, and the vacuum cleaner's (aka James Leadbitter) live art practices including *The Ship of Fools* (2011), *MENTAL* (2013), and *Madlove* (2014–19) form the focus of the chapter. The works span two countries,[6] 52 years (though *Titicut* was actually banned and therefore largely unseen until 1991), and at least three aesthetic practices, not to mention straddling the radical shifts in the history, policy, and approaches within formal psychiatric care. Indeed, the works in some ways map messily onto the broad brushstrokes of these latter movements. If *Titicut* holds asylum life in filmic suspension, then *Blue/Orange* captures a form of hospital bureaucratic managerialism in aspic, while Leadbitter's projects intervene in the contemporary values and shapes of community care. The language here is not to suggest that the two former pieces are fixed and over-determined; rather it is to point to the particularity of both Wiseman and Penhall's focus and the historicised gestures housed therein, and also to signal the currently unfurling, unfinished, and expansive nature of Leadbitter's work. Far from congealing the meaning of Wiseman and Penhall's work, I simply aim to draw attention to the distinction between the (relative) conceptual certainty of the asylum and hospital as opposed to the amorphous multivalence of 'community' and consider the consequences of this for the form and politics of the art works. Nevertheless, while marked divergences provide valuable points of tension between these works, keen similarities are as abundant. Indeed, in key manners the works shudder in political unison. The works share thematic preoccupations with human expression, power, authority, knowledge, voice, and shame. All three artists question what it means to care, what constitutes a community, and how far the political capacity to be heard is conditioned through interlocking, authoritative discourses. Echoing Foucault here, the artists sound a clarion note that madness and its discontents are inscribed in discursive formations.[7] Taking each artist in turn, this chapter will sketch the ways in which the works politically engage with spaces of madness and cultures of harm. The chapter will argue that, through aesthetic means, the three attempt to redistribute the locus of knowledge about madness, widen the aperture of perceptual realities, and decentre the question of where to 'put' madness. In their interrogations of space and place, they provoke new and vital considerations as to what a hospitable community of support might actually feel like.

The less we say about it the better

Psychiatric history is a cannibal. The standard grand narrative of institutional life is one of flawed progress, but progress nonetheless. In this sense, the horrors of the past

are quickly self-devoured in the appetite for present success, and belched as aber-
rance. We have moved from barbarous chains through dismal loony bins through
unworkable hospitals to the fuzzy promise of community. However, as Andrew Scull
is right to point out, the tendency to pour scorn on our predecessors is rife in the
canon of psychiatric history. He notes the zeal of the nineteenth-century lunacy
reformers who 'pictured the preceding age as mired in ignorance and cruelty, conjuring up indelible images of monstrous madhouse-keepers beating their patients
into submission, chaining them up like wild beasts in foul holding-pens filled with
shit, straw, and stench.'[8] Scull here is not offering a recuperation of the long eighteenth century as a bastion of compassionate care; rather he is, following Roy Porter's
Mind Forg'd Manacles, simply disturbing the Whiggish castigation of *then* in the cel-
ebration of *now*.[9] Observing the rhetoric of the asylum movement which cast the
family and community as an inadequate space to contain madness, Scull notes 'how
consistently those in charge of the system, indeed society as a whole, sought to
deflect attention away from the horrors of the present by resurrecting the tales of the
barbarities of the past.'[10] Moreover, this pattern persists through the twentieth century. Deinstitutionalisation, for a period, rode high on the crest of a wave of long-
awaited progress that 'would finally liberate mental patients from the shackles of the
past.'[11] Indeed, between the late-1950s and mid-1970s there was 'a veritable flood of
social scientific research [which] elucidated the baneful effects of confinement in an
institution.'[12] The point again here is not to suggest that asylums and hospitals were
actually fine and in no need of reform. It is merely to caution against neat tales of
progress. The wild optimism of the asylum movement meets its match in the wild
optimism of the decarceration movement. While psychiatric history may, at times,
appear to eat its own tail, it is indisputable that space and environment have held a
central position in the debates. As James E. Moran and Jonathan Andrews articulate:

> Spatial separation has been one of the most frequent social responses to mad-
> ness. From the early modern period to the present, designing and creating alter-
> native spaces, whether conceived as curative, healing, managerial, or custodial,
> has dominated the Western response to those considered mentally troubled.[13]

While it is beyond the scope of this chapter to offer a comprehensive account of
this history, I will briefly sketch the key developments that pertain to this study of
Wiseman, Penhall, and Leadbitter.[14]

Containing history

Throughout the seventeenth and much of the eighteenth century, the 'management' of madness remained a largely community and family affair. Foucault's claims
regarding 'the great confinement' in *Madness and Civilisation* have been roundly and
rigorously disputed: 'Not only does his genealogical narrative of the confinement
of the mad in early modern Europe include some extravagant historical inaccura-
cies but his concern with the high politics of knowledge and the architecture of

institutional power reduces the cast of historical players to a few seminal figures and obscures the complex world of institutional conventions and community preferences.'[15] Indeed, it is not until the nineteenth century that one can witness a coordinated and state-led model of detention for those they called mad. Within this regime, the professionalization of care emerges and thereby the expert rises. If in the eighteenth century it was assumed that madness was visible, the nineteenth century saw it burrow inside. This shift required the professional eyes of the psychiatrists to unlock the secrets of a soul undone. On both sides of the Atlantic, by mid-century, the stage was set for a model of care that would endure for over a hundred more years. As Gerald Grob states:

> In 1840 eight asylums admitted an average of 180 patients; a decade later twenty-two institutions admitted nearly 329 persons... This process of expansion would continue for more than a century; not until 1955 did the total inpatient population peak at nearly 559,000.[16]

The UK asylum archives tell a broadly similar tale of expansion. In 1845, there were around 95,600 asylum patients rising to around 155,000 in 1954.[17] Moreover, the emptying of the bins – though more rapid in North America – occurs in tandem and is woven around shared humanitarian rhetoric of better care for mentally ill persons. Between 1955 and 1991 the UK asylum population fell from 150,000 to 43,000. American hospital populations halved between 1955 and 1974.[18] The asylum, which had in part marked a rejection of the family and community as capable carers, was decisively abandoned in favour of the community and family. Of course, as Peter Bartlett and David Wright point out, in the asylum era 'the household remained an important locus of care for the insane, and families maintained a central role in the decisions over treatment.'[19] Moreover, discharged patients in the nineteenth century were often observed via a 'long leash' discharge and thus 'the practice of monitoring ex-patients in the community is as old as the asylum itself.'[20] Thus, while the shift in the 1950s towards community was a radical break, it is misleading to conceive of the asylum and the community as strangers. Further, as Scull argues, anti-institutional campaigns were very present in the nineteenth century and so one has to consider why such battles were lost at that time but were won in the next century.

Bartlett and Wright suggest that care in the community 'holds the dubious distinction of being universally supported in principle, and universally condemned in practice.'[21] It is often assumed that the move toward community care was heralded by the pharmacological revolution of the mid-1950s. However, authors such as Scull have contested the chronology of this claim and instead point toward the interlocking forces that fuelled the change: fiscal, ideological, psychiatric, social, legal. If the anti-asylum movement failed in the nineteenth century, it was owing to a number of reasons: the recentness of the vast finances invested made people reluctant to tear asunder their ventures; the lack of a welfare system; the ghoulish shadows of eighteenth-century treatment; and relief for some that the 'burden' of care had shifted off their shoulders. However, the terms of the debate had altered by the 1950s. The rise of welfare support, the unionisation of hospital staff, the upkeep of failing buildings, and the declining ability to exploit patients as internal labour force in both nations rendered asylum care vastly expensive. Indeed, the revival of anti-institutional activism and discourse was now useful to governments insofar as it allowed them 'to save money while simultaneously giving their policy a humanitarian gloss'.[22] When combined with the humanitarian discourses – perhaps most notably Erving Goffman's *Asylums* – and the development of drugs, the argument for change was won.[23] The appalling aftermath of this policy, however, is far from triumphant. Care in the community has, all too frequently, meant poor or non-existent care, ghettoisation, social isolation, and homelessness. As Peter Sedgwick has written, 'In Britain no less than in the United States, "community care" and "the replacement of the mental hospitals" were slogans which masked the growing depletion of real services for mental patients.'[24] Indeed, particularly in the early decades of the policy:

> Deinstitutionalisation of the mentally ill, while securing the negative right to be free of organised interference in one's life, has all too often meant the denial of the positive right to care and attention. As a result, for the majority of those affected with chronic mental illness, what has changed is the packaging rather than the reality of their misery.[25]

It is clear that planning and practices of care in the community have improved since their hasty introduction. Moreover, research suggests that there is some clear patient support for treatment in non-hospital contexts where possible. What is less clear is how far the fundaments of the practice have been properly interrogated. Precisely what constitutes a 'community' in this care framework? How has the move to community affected the individual's experience of discharge and illness narrative? How does the ever-expanding use of Community Treatment Orders [CTO] impact on one's sense of autonomy?[26] As Bean and Mounser suggest, 'Patients simply have their status as a patient reactivated at the switch of the community treatment programme.'[27] Or, as one patient put it: 'once under the surgeon's knife, always under the surgeon's knife.'[28] Yet while there is certainly widespread support from psychiatrists for CTOs given their ever-increasing use, the evidence for their efficacy, as we saw in the introduction, is not robust.[29] It is outside my disciplinary training to offer any sustained interrogation of the clinical literature. However, it is reasonable to suggest that the state of mental health care is inadequate, too reliant on pharmacology, and experienced as coercive, punitive, and dehumanising by a significant proportion of the population with a mental health diagnosis. Moreover, critiques of community care tend to be overly preoccupied with procedure and bureaucracy as opposed to a more conceptual exploration of what community, care, and wellness might actually mean for people. As Diana Gittens uncovered in her study of staff and patient experiences of Severalls Hospital: 'Drugs provide a relatively cheap, and easily administered, solution to controlling violence and acute distress, even if they do not cure. Almost all of the patients I spoke to, however, felt that factors such as a beautiful and spacious environment, time, psychotherapy, religious belief and, above all, love, were ultimately what helped them most towards recovery.'[30] Embedded within this summary are core issues around class (beauty and space), listening (time and therapy), and value (belief and love). And while the purpose of this chapter is certainly not to suggest that 'all you need is love', and that this is literature's cosy offer, I would suggest that we dismiss such tenets of humanity at our peril. This chapter argues that, in fact, these art works invite us to think rigorously, politically, and conceptually about our feeling responses to madness. The focus on the surface 'packaging' marks a failure to listen to the depth and breadth of experience. I propose that these creative works mark a sustained and careful engagement with patient-led alternatives to current practice.

Being direct

Frederick Wiseman was a key figure in the Direct Cinema movement in America in the 1960s and 1970s. A satellite figure of the Drew Associates, Wiseman adopted the practices of a stripped back form of cinematic framing. As Jillian Smith summarises:

> None of Wiseman's films include interviews, music, or voice-overs, no narration, no external method of explanation, no Edward Murrow essays to launch us off or catch us as we land. The films are intensive exercises in location; sound and lighting are found, never supplied.[31]

Unlike their European Cinéma Vérité counterparts who, in Brechtian gestures, foregrounded the apparatus of cinematic telling, the exponents of Direct Cinema sought to dissolve personnel and technology in pursuit of objectivity. Wiseman describes this desire for a filmic vanishing act: 'The way I try to make a documentary is that there's no separation between the audience watching the film and the events in the film. It's like the business of getting rid of the proscenium arch in the theater.'[32] Much research at the time, and in the intervening years, has exposed the luminous flaws in such claims and Direct Cinema's truth claims overall, not least with respect to questions of neutrality, ethics, and the editing 'reality'.[33] However, what Wiseman intends and claims for his work and how one understands the work need not marry. For the purpose of this discussion, our attention, therefore, will turn away from the movement's ambitions to questions of gaze, shame, and bureaucracy in *Titicut Follies*.

Wiseman's starting impetus to make *Titicut Follies* was to educate the trainee prosecutors he was teaching at Boston University Law School about where they were potentially sending their clients. Filmed at Bridgewater State Hospital in 1966 with the permission of the then Superintendent, Charles Gaughan, the film offers a fragmented vision of institutional life. After some initial screenings in New York in 1968, the film was stopped in its tracks and the state of Massachusetts fought and won a legal battle to have the film banned on grounds of breach of contract and inmates' rights to privacy. Revealingly, some staff also launched claims that their privacy had been breached insofar as it was not always clear who was a patient and who was staff. The original case ordered not only that the film be banned but also that it must be permanently destroyed. Wiseman successfully appealed and this saved the negatives from the furnace and also permitted a select group of professionals to be able to see the film, on condition that they signed an affidavit to the effect that they were on the list of appropriate professions (such as psychiatrists, doctors, social workers, and so on) who were deemed suitable viewers.[34] The ruling was finally overturned in 1991, and the film was aired on the American television channel PBS on 4 September 1992 and on BBC2 on 27 March 1993.

May not be suitable for all viewers

As Jillian Smith notes, the mad themselves are notable by their absence from the list of proper viewers for *Titicut Follies*:

> the primary movement against the distracted mind is in establishing a coher-ent subject/object relationship, wherein the practising subject's practice assumes and maintains authority and anteriority and distance over the sub-ject/object. All of this becomes strikingly clear when we consider who is not on the list of authorized viewers: the insane themselves.[35]

In his summary of the case, the judge said of Wiseman, 'he abused the privilege [of making the film] showing identifiable inmates naked or in other *embarrassing situations*.'[36] What is particularly striking here is the locus of shame in tandem with the distribution of knowledge. The ruling tacitly suggests that the inevitable gaze of viewers is one of pity. Viewer and viewed are caught in a mutual and reciprocal act of shame and shaming. The act of looking and the captured behaviours are what are cast as shameful here rather than the structures that produce such conditions of despair and degradation. The 'excessive nudity' is thus cast as a problem of gaze and not of routine, systemic abuse.[37] This is not to suggest that there are no questions of consent at stake here for the institutionally looked upon in *Titicut Follies*. However, what is vital to apprehend is how far the judge's summary relies upon already agreed social scripts regarding the shameful nature of madness. For shame, we ought to look away. A paradoxical dignity is presumed conferred by turning away from bruised life. And what is more, it is then kept in its private place.[38] Moreover, only 'expert' eyes can properly decipher such improper scenes. The judge reasoned that 'because of the character of such audiences, the likelihood *of humiliation*, even of identifiable inmates, is greatly reduced.'[39] It is the conten-tion of this chapter that, in fact, the film's refusal to tidy away and metaphori-cally 'clothe' madness offers not only a searing critique of the asylum system but also forms a valuable counterpoint to the sanitised nature of much contemporary anti-stigma campaigning.

The ruling related not only to content but crucially to form. The judge summarised that:

> The film is 80 minutes of sordidness and human degradation. It is a hodge-podge of sequences, with the camera jumping, helter-skelter…There is no narrative accompanying the film, nor are there any subtitles, without which the film is a distortion of the daily routine and conditions at the institution. Each viewer is left to his own devices as to just what is being portrayed.[40]

In short, knowledge is not organised for the viewer. And indeed, the judge is correct in this sense. As a viewer, one's coordinates are deliberately disturbed. For example, in the opening of *Titicut Follies* the camera cuts from the follies (institutional cabaret/revue) to strip searches to a patient interview without establishing context or deploying conventions, such as regular edit lengths or direct to camera address. This form, as Smith argues, means that 'the whole film unrolls in long takes that never offer holistic consideration' and suggests that such strategies work to 'flatten the fields of the viewer and the viewed by destabilising the familiar hierarchy.'[41] Moreover, the choice to begin the film with the follies performance immediately invites a theatrical gaze. If, in theatre (as we will discuss at length in Chapter 4) things and people are simultaneously absolutely and not at all what they appear to be, then to open a documentary that promises authenticity with a scene of hyperbolic theatrical performance signals a desire to unsettle visual certainty. The collision, here, of a documentary register with a performative dynamic invites the notion of possibility into the frame in political manners. It is both *the way it is* and *constructed*. If this is the case, then the way it is could become the way it was. Change thus becomes an undercurrent in *Titicut*, that politically curves the documentary lens in order to see the alternatives that might lie round the bend.

Time wasters

Alongside this drubbing of orders of power through form, the visual tessellation of the film creates an asphyxiating sense of time. The looping 'helter-skelter' form paradoxically draws attention to causality and continuity and, in so doing, offers an affective expression of the doubled time signature of institutional life; at once regimental and bloated. One's time is there to be exhausted via the routines set by others. Writing in 2011 about patients' experience of compulsory treatment, it is sobering that the following still apparently needs stating: 'offering patients choice over some aspects of their involuntary stay (i.e. type of medication, involvement in activities in the ward, control over sleeping/eating routines etc.) might increase their sense of control in their lives.'[42] The neo-absurdist exhaustion of time witnessed in *Titicut Follies* through regimes of washing, shaving, singing, searches, observations, and so forth creates a mood of banal horror.

FIGURE 2.1   Exercise yard in *Titicut Follies*

The long slow pan of the camera across the exercise yard, for example, captures men filling time in order to waste it (Figure 2.1).

Moreover, as one man, Vladimir, vigorously and clearly explains, he only came down for observation [from prison] and has been here for 18 months and is deteriorating because of the environment and because 'the medication has harmed me.'[43] After pleading to the doctors during his case conference, the decision is taken to up his dose of tranquilisers to help 'tone this down'.[44] As the narrator of Susanna Kaysen's novel *Girl, Interrupted* reminds us, time is often violently destroyed in hospital:

> When digital watches were invented years later they reminded me of five-minute checks. They murdered time in the same way – slowly – chopping off pieces of it and lobbing them into the dustbin with a little click to let you know time was gone. Click, swish, 'Checks,' swish, click: another five minutes of life down the drain. And spent in this place.[45]

Wiseman's lingering, irregular time signature in this way mimics the felt experience of institutional detention in Bridgewater Hospital and thereby invites us as viewers to sit and feel the passing of time, to sit between the tick and the tock, killing time.

The other striking element of time for *Titicut Follies* lies in the queer temporality of its belated release. The temptation is, of course, to read its barbarities as historic. Writing in *The Independent* in 1993, for example, Nady Gill described it as a 'howl from the Dark Ages of psychiatric practise [sic].'[46] However, one ought to caution against the neatness of retrospect. Indeed, Wiseman's wry final scene titles themselves warn against setting too much store in progress (Figures 2.2 and 2.3).

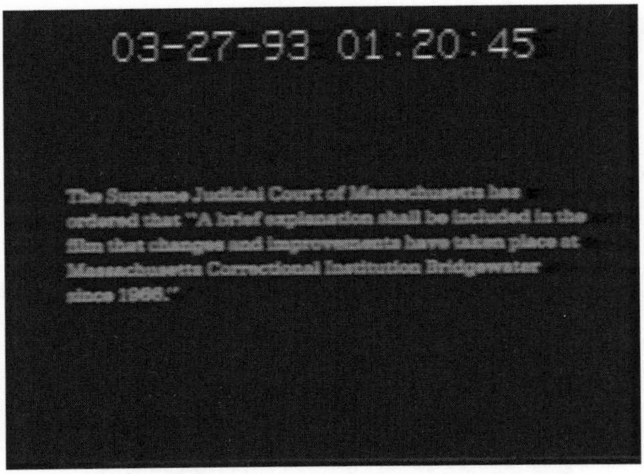

FIGURE 2.2 Final titles from *Titicut Follies*

FIGURE 2.3 Final titles from *Titicut Follies*

Now fifty years on from its recording, we can be confident that some of the extremities of cruelty witnessed in the film are rare in both Britain and America. Nevertheless, the themes and moods it burned onscreen remain unresolved. Snaking through a wide range of contemporary literature (from medical research to memoir) are the same concerns with autonomy and coercion, respect and humiliation, power and impotence. Thus, while *Titicut Follies'* past howls, our present also roars.

What are you looking at?

Perhaps the most remarked-upon scene from *Titicut Follies* is the force-feeding of a naked, emaciated patient by a smoking Doctor whose fag ash teeters nonchalantly over the funnel of liquid (Figure 2.4).

FIGURE 2.4   Doctor administering force-feeding in *Titicut Follies*

Paula Rabinowitz remarks: 'The sheer casualness of the scene, the regularity with which this must've happened, is clear from the relaxed banter; nothing out of the ordinary here.'[47] The passive man is called a 'veteran' by the doctor and praised for being a 'very good patient, very nice' and staff joke that he should 'chew his food' and ask if they should use 'the same stuff for the other guy'.[48] The still picture of his resigned body is only disrupted by his 'convulsively shuddering throat'.[49] It is an unremarkable hospital scene. Wiseman intercuts the feeding with shots of the same man being embalmed and placed in the morgue. The editing here allows the earlier stillness of the man's body to be visually echoed in his final stillness. Wiseman thereby creates a living ghost, and one that accuses us all in his passing. The camera viewpoint positions us in the feeding circle surrounding the man and through this we, as viewers, exchange glances with other men. We too stand by and do nothing. Indeed, throughout the film there are numerous scenes of people watching; watching things, watching people, watching procedures, reminding us of our own act of looking. Rabinowitz again suggests that hospitals such as Bridgewater are 'shameful places because they are so shameless in their guilelessness, their arrogance.'[50] While one can agree that the apparently invisible violence of the scene actually exposes the cruelty of the regime and its staff, one also has to question our desire to see such pain. Should we look away here? Should we look away later as another naked man called Jim is bullied by staff about the cleanliness of his room until he is so agitated that all he can do is stomp his feet over and over and over? Should we look away then? As Susan Sontag questioned, how should one properly regard the pain of others?[51]

In many ways, *Titicut Follies* is part of a long-standing exposé tradition. From Dorothea Dix to Nellie Bly to Clifford Beers to Albert Q. Maisel to David Rosenhan to Susan Sheehan, Irma Kurtz, Peter Thomson, Clifford J. Levy and others, undercover or post-discharge exposés of asylums and hospitals are a well-worn literary genre.[52] Indeed, films such as Samuel Fuller's 1963 *Shock Corridor* are structured around such an exposé plot. Scull has been critical of the value of many exposés arguing that they are often neither bold nor effective: 'one must ask what all these assaults amounted to, in what respects they were novel, and how far they contributed to the dissolution of the segregative approach to mental illness.'[53] Furthermore, he remains somewhat sceptical overall about the contribution of art and literature to the psychiatric debates around care and treatment.[54] Under such a view, art is a rather limp opponent to psychiatry. Thus, the justification for looking at bodies in distress in works like *Titicut Follies* becomes rather strained. However, as Sharon L. Snyder and David T. Mitchell propose in their study of disability:

> Because most people have the majority of their interactions with disability through written and visual materials, the analysis of this domain can provide significant interventions into the public representation of bodily, sensory, and cognitive difference. While such an analysis often entails exposing debilitating depictions, this cultural work is necessary and even paramount to influencing the ideological agenda of disability.[55]

Imogen Tyler similarly argues for the corrosive capacity of negative social representation suggesting that 'symbolic violence is converted into terms of material violence that are embodied and lived.'[56] If we accept that artistic practice shapes social, perceptual, and ideological realities, then its effect on our looking becomes rather more urgent than Scull affords. Indeed, it is precisely in his refusal of the logic and dynamics of shame in his unflinching camerawork that, I propose, Wiseman presses his most radical statement.

Someone like you

Sara Ahmed discusses the dual dynamics of exposure and concealment that attend on shame and suggests that shame demands a covering over in the very moment of being revealed. Moreover, she observes how shame turns the body against itself and yet is always relational: 'Shame becomes felt as a matter of being – of the relation of self to itself – insofar as shame is about appearance, about how the subject appears before and to others.'[57] Shame experiences necessarily involve, then, 'intercorporeality and sociality.'[58] The initial attack upon *Titicut Follies* by the authorities turned on an axis of shame and privacy: these were people and situations to be protected from our shaming eyes. If we turn to contemporary anti-stigma campaigning such as that led by Time to Change and See Me, much of this too, I suggest, inadvertently turns on dynamics of shame. We are encouraged to be open and talk on the basis that there is nothing to be ashamed of. We are encouraged to refuse the social experience of shame by heading it off at the pass with defiant self-respect. While this approach totally overlooks the structural and systemic production of shame, one can follow and embrace a campaign that supports and encourages the demystification of psychological distress and difference. However, if one lingers on the terms of the demystifying project, a more problematic picture of anti-stigma campaigns emerges. The will to both normalise and medicalise that characterises a significant proportion of the anti-stigma work is problematic, I argue, on three grounds. Firstly, likening, for example, depression to a broken leg is unhelpful. Countless popular articles about depression recirculate this thinking: 'The only difference between having a mental illness and having a broken bone or the common cold, or cancer is that the latter are physical.'[59] Depression is not like a broken leg and such a characterisation actually serves to further obscure the experience of depression by flattening its complexity and turning a blind eye to the very stigma it aims to counter. Secondly, it places mental illness in polite soft focus. Only a select range of madnesses are visible in these campaigns and one risks, thereby, creating further categorisation of 'good' and 'bad' madness. Thirdly, the objective appears to be to reassure *them* that *we* are OK. Time to Change's *Schizo* the movie campaign usefully sought to counter the cinematic mad-axe-man stereotype but did so by presenting a figure who embodied a set of normative values. A white, middle-class, middle-aged, heterosexual man functioned to prove schizophrenia was just another illness. Moreover, the contrast between the heightened aesthetics in the film and the weakness of the delivery of the dialogue creates an image of vulnerable victim-hood in problematic manners. While I appreciate the impetus behind the project, it is my contention that the strategy to disprove a stereotype actually loops back to, and indeed relies upon, a set of normative values which exclude and marginalise. The tacit 'just like you' model enacts a symbolic violence against all of those who are not and cannot, or who will not, pretend to be normal.

Titicut Follies makes no effort to normalise or soften. In its child-like willingness to stare, it could be presumed rude. Furthermore, in its rejection of contextual information it risks homogenising its subjects. Yet, as Smith contends, the men remain defined: 'it is easy to generalise them as emblems of their situation, ignoring their utter singularity. But Wiseman's subjects are absolutely singular, utterly specific, and they resist being emblems because they resist being abstracted from the material field in which they are embedded.'[60] While there remains a problem of making bodies 'speak' through the documentary frame, a position which is particularly acute for an already over-observed and deciphered asylum population, Wiseman's apparent desire to make these men be anything other than what they are is a political *gesture*. Further, as Raymond Williams suggested, 'There are in fact no masses; there are only ways of seeing people as masses.'[61] Wiseman offers a doubled frame then: one that perceives individuals within a system of mass. These are edited realities, of course, but Wiseman is steadfast on our behalf in his refusal to look away. In this way, we are invited into a more complex but more radical contract with mental alterity. By remaining within the frame, Wiseman's complex subjects broaden the aperture of human experience. Moreover, by zeroing in on the men's lived experiences of the hospital, Wiseman redirects our gaze from bureaucracy and architecture to the bodies that matter.

Stage left

British dramatist Joe Penhall came to prominence in the 1990s amidst a wave of new writers such as Sarah Kane, Mark Ravenhill, and Phillip Ridley. While being a more conventional playwright than his contemporaries, he shared their collective engagement with social politics. Indeed, in the introduction to his first collection of plays, Penhall explains the political impetus behind the composition of his dramatic works that examine mental illness. It was, in part, a response to the inadequacy of his then current occupation – a journalist: 'I felt strongly that newspaper articles weren't enough to convey the true misery and loneliness of schizophrenia.'[62] For Penhall, it seems clear that theatre is a site of feeling in particular and politicised manners insofar as the form gives three-dimensional, emotional shape to arguments of resistance. Theatre appears to promise a more affective encounter with discrimination than is available in print media. However, as Alan Read's *Theatre, Intimacy, and Engagement: The Last Human Venue* has suggested, all human activities are politicised: 'The error has precisely been to leave these two terms [theatre and politics] bonded in a fantasy of expectation and hope while patronising them both with the commiseration of a failure.'[63] Read's argument proceeds to suggest that 'theatre has no political power. But it does have ethical effect.'[64] What Read troubles in his book is the presumption that self-proclaimed 'political theatre' is efficacious on the basis that it is self-consciously engaged with real society. Read suggests that 'political theatre' like Penhall's is anything but because: 'The more it seeks relations with the world, the more singular and isolated from that world it seems.'[65] If one accepts Read's premise, it, perhaps peculiarly, allows the political vibrancy of Penhall's plays to shine more sharply. Works such as *Blue/Orange* and *Some Voices* are certainly not radical acts, they are, however, feeling arguments about the state of things. If *Titicut Follies* turned our gaze towards looking carefully at Wiseman's excessively visible subjects, Penhall's work in many ways makes invisibility day-glo bright. The men in both plays, Ray in *Some Voices* and Christopher in *Blue/Orange*, disappear behind towers of paperwork, diagnostics, and discourse. Language in these plays constitutes place, reality, and power. By turning our attention to script and scripting, Penhall illustrates how humans are wounded in the bureaucratic violence of discourse. While the physical regime of coercive control that one witnesses in Wiseman's film has been dismantled, Penhall makes plain how far knowledge and authority remain vertically distributed and confining. Moreover, there remains, for Christopher at least, no place, or no safe place to be.

Economy of language

Some Voices charts the post-discharge life of Ray after a compulsory section two in a psychiatric hospital.[66] The play was first performed at the Royal Court Theatre Upstairs in September 1994 and has been revived multiple times and adapted for the screen by Penhall in 2000 starring Daniel Craig as the central character. Ray, the play's protagonist, is released into the care of his brother Pete and the drama is self-avowedly concerned with the politics and pitfalls of community care. As Penhall notes, 'Ray is a product of legislation which was at best ill-advised and at worst an exercise in cruelty and greed unparalleled in post-war England.'[67] The play is acutely alive to the procedures of mental health care. The language jangles with stigmatising slang and is also intruded upon by business vocabulary that exposes the bleeding of consumerism into care practices following the 1990 Community Care Act, which introduced an internal market for care services. Ray refuses to take his medication because the pharmacological intervention dulls his experience of living. An audience encounters cruelty and paranoia in the character of Dave and thereby encounters questions regarding the distinction between reason and unreason, between badness and madness, and, moreover, the place of poverty and paucity of opportunity in the social aspects of distress. The play closes with a scene of informal occupational therapy as Pete teaches Ray to cook and presents the possibility of familial rehabilitation. In short, *Some Voices* is a conventional but considered anatomisation of mental ill-health in Britain at the close of the twentieth century.

The contemporary language of the mental health services is exposed as alienated from the actual experiences and processes to which it refers. Shortly after Ray arrives at Pete's home, Pete urges Ray to 'go and see that / woman today … The one they fixed you up with to sort out the thingie for / your whatsit.'[68] The 'whatsit' it transpires is the post-discharge follow-up care, or, as Pete describes it, the 'After-sales service.'[69] While Pete is clearly using language to circumnavigate discussing the reality of the situation, his terminology evidences the shift from a register of care to a register of consumerism that has taken place in the British mental health system in the last thirty years. The shift from patient to client to service-user (and consumer in North America) in mental health practice and literature linguistically marks the infiltration of the market economy into the care system. Later in the play, as Ray's behaviour begins to jar with Pete's, the fiscal tone intrudes once more:

PETE   And…for the rest of my life. I mean how weird are
          things gonna get? You been out two weeks and you haven't
          done any of the things you're supposed to do. I'm keeping my
          end of the deal what about yours?

RAY   Don't talk to me about deals – I'm not doing any more deals.[70]

Here again one can perceive language in a vector of retreat from that which it attempts to capture. The relocation of therapy and care into a language of transaction is historically accurate and, therefore, again, allows Penhall to proceed in a naturalistic tone. However, by placing this language in the mediated form of theatre, Penhall draws our attention to it and thereby places its legitimacy in question. The rhetoric of economy serves to underscore its own artificiality in a care setting. This is not necessarily to advocate a return to the paternalistic language of 'patient' (though perhaps this would be a more honest appraisal of the internal power dynamics within many care practices), but rather to note that Penhall here is attempting to trouble the manner in which language congeals around a concept, and to question what exactly the nature of that coagulation reveals about the ideology of a given society. In these ways, Penhall productively shackles language to context and asks what is politically at stake in a name, phrase, or register.

The economic terminology in *Some Voices* is also engaged with the Thatcherite politics of individualism. The care contract that Pete has undertaken with the National Health Service is gradually eroded as a sustainable mechanism of support. Pete proves ill-equipped and disinclined to cope with the care of his brother Ray. As he demands that Ray leave, Pete desperately remarks in tellingly entrepreneurial terms, 'It's none of my business. It isn't and I cannot make it my / business no matter who says I should. I have my own business.'[71] Penhall does not appear to be suggesting that community care is an impossible concept, but rather he is exposing the transactional framing of social responsibilities affected under a neoliberal care context. The problem is further crystallised in Pete's extended speech to Laura, Ray's girlfriend, about the social and personal consequences of the bureaucratisation of health:

> I went in there. I went and saw this woman he's been
> seeing. Turns out he hasn't been seeing her – what am I talking
> about – I knew he hadn't been seeing her. They never even
> heard of him. I say 'How come you never heard of him?' They
> say 'Because he didn't fill out the form.' 'What are you talking
> about?' I say. 'I filled out the form.' 'No you filled out *your*
> form', they say. 'He's supposed to fill out his form and take it to
> a different building.' 'I filled out the fucking form', I say. 'I did
> everything to the letter.' 'No', they say, 'you filled out the form
> to say he filled out his form. If he didn't fill out his form then it's
> null and void.' *(Beat.)* Then they gave me more forms.[72]

Some Voices is then stridently concerned with contemporary political arguments about community care, mental health, and economics. Penhall's decision to stage these issues is indicative of his politicised desire to challenge received public narratives of mental ill-health. By placing a frame around the public language of care he explodes the rhetoric as a sham. As Scull suggests, successive political regimes have long issued 'Orwellian bleatings about "Better Services for the Mentally Handicapped" (Department of Health and Social Security, 1971) while systematically adopting policies designed to produce precisely the opposite effect.'[73] By placing such registers in an altered context (that is to say not broadcast media) Penhall amplifies their inadequacy.

Seeing blue

Penhall's more recent play about psychiatry, *Blue/Orange*, was first staged at the National Theatre in 2000. It has been performed extensively to critical acclaim both in the UK and across North America and, like *Some Voices*, was adapted for the screen by Penhall and Howard Davies in 2005. *Blue/Orange* portrays the intellectual and egotistical battle between two psychiatrists, Bruce and Robert, over the diagnosis and discharge of a service-user, Christopher. Moreover, like *Some Voices*, it too is a play of language. The sparse set is comprised of a 'transparent water cooler' and 'a glass bowl containing three oranges' and there is scant action – three men sit, stand, talk.[74] The original production at the Cottesloe had raked seating on four sides evoking a boxing ring. Language spars create the architecture of psychiatry here. In this densely verbal play, we witness Christopher being folded away inside sheets of language, dwarfed while his psychiatrists balloon. One is left in no doubt at the play's conclusion that power is a fundamental to psychiatric practice. In their discussion of disability, Snyder and Mitchell consider: 'If, for Virginia Woolf, women historically function as a device to reflect the image of men back to themselves at twice their normal size, should we suggest something similar with respect to the cultural function of disability for subjects seeking to establish, by contrast, their abilities?'[75] *Blue / Orange* would appear to answer clearly – yes.

Thematically, the play gestures towards the over-representation of African and Caribbean men in British mental health services as well as staging debates around cultural relativism and, as we saw in Chapter 1, debates around anti-psychiatry. *Blue / Orange*, along with other plays of the period such as Wayne Buchanan's *Under Their Influence* or Zindika's *Leonora's Dance*, is self-consciously preoccupied with the potential neo-colonial politics of psychiatric care in Britain. Indeed, the programme for *Leonora's Dance* details the 'disproportionate number of black, mainly Afro-Caribbean people in Britain diagnosed as mentally ill.'[76] Likewise the notes at the end of the published play text for *Under Their Influence* form an almost statistical epilogue to the drama: 'Black men are up to 10 times more likely to be diagnosed on first admission to hospital with schizophrenia than their white counterparts. Black men are more likely to be given higher doses of medication, and less likely to be offered counselling, than their white counterparts.'[77] The programme for *Blue / Orange* likewise had a statistical section regarding the disproportionate presence of black men in psychiatric services. However, while Christopher is the ostensible focus he is in fact lost in the fray. Indeed, he is frequently sent off stage during discussions:

BRUCE   Christopher is a Schizophrenic.
                Pause.
                Did you hear me?
ROBERT   No, he's BPD.
BRUCE   If you Section 3 him I can keep him here until he's properly diagnosed.
ROBERT   No. Absolutely not.
BRUCE   He's Type I Schizophrenic with Positive
                Symptoms including Paranoid Tendencies. Probably Thought Dis-
                order as well.
                [...]
BRUCE   Give me time and I'll show you.
ROBERT   You haven't got time. He's been here a month. He's been steadily
                improving – it's therefore a brief Psychotic Episode associated with
                BPD. Nothing more insidious.

BRUCE	He's paranoid. You heard him.
ROBERT	How does BPD with Paranoia sound? Stick to the ICD 10 Classification.
BRUCE	You love the ICD 10 don't you? All the different euphemisms for 'He's Nuts' without actually having to admit he's nuts. It's like your Linus blanket.
ROBERT	OK. BPD and A Bit Nuts.[78]

As the play progresses, Christopher's footing in the discussions swirling above, at, and about him becomes precarious: 'I don't know what to think any more. When I do think, it's not my thoughts, it's not my voice when I talk. You tell me who I am.'[79] Moreover, the play dramaturgically relies on a problematic expectation of a 'reveal' as to whether Christopher is *really* mad or not. In so doing it replicates an idiom of truth. Elsewhere the dialogue is lively, funny, and awash with professional abbreviations – BPD (Borderline Personality Disorder), ICD 10 (International Classification of Diseases) – that purposefully amplify the implied absurdity and reductionism of psychiatric theory, and its haphazard application. However, there is a further dynamic of scripting that takes place that returns us to *Titicut Follies* and language as a core disciplinary strategy in psychiatry's armoury.

Learning lines

There is a brutalising sequence in *Titicut Follies* in which a naked man, Jim, is taken from his bare cell to be shaved, roughly, before being returned and locked in his room. In the course of the three and a half minute sequence the guards ask Jim almost twenty times if his room will be tidy tomorrow: 'how's that room gonna be, Jim?'[80] In the same sequence, they ask Jim to repeat himself or speak up at least 26 times: 'What's that, Jim?'[81] This is evidently a daily routine – as one of the guards remarks 'you told me that yesterday' when Jim promises to have his room spick and span.[82] It is an uncomplicated picture of grotesque bullying. In the opening act of *Blue/Orange* Christopher is asked eight questions about why he can no longer drink Coke, four about why he can no longer drink alcohol, two about coffee, and advised once not to walk too much, 'you must try and control it'.[83] The point here is not to suggest that these scenes are interchangeable, or that it may not be good advice for Christopher to cut back on caffeine; rather it is to direct attention toward the performance of power and the persistence in the line of questioning in both pieces. As Ariel Watson points out all too often Dr/patient dialogue is in fact not dialogue at all but learning the right words to say 'until the right answer is given, the scripts are followed, the roles taken up.'[84] One watches, here, a performance of hospital citizenship in which compliance is the hinge on which being a 'good' patient turns. Repetition functions, then, as a form of performative coercion:

| **Bruce** | What's wrong with drinking Coke? |
| **Christopher** | But I'm going home. |

Bruce	Christopher. Come on you know this, it's important. What's wrong with Coke?
Christopher	It rots your teeth.
Bruce	No – well, yes – and …? What else does it do to you?
Christopher	Makes my head explode.
Bruce	Well – no – no – what does it do to you really?
Christopher	Makes my head explode – oh man – I know – I get you.
Bruce	It's not good for you, is it?
Christopher	No. It's bad.[85]

What is at stake here is that in its exposure of the scripting of relatively banal choices – whether to drink Coke – *Blue/Orange* invites us to perceive other scripts of codified behaviour. In so doing, we are returned to the terms that condition normalcy and, moreover, able to see who authors and polices such coordinates. As Snyder and Mitchell ask: 'What can we learn about disability by beginning with the premise that our understanding of human variation has been filtered through the perspectives and research of those who locate disability on the outermost margins of human value?'[86] Penhall's acute interrogation of language makes audible the grinding refrains of rusted power: 'You see, sick people come to me. All creeds and colours. They are suffering. They go away again and they no longer suffer. Because of me. All because of me.'[87] Indeed, only on condition of learning Robert's lines (in the guise of the complaint letter) is Christopher able to attain his longed-for freedom.

If *Titicut Follies* was immovably located, heavy in its specificity, *Blue/Orange* cuts a somewhat more capricious shape. It is both somewhere (a London hospital) and nowhere (a discursive anteroom). By placing the locatedness in recession and foregrounding language *as* place, Penhall quietly exposes how far rhetoric can obscure realities. As the two psychiatrists fight over where to put Christopher, it becomes apparent that in fact there is nowhere to go. There is no place for him. On the one hand, 'we don't have the beds' so Christopher cannot stay where Bruce argues he should be.[88] On the other hand, the community to which Robert wishes to send Christopher is hardly what one might call caring: 'I don't have a home … I don't have any friends … QPR supporters … With bananas … Pissing through the letter box, fires, firestarting on the front step.'[89] Thus, while the arguments clatter on what gets lost in the chatter is any sense of what home, place, care, and safety might actually mean. Indeed, the single request that Christopher makes to help him find some peace at night is rebuffed out of hand: 'Well you know, Chris, I can't provide you with double glazing. It's not part of my remit. If you want double glazing … Go to the council.'[90] In all the sound and fury what evaporates, Penhall argues, is the capacity to hear when someone tells you what they need.

I will if you will

Sara Ahmed's political study of the concept of wilfulness asks not only 'what is wilfulness doing?' but also 'what are we doing when we are being wilful?'[91] She writes that we 'become willing by learning not to be conscious of an agreement'.[92] We, in effect, sleepwalk in consensus. Wilfulness, on the other hand, becomes a wakeful and spatialised notion: the wilful subject walks a different path.[93] Artist and activist the vacuum cleaner (James Leadbitter) is a wilful subject.[94] His protests and art works disrupt orthodoxy and consensus and put naturalised social and political contracts in bright lights. His practice thereby asks if there might be different ways to live. A common critique of the wilful subject is that their acts form an inherently selfish gesture:

> The acquisition of good will, as the will in pursuit of the right ends, becomes a way of creating social harmony: a good will is in agreement with other wills. Wilfulness as ill will is often understood as a will that is in agreement only with itself: a willing of what is agreeable *to* the self.[95]

In this reckoning, the wilful subject herself is framed as the problem as opposed to the ideological structures under which she currently operates. One is put in mind here of Slavoj Žižek's critique of the ideology glasses in the 1988 film *They Live*. Žižek argues that the extended fight sequence in which John Nada attempts to get his friend to put on the ideology glasses (and thereby see the truth of what is happening) alerts us to how far we do not want to see. Likening ideology to a trash can, he argues:

> The material force of ideology makes me not see what I am effectively eating. It is not only our reality which enslaves us. The tragedy of our predicament, when we are within ideology, is that when we think that we escape it into our dreams, at that point we are within ideology.[96]

Moreover, he concludes the comfort of ideology is that 'we, in a way, enjoy our ideology'.[97] Thus comes the radical paradox of 'the extreme violence of liberation... Freedom hurts.'[98] Leadbitter's wilful work pursues forms of political freedom. It asks us to see how power, freedom, and autonomy are afforded to some and not others. Vitally, however, at the core of this project is a critical engagement with community. This is not in a cosy gesture of roseate sharing; rather he contests the meaning of space and inter-relationality in order to ask a core question of ethical life: how can we live together? Leadbitter's work persistently foregrounds collectivity in the forging of radical alternatives in mental health support. In this way, far from selfish, his practice is characterised by wilful generosity.

Spring watch

It is late spring 2011. James Leadbitter is struggling. He is depressed, anxious, and suicidal. As he wryly jokes in his later performance piece *MENTAL* about this period: 'My yearly cycle of getting ill is upon me, or spring as you call it.'[99] Reluctant to be admitted to a psychiatric ward, James, with the help of friends and a 'fucking brilliant' mental health lawyer, decides (and manages) instead to write his own mental health act and detain himself on its terms in his own flat. His previous experiences of admission had been 'more traumatic than my already mentally distressed state'.[100] *The Ship of Fools* then, was, at heart, an attempt to navigate a creative route through profound distress as an antidote to toxic hospitalisation (Figure 2.5).

The Ship of Fools

A project/residency with the vacuum cleaner.

Anti-Section 1 of the vacuum cleaner's Mental Health Act; 2011

i: From now (10th May 2011) and for the next 28 days, artist/activist the vacuum cleaner has committed himself to the self-made mental health institution the Ship Of Fools (his flat in Hackney, London).

ii: The Ship Of Fools will function as an inter-section between mental sanctuary and creative liberty. As part of this time the vacuum cleaner seeks creative residencies at the Ship Of Fools: both artist and non-artists alike in an attempt to find creativity in madness. Artists can use the residencies for making, researching, reflecting or anything else that they need time and space for. The only condition is that the residencies must involve the vacuum cleaner in some way – as material, as collaborator, as helper, as observer or as anything else that is creative and useful to both/all.

iii: During this time the vacuum cleaner will also attempt to create work and you are invited to join this process, should you wish.

iv: The Ship Of Fools will offer a small honorary fee, space to work, computers, fast internet access, stills camera, video camera, screen printing facilities, cake and cups of tea, maybe even some lunch. Residencies can last anywhere from one day to the full twenty-eight.

v: What happens at the residency is totally open but is dependent on a mutually beneficial relationship between the vacuum cleaner and the resident. Material from the residency may be collected and presented in some form in the future.

vi: Participants of the residency should be aware that this may be a challenging experience and willing to work with the artist to find mutually respected boundaries.

vii: Applications, however small or large, mental or not are welcome. Submissions are open from now until the 24th of May. Include a brief description of what you would like to do, some form of documentation of previous work and a timeframe for when you would wish to undertake the residency. Submissions can be in any format, digital, hard copy or in person. fools@thevacuumcleaner.co.uk (email to arrange in person submission)

the vacuum cleaner
Toynbee Studios
28 Commercial St
London, E1 6AB
(Don't post anything you want back)

www.thevacuumcleaner.co.uk/shipoffools

This project is supported by Arts Council, Artsadmin and Live Art Development Agency.

FIGURE 2.5 The vacuum cleaner's Mental Health Act/Artist Call-Out. Image credit: the vacuum cleaner

FIGURE 2.6   *Ship of Fools* exhibition, Blue Coat Gallery Liverpool. Photo credit: the
vacuum cleaner

In the course of the 28-day section, he was visited by 12 people.[101] Together with
Leadbitter they made a range of creative works that were later part of a touring exhibition of *The Ship of Fools* project. The art works ranged from a sermon
on a mount from the Reverend Janet Ashton, to the installation of a number
of shoelace nooses on some railings adjacent to a children's playground, to cus-
tomised t-shirts with messages such as 'I went mental and all I got was this lousy
t-shirt' and 'psychiatrists tried to make me go to the nut house and I said no, no,
no' (Figure 2.6). What is arresting about the project is how far the principles of
community are nested within the creative responses to distress. Moreover, community functions in triplicate in this work. There is the internal, dialogic, making
community of the artists in residence with Leadbitter who talk, and walk, and
make. This collective is tucked inside a wider community that is engaged via the
creative interventions in public, shared spaces. From the painting of the letter box
of a cherished closed-down café (kicked out by property developers) with gold
and block lettering reading 'Paradise Lost', to writing 'barking mad' on a tree
trunk or 'your enthusiasm' on a curb in marker pen, to the homeless puppet left
in a park only to be weed on by a passing dog, the community is a core aspect
of the methodology. Further, the project's museum afterlife allows the hospitable
embrace of others to extend to a much wider 'us'. Community is not a fluffy
conceptual ideal here. Nor am I suggesting that *The Ship of Fools* argues straightforwardly *for* a model of community-based support; rather I am arguing that the
dialogic relationships that it establishes between self and others and objects precisely invites us to not only think about what community means but also what
it feels like and perhaps most importantly what it can do. Community here shifts
from a spatial notion to a relational and emotional one. Here we return to Ahmed
who argues that:

emotions are not simply something 'I' or 'We' [the crowd] have. Rather, it is through emotions, or how we respond to objects and others, that surfaces or boundaries are made: the 'I' and 'we' are shaped by, and even take the shape of, contact with others.[102]

While Ahmed's and my arguments may not appear new following Benedict Anderson and others,[103] it is important to note how far Leadbitter's work renders the politics of emotions newly legitimate in ways that remain, sadly, radical in the context of mental health care. If those living with a mental illness diagnosis experience some of the highest degrees of regulation by authorities (emotional, physical, civic), then Leadbitter's horizontal model of mutual care in which emotions are not there to be fixed is urgent and overdue. Moreover, his acute appreciation of community as performatively produced through intervention, networks of support, and participation acts as a dynamic rejoinder to the leaden notion of community as simply space in which care is 'delivered'.

Truly, madly, deeply

The Ship of Fools kept Leadbitter alive and out of hospital. However, he explained that it had placed a great deal of strain on his friendships during the period owing to the levels of support they offered.[104] Following the project, he had an email from someone else in pain asking if Leadbitter could recreate the process for him to help him get through. This exchange, in turn, helped nurture the seeds of what would emerge as Leadbitter's current initiative *Madlove: A Designer Asylum*, which is a creative research process aimed to reimagine psychiatric in-patient spaces. During *The Ship of Fools*, Leadbitter's psychiatrist had tried to place him under a section and Leadbitter explained that the project itself was hidden from the home treatment team. For example, rather than suggesting he had written an alternative mental health act and sectioned himself under it with the support of artists (almost certain, he felt, to accelerate the push to detain him), he told them: 'my friends are coming round to do some art.'[105] This returns us to the questions explored in relation to language and dialogue in *Blue/Orange* insofar as it further exposes how far often what is framed as dialogue is, in practice, monologic. Indeed, critiques of the current recovery model often observe how far it represents a further articulation of a normative set of expectations, behaviours, and political categories of selfhood. Recovery becomes, therefore, a rehabilitation to an agreed upon set of values authored by a very limited demographic. Writing one's own mental health act, despite being a transformative and life-saving action, is unlikely to have been an acceptable goal under such a model. Leadbitter instead advocates a 'discovery' model, which seeks ways to live with and through our experiences rather than recovering to a 'normal' position. While, of course, a desire to be 'normal' or free from the debilitating aspects of madness ought not be diminished, Leadbitter's prototype is not unbending in form and thus extends to accommodate such thinking.

FIGURE 2.7   *Madlove*, Newcastle Workshop Drawing, illustration by Michael Duckett.
Photo credit: the vacuum cleaner

The project, to date, has comprised a series of workshops in Britain and Europe that have principally examined the following questions: 'What does good mental health feel like?', 'What does good mental health care look, feel, taste, smell, sound like?' and 'If you could design your own asylum what would it be like?'[106] A pilot installation that responded to the initial findings was presented at FACT (Foundation for Art and Creative Technology) in Liverpool as part of the *Group Therapy: Mental Distress in a Digital Age* exhibition and more recently as part of the *Bedlam* exhibition at the Wellcome Trust.[107] The next stage of the project will examine the logistics and processes in running such an environment. Here Leadbitter and his participants will ask such key questions as 'how are decisions made in this environment?', 'who is this space *for*?' and 'who facilitates this space and how?' The final outcome will be a temporary hospital that will run as a day unit for six weeks in 2019. *Madlove* will also have an online resource for people in distress and those supporting them to draw upon (Figure 2.7).

Madlove's principal aim to find an alternative to acute in-patient care is not a new idea. As we explored in Chapter 1 in relation to R. D. Laing and the therapeutic community movement more broadly (let alone myriad other historical attempts to find the 'right' place for madness), examples are not in short supply. However, influenced by the thinking of Paolo Friere's *Pedagogy of the Oppressed* and *Pedagogy of Freedom*, Leadbitter asks the question, 'how do you formalise mutual care while still dissolving power?'[108] Indeed, the principle of *Madlove* is a bottom-up, patient-led, horizontal process of research and knowledge exchange. As Andrew Scull maintains: 'Uncomfortable as it may be for some to accept the obvious, I insist that issues of power and social control, broadly conceived, are indeed central and necessarily so, to any balanced understanding of the psychiatric realm.'[109] Leadbitter's decentred, wide-angle lens approach, then, expands the horizon of perceptual realties and thinking as to what constitutes not only good support and treatment, but also what constitutes good mental states. In this way, through the redistribution of knowledge (and thereby power), Leadbitter is steadily digging a fertile space for alternative categories of political life and structures of support. While this may sound utopic, it is difficult to imagine a project that seeks to radically reimage the horizons of what is thinkable that is not wilfully optimistic, especially when one's opponent is orthodox psychiatry. Furthermore, while Leadbitter's unequivocal aim is to have a direct legacy on the actual lived conditions and structures of mental health care and support, he is not unaware that a holographic room and feral cats may not always make the final edit: 'It's like Vivienne Westwood. You wouldn't wear it, but you're inspired by it and incorporate some of it into your life.'[110] Leadbitter's foregrounding of emotions, sensations, and bodies as at the heart of political life in the context of psychiatry is a bold invitation to change not just packaging but the feeling and lived experience of care.

Disco fever

Imogen Tyler's book *Revolting Subjects: Social Abjection in Neoliberal Britain* astutely observes that the creation of 'waste populations' serves a dual function of providing a socio-political scapegoat as well as a source of revenue for business. For example, the gypsy and traveller communities in Britain have been transformed into political capital to be blamed for social ills while also providing financial capital for the global entertainment industry via programmes such as *My Big Fat Gypsy Wedding*.[111] She writes: 'Waste populations are in this way *included through their exclusion*, and it is this paradoxical logic which the concept of abjection describes.'[112] Moreover, as Sara Ahmed observes, 'there can be nothing more dangerous to a body than the social agreement that *that* body is dangerous.'[113] This creation of dangerous bodies as excludable limit cases for acceptable normalcy is not unfamiliar practice in the field of madness studies. And as Snyder and Mitchell argue, deviance is not an excursion from normalcy; rather it is its ultimate product.[114] If we accept that 'fear works to restrict some bodies through the movement or expansion of others' then what is a viable gesture of resistance to such restrictions?[115] Ahmed suggests that: 'It is the regulation of bodies in space through the uneven distribution of fear which allows spaces to become territories, claimed as rights by some bodies and not others.'[116] How might a piece of theatre mark a challenge to such regimes? How might theatre enact the deregulation of space and de-constrict bodies? Leadbitter's intimate performance of pain, *MENTAL*, offers a keen example of how artistic practice enables alternative modes of thinking about political freedom. Spun around a tender skeleton of disco tracks, *MENTAL* embodies resistance in a vulnerable, powerful body and thereby reconceives pain as a legitimate political register. *MENTAL* offers a portrait of protest through strains of story, disco, and cake.

In the beginning was the end

MENTAL starts at the finish: 'And this is how the stories ends, with me sat in front of you.'[117] The story that James tells is of his experiences as a protestor, or 'domestic extremist' as the police call him, and as a psychiatric patient between 1999 and 2011. He obtained his police and medical records through a Data Protection request and these form a core dramaturgical element, structuring an audience's encounter as documents are regularly projected on an OHP.[118] The piece is performed in non-theatre spaces (usually houses) to small audiences who take off their shoes, have a cup of tea and a piece of carrot cake together, and enter the space as a group.[119] The slow-paced pre-show ushers in a careful sense of shared, deliberate activity. Moreover, the literal path that one takes to attend the performance re-routes one away from the familiar roads to the local theatre door and leads you elsewhere in the city. Again, one's deliberate intention to attend is foregrounded here and invites a more wakeful sense of doing. Leadbitter is somewhat sceptical of theatre and its representational trappings and thus the James we are presented with impresses upon us his authenticity – whether through the documents, or exposing the wounds that are cut into his back saying 'this civilisation is fucked', or the self-talk that textures the piece:

> Just say something. Well done. Now. You have done this before, they've paid for a ticket, they expect a show. Yeah, that's right. Just don't spend ages apologizing. It's okay, if you have a panic attack, if your mood swings are too much, that's ok.[120]

While, of course, there is a representational quality to the piece, nevertheless, this remains an unambiguously autobiographical encounter. The point of significance here is that to disassemble the promise of authenticity here would be to misapprehend the politics of the work. If the pain *is* the politics and the pain is James' then to set about an academic dilution of *MENTAL*'s claims to reality is to neuter its power. Moreover, the violent need to hear survivor voices is paramount. *MENTAL* legitimates otherwise illegitimate voices:

> Suicide can be a hard thing to talk about, but it isn't a hard thing to understand. Imagine you're in utter pain, and this pain out weights what you may be able to cope with. That's all it's really about. Being unable to cope with the pain you are in is perfectly normal.[121]

In short, the wilful contract with authenticity that takes place in this work, I argue, has political effect. In a piece that is evocatively and sensately concerned with the practices of mutual care and responsibility, it is paramount that the encounter is understood as genuine. Indeed, the locatedness of the story within James' body ought not be critically abstracted. He is, in this way, the tender site of the personal and political struggle.

Me sat in front of you[122]

Alongside its excavation of an echo chamber within which to speak and hear pain, *MENTAL* performs intimacy. In a bedroom somewhere, socks off, tucked underneath the edges of James' duvet, a room of watching bellies, warm with tea and sated on cake, sit together and listen. This sensate affair is matched by the direct address, ambient lighting, and ballad-slow pace. Such strategies and dramaturgical choices form a stark counterpoint to the accumulating factual papers and prescription boxes that bureaucratically, legalistically, and medically attempt to capture, describe, and diagnose James Leadbitter. Notably, the more these pages and prescriptions offer accounts, descriptions, and evidence the more they are exposed as wholly inadequate to their task of *knowing* (Figure 2.8). The show relates a decade of free fall through the psychiatric system. Eventually, James is told that he has, and always has had, a diagnosis of Borderline Personality Disorder:

> I say that I don't really know what this diagnosis means, I'm told that this shouldn't be a shock, "you did spend a year in a specialist unit for personality disorders." But it is a surprise… I go home and smash plates.[123]

FIGURE 2.8 Leadbitter in *MENTAL*. Photo credit: Hannah Hull

The diagnosis, he says 'gives me a framework, and that helps'.[124] However, theatrically, we come to an understanding of James' experiences via a different route. Indeed, as James relates the journey to his suicide attempt, our involvement becomes gut-wrenching: 'It's raining so hard as I cycle towards hackney marshes. I stop and buy myself the last thing I'm going to eat, which is a piece of carrot cake.'[125] There is a queasiness to our retroactive encounter with the cake we have consumed. The delicious treat is skewered with sadness. Lumps form in throats. The cake enacts a double tide of remorse and sensual intimacy. I am not suggesting here that what *MENTAL* offers in this gesture is either blame or a pseudo-suicidal experience; we are not simply accused nor do we *know* what James has experienced by virtue of eating a bit of cake. Instead, I think, what takes place here is an extension of a broader narrative structure in the piece which offers a theatrical engagement with pain as encounter. The intimacy of taste simply shuffles me a little closer to his story. Moreover, it is the juxtaposition of intimacy and administration witnessed through the reams of documents that signals the politics at stake in *MENTAL*. In the therapeutic cloister of the bedroom, *MENTAL* flattens the hierarchies of knowledge and redistributes the capacity for care, support, and expertise amongst the audience. This is not in a revolutionary bid to disband psychiatry altogether; rather it is merely to suggest that there are different ways to hear, respond to, and be with the pain of others.

Adjusting the lens

The move away from a predominantly segregative system of mental health care since the 1960s is incomplete. While many hospitals and asylums have closed or been repurposed as luxury gated communities where you now pay for the privilege to stay inside, and hundreds of thousands of patients have been dispatched into 'the community', it is abundantly clear that we do not have an adequate understanding of what community means or how it is produced. Nor has there been a dismantling of the invisible walls of segregation enacted by ghettoisation, surveillance, and social marginalisation. Art does not have all the answers. But, vitally, nor does psychiatry (broadly conceived). As Sedgwick suggested, altering the packaging of support is insufficient if it is not enacted in tandem with a sustained and radical engagement with the lived experience of madness, detention, and care. There is tireless work taking place across hospitals, day units, GP surgeries, drop-in centres and elsewhere with psych discipline staff battling to meet the needs of their patients. However, in order to reform care practices so that they meet people's needs without coercion, disempowerment, and punishment being commonly felt responses to treatment it is evident that we need to listen to the voices of patients and redistribute knowledge, power, and expertise. The three works under discussion in this chapter cumulatively expose the persistence of key themes in the experience of psychiatric space: autonomy, language, knowledge, emotions. Collectively, the works shift the focus away from the bricks and bureaucracy and towards the bodies and behaviours housed therein. If *Titicut Follies* interrogates how we see difference, then Joe

Penhall's work critiques how we speak difference, and Leadbitter's practice shows us how we feel difference. For all three artists, however, there is a tacit invitation to expand our thinking with regard to the parameters of personhood, in-patient care, and community. *Titicut Follies*, *Some Voices*, *Blue/Orange*, *The Ship of Fools*, *Madlove*, and *MENTAL*, when heard in unison, urge that we need new, more tender structures through which to understand, value, and hold emotion and experience. It is only through a horizontal confluence of voices that having a place, and a safe place to be, will emerge as a possibility for all.

Notes

1 Talking Heads, 'This Must Be the Place', *Speaking in Tongues*, Sire Records, 1983.
2 Nathaniel Lee, quoted in Roy Porter (ed.), *The Faber Book of Madness* (London: Faber, 1991), p. 1.
3 For an extended discussion of space and madness in relation to popular culture and film please see Anna Harpin, 'Revisiting the Puzzle Factory: Cultural Representations of Psychiatric Asylums' in *Interdisciplinary Science Review*, 34: 4, pp. 335–50. For an extended discussion of metaphors of madness and their relationship to British theatre and dramaturgy please see 'Dislocated: Metaphors of Madness in Contemporary Theatre' in Anna Harpin and Juliet Foster (eds), *Madness, Performance, Psychiatry: Isolated Acts* (Basingstoke: Palgrave, 2014).
4 For example, please see Thurstine Basset and Theo Stickley (eds), *Voices of Experience: Narratives of Mental Health Survivors* (Oxford: Wiley-Blackwell, 2010) and Juliet L. H. Foster, *Journeys Through Mental Illness: Clients' Experiences and Understandings of Mental Distress* (Basingstoke: Palgrave, 2007).
5 There is, however, a growing body of examples that counters this generalisation. See, for example, Diana Gittins, *Madness in Its Place: Narratives of Severalls Hospital, 1913–1997* (London: Routledge, 1998), or Joseph Melling and Bill Forsythe, *The Politics of Madness: The State, Insanity and Society in England, 1845–1914* (London: Routledge, 2006), Peter Bartlett and David Wright, *Outside the Walls of the Asylum: The History of Care in the Community 1750–2000* (London: The Athlone Press, 1999), or Rhodri Hayward's *The Transformation of the Psyche in British Primary Care* (London: Bloomsbury, 2014) and *Psychiatry in Modern Britain* (London: Bloomsbury Continuum, 2013) to name but a few.
6 *Blue/Orange* is a British play but has been extensively performed across North America since its premiere in London in 2000. This points interestingly to the portability of the debates staged within the piece across psychiatric regimes.
7 While Foucault's *Madness and Civilisation* had been widely and robustly critiqued, his contribution to the consciousness-raising of the subject and his theorising of bio-power ought not to be overlooked. See Andrew Scull, *The Insanity of Place/The Place of Insanity: Essays on the History of Psychiatry* (London: Routledge, 2006) for a detailed interrogation of Foucault.
8 Andrew Scull, *The Insanity of Place*, p. 41.
9 Roy Porter, *Mind Forg'd Manacles: A History of Madness in England from the Restoration to the Regency* (London: Penguin, 1990).
10 Andrew Scull, *Social Order/Mental Disorder: Anglo-American Psychiatry in Historical Perspective* (London: Routledge, 1989), p. 306.
11 Scull, *Social Order*, p. 301.
12 Ibid., p. 308.
13 James E. Moran and Jonathan Andrews (eds), *Madness, Architecture and the Built Environment: Psychiatric Spaces in Historical Context* (London: Routledge, 2007), p. 1.
14 See, for example, important studies in the history of psychiatry including: David Healy, *The Anti-Depressant Era* (Cambridge, MA: Harvard University Press, 1997), Roy Porter,

A Social History of Madness: Stories of the Insane (London: Weidenfeld and Nicolson, 1987), Andrew Scull, *Madhouse: A Tragic Tale of Megalomania and Modern Medicine* (London and New Haven, CT: Yale University Press, 2005), Edward Shorter, *Before Prozac: The Troubled History of Mood Disorders in Psychiatry* (New York: Oxford University Press, 2009), Carla Yanni, *The Architecture of Madness: Insane Asylums in the United States* (Minneapolis: University of Minnesota Press, 2007), Peter Bartlett and David Wright (eds), *Outside the Walls of the Asylum: The History of Care in the Community 1750–2000* (New Brunswick, NJ: Athlone Press, 1999), Peter Barham, *Closing the Asylum: The Mental Patient in Modern Society* (London: Penguin, 1992), and Gerald Grob, *Mental Institutions in America: Social Policy to 1875* (New Brunswick, NJ: Transactions Publishers, 2009 [1973]). These authors all offer numerous important and politically diverse scholarship on this subject.

15 Joseph Melling and Bill Forsythe, *The Politics of Madness: The State, Insanity, and Society in England, 1845–1914* (London: Routledge, 2006), p. 3.

16 Gerald N. Grob, *The Mad Among Us: A History of the Care of America's Mentally Ill* (Cambridge, MA: Harvard University Press, 1994), pp. 48, 49.

17 Andrew Scull, *Decarceration: Community Treatment and the Deviant – A Radical View*, 2nd edn (Cambridge: Polity Press, 1984), p. 65. The histories offer a range of figures for asylum populations from Scull's 148,000 patients to others such as Philip Bean and Patricia Mounser who place the figure at 165,000 in their book *Discharged from Mental Hospitals* (Basingstoke: Macmillan, 1993), p. 19. I have opted, therefore, to offer an average figure in the middle of these necessarily uncertain estimates.

18 Scull, *Decarceration*, p. 68.

19 Bartlett and Wright, p. 4.

20 Ibid., p. 13.

21 Ibid., p. 16.

22 Scull, *Decarceration*, p. 139.

23 Erving Goffman, *Asylums: Essays on the Social Situation of Mental Patients and Other Inmates* (London: Doubleday, 1961).

24 Peter Sedgwick, *Psychopolitics* (London: Pluto Press, 1982), p. 193.

25 Scull, *Decarceration*, p. 174.

26 These are called Outpatient Commitments in North America.

27 Bean and Mounser, p. 14.

28 Anonymous, quoted in Christina Katsakou *et al.*, 'Psychiatric Patients' Views on Why Their Involuntary Hospitalisation was Right or Wrong: A Qualitative Study' in *Social Psychiatry and Psychiatric Epidemiology*, 2011, 47:427, pp. 1169–79, p. 1174.

29 See Delphine Coyle *et al.*, 'Compulsion in the Community: Mental Health Professionals Views and Experiences of CTOs' in *The Psychiatrist*, 2013, 37:10, pp. 315–21. This article also argues that of the sample studied 83% of psychiatrists were in favour of CTOs as compared to 67% of other mental health workers (nurses, social workers and so forth). The latter front line group raised concerns about the coercive nature of the practices.

30 Diana Gittins, *Madness in Its Place: Narratives of Severalls Hospital, 1913–1997* (London: Routledge, 1998), p. 221.

31 Jillian Smith, 'The Politics of Tactility: Walter Benjamin Materialized by Way of Frederick Wiseman's *Titicut Follies*' in *Studies in Documentary Film*, 2008, 2:2, pp. 103–22, p. 107.

32 Frederick Wiseman quoted in Thomas R. Atkins, *Frederick Wiseman* (New York: Monarch Books, 1976), p. 44.

33 See, for example, Michael Renov's *Theorizing Documentary* (London: Routledge, 1993), Dave Saunders, *Direct Cinema: Observational Documentary and the Politics of the Sixties* (London: Wallflower Press, 2007), Paula Rabinowitz, *The Must Be Represented: The Politics of Documentary* (London: Verso, 1994), and Thomas W. Benson and Carolyn Anderson, *Reality Fictions: The Films of Frederick Wiseman* (Carbondale, IL: Southern Illinois University Press, 1989).

34 The full list of sanctioned professions is 'legislators, judges, lawyers, sociologists, social workers, doctors, psychiatrists, students in these or related fields, and organizations dealing with the social problems of custodial care and mental infirmity', Massachusetts

Superior Court, 356 Mass. 251, Commonwealth and Others v. Frederick Wiseman and Others, May 6 1969 to June 24, 1969, Suffolk County, p. 262.

35 Jillian Smith, pp. 119–20.

36 Massachusetts Superior Court, emphasis mine.

37 Superintendent Charles Gaughan quoted in Massachusetts Superior Court, p. 254.

38 The court judgement makes frequent reference to the 'private' nature of the inmates' situations.

39 Massachusetts Superior Court, p. 263, emphasis mine.

40 Ibid., p. 254.

41 Jillian Smith, p. 107, p. 110.

42 Katsakou *et al.*, p. 1179. Byron Vincent's 2013 play *Talk About Something You Like* offers a hilarious and moving portrait of his experiences of suggested activities on an NHS psychiatric ward which included 'talk about something you like'.

43 Vladimir in *Titicut Follies*, 01:02:55, dir. Frederick Wiseman (Zipporah, 1968) [BBC2 Broadcast]. Hereafter, *TF*.

44 Psychiatrist in *TF*, 01:04:38.

45 Susanna Kaysen, *Girl, Interrupted* (New York: Vintage, 1993), p. 55.

46 Nady Gill, *The Independent*, 29 March 1993.

47 Paula Rabinowitz, *They Must Be Represented: The Politics of Documentary* (London: Verso, 1994), p. 154.

48 *TF*, 46:06.

49 Jillian Smith, p. 107.

50 Rabinowitz, p. 53.

51 Susan Sontag, *Regarding the Pain of Others* (London: Penguin, 2003).

52 See, for example, Nellie Bly, *Ten Days in a Madhouse* (West Valley City, UT: Waking Lion Press, 2013), Clifford Beers, *A Mind That Found Itself* (London: Longmans, Greens, and Company, 1913), Albert Q. Maisel, 'Bedlam 1946' in *Life Magazine*, 6 May 1946, Susan Sheehan, *Is There No Place on Earth For Me?* (Boston: Houghton, Mifflin, Harcourt, 1982), Irma Kurtz, *Nova Magazine*, October 1968, Peter Thompson, *Back From Broadmoor* (London: Mowbray, 1974), Clifford J. Levy, 'The Operators', 'Where Hope Dies' and 'Final Destination' in *New York Times*, pp. 28, 29, and 30 April 2002.

53 Scull, *The Insanity of Place*, p. 98.

54 Ibid., pp. 137–8.

55 Sharon L. Snyder and David T. Mitchell, *Cultural Locations of Disability* (Chicago: Chicago University Press, 2006), p. 201.

56 Imogen Tyler, *Revolting Subjects: Social Abjection and Resistance in Neoliberal Britain* (London: Zed Books, 2013), p. 26.

57 Sara Ahmed, *The Cultural Politics of Emotion*, 2nd edn (Edinburgh University Press, 2014), pp. 104–5.

58 Ibid., p. 105.

59 Catriona Harvey-Jenner, 'Why we need to STOP treating mental health as such a taboo' in *Cosmopolitan*, 4 February 2016. While one may be tempted to dismiss this article as simply misinformed, it is framed as a think-piece in dialogue with Time to Change and its wide readership ensures the circulation of this model of thinking.

60 Jillian Smith, p. 110.

61 Raymond Williams, *Culture and Society 1780–1950* (London: Doubleday, 1960), p. 319.

62 Penhall, 'Introduction', in *Plays: One* (London: Methuen, 1998), p. x.

63 Alan Read, *Theatre, Intimacy, and Engagement: The Last Human Venue* (London: Palgrave, 2008), p. 7.

64 Ibid., p. 53.

65 Ibid., p. 38.

66 A section two detention is a compulsory admission to a hospital for assessment for a period of up to 28 days (maximum).

67 Penhall, 'Introduction', p. xii.

68 Penhall, 'Some Voices', *Plays: One*, I.2, p. 11.

69 Ibid., I:2, p. 11.
70 Ibid., II:1, p. 51.
71 Ibid., II:5, p. 69.
72 Ibid., II:7, p. 76, emphasis original.
73 Scull, *The Insanity of Place*, p. 27.
74 Joe Penhall, *Blue/Orange* (London: Methuen, 2013), p. 5.
75 Snyder and Mitchell, p. 21.
76 Programme for *Leonora's Dance*, quoted in D'Monté and Saunders, p. 99.
77 Wayne Buchanan, *Under Their Influence* (London: Aurora Metro Press, 2001), p. 94.
78 Penhall, *Blue/Orange*, I, pp. 26–7.
79 Ibid., III, p. 102.
80 *TF*, 26:08.
81 *TF*, 25:06.
82 *TF*, 26:18.
83 Penhall, *Blue Orange*, I, pp. 6–8, p. 16, p. 35.
84 Ariel Watson, 'Cries of Fire: Psychotherapy in Contemporary British and Irish Drama' in *Modern Drama*, 2008, 51:2, pp. 188–210, p. 200.
85 Penhall, *Blue/Orange*, I, p. 7.
86 Snyder and Mitchell, p. 21.
87 Penhall, *Blue/Orange*, III, p. 115.
88 Ibid., I, p. 22.
89 Ibid., II, p. 57, p. 58, pp. 63–4.
90 Ibid., II, p. 59.
91 Sara Ahmed, *Wilful Subjects* (London: Duke University Press, 2014), p. 12.
92 Ibid., p. 75.
93 Ibid., p. 21.
94 While his professional name is the vacuum cleaner for ease of prose, I will refer to him as Leadbitter in the course of the discussion.
95 Ahmed, *Wilful*, p. 95.
96 Slavoj Žižek in *The Pervert's Guide to Ideology*, dir. by Sophie Fiennes. Zeitgeist Films, 2013, 00:53.
97 *Pervert's*, 05:40.
98 *Pervert's*, 06:53.
99 James Leadbitter, *MENTAL*, unpublished manuscript, p. 13. The piece was first performed at In Between Time in Bristol in 2013. The piece has subsequently toured both nationally and internationally.
100 James Leadbitter, *The Ship of Fools* exhibition video.
101 Everyone was accepted who applied except for two people. James felt that they were unprepared for the mutual responsibility of the situation. One psychiatrist visited on the final day (not James' own). His home treatment team continued to visit in the course of the section.
102 Ahmed, *Cultural Politics*, p. 9.
103 Benedict Anderson, *Imagined Communities* (London: Verso, 1983).
104 Leadbitter, personal interview, 18 June 2015.
105 Ibid.
106 At the time of writing workshops have taken place in London, Birmingham, Nottingham Liverpool, Newcastle, and Zurich.
107 The exhibition ran from 5 March to 17 May 2015.
108 Paolo Friere, *Pedagogy of the Oppressed,* trans. by Myra Bergman Ramos (London: Continuum, 1970) and *Pedagogy of Freedom: Ethics, Democracy and Civic Courage*, trans. by Patrick Clarke (Lanham, MD Rowman and Littlefield, 1998).
109 Scull, *The Insanity of Place*, p. 111.
110 Leadbitter, personal interview, 18 June 2015.
111 Tyler, pp. 141–8.
112 Ibid., p. 20, emphasis original.

113 Ahmed, *Cultural Politics*, p. 212, emphasis original.
114 Snyder and Mitchell, p. v.
115 Ahmed, *Cultural Politics*, p. 69.
116 Ibid., p. 70.
117 Leadbitter, *MENTAL*, p. 1.
118 See also, Dylan Tighe's alternative opera *RECORD*. For a discussion of this unpublished piece see Tighe in Harpin and Foster (eds), 'Start Making Sense', pp. 111–36.
119 The Edinburgh 2014 performances were in an office space.
120 Leadbitter, *MENTAL*, p. 1.
121 Ibid., p. 2.
122 Ibid., p. 13.
123 Ibid., p. 10.
124 Ibid., p. 10.
125 Ibid., p. 8.

3

'IT WAS A BRILLIANT CURE BUT WE LOST THE PATIENT'[1]

Treating Madness

In the Gospel according to Luke, we are advised: 'And as ye would that men should do to you, do ye also to them likewise.'[2] This moral sentiment of spiritual generosity and mutual care impresses upon its listener the virtues of empathy. One is invited to behave 'properly' towards another by imagining what one might want and need if shoes were swapped and positions altered. How we treat an Other, then, is framed as a question of esteem, commonality, and equality. A tacit assumption of sameness slinks through this command: I will treat you kindly because that is what *I*, and by extension *you* and therefore *we*, deserve. As a theoretical moral principle (irrespective of its Christian associations), it is difficult to disagree with. One finds a related feeling of common vulnerability above some asylum doors: 'there but for the grace of God go I.' Again, what is acknowledged here is our shared vulnerability; we are alike in our susceptibility to hardship. While it is often suggested that madness is stigmatised because of its alarming unknowability, I would counter that it is in fact precisely its familiarity and affective proximity that feels fearful and dangerous. As Sander L. Gilman suggests, any spectre of health or disease places us in the position of observers of our own bodies, 'bodies inherently in danger of illness.'[3] Other examples of religious or philosophical arguments for fair and humane treatment of selves and others are not in short supply, from Confucianism to Oprah. However, in practice, how humans treat each other exposes manifold hierarchies of power, value, and agency.

If we turn away from this somewhat fuzzy burrow of common humanity and specifically towards psychiatric treatments, the picture becomes both sharper and more stark. I am not straightforwardly equating a generalised notion of 'treating someone right' with 'psychiatric treatments' in an uncritical manner. I am, however, suggesting that within both contexts submerged or capsized ideological values are washing around. The aim of this chapter is, therefore, to examine psychiatric treatments, as portrayed on stage and screen, in a bid to spotlight the relationship between treatment and socio-political value. I am interested in how the artists reveal the ideological values streaked through mental health care practices and what the implications of this might be for future developments in treatment approaches. How is care practised, experienced, and represented? And how does artistic work allow us to think in dynamic, multi-dimensional manners about how to understand and respond to human problems and distress? If the previous chapter considered the interactions of place and experience, this chapter makes space to try and understand what treating mad people 'right' might mean and entail.

As with Chapters 1 and 2, three primary works will form the core of this chapter. I will examine Miloš Forman's 1975 film adaptation of Ken Kesey's novel, *One Flew Over the Cuckoo's Nest*, Terry Johnson's 1993 play, *Hysteria*, and Brian Yorkey and Tom Kitt's 2008 musical, *next to normal*. The chapter will examine a range of treatments including electroconvulsive therapy (ECT), lobotomy, drugs, and talking therapies. All three works are, broadly conceived, populist, mainstream, realist works with strong comic registers (even if shot through with tragedy). It follows that the discussion is concerned less with the perceived accuracy or inaccuracy of the procedures and practices portrayed than with the politics of representation in popular entertainment. Indeed, I am attempting to understand how the activities of mental health and therapeutic systems are figured in conventional artistic forms (the Hollywood film, the farce, the musical) to grasp the role of such work in political critiques of psychiatric care. In this chapter, I foreground a dimensional, as opposed to categorical, understanding of mental distress alongside a radical reengagement with psychosocial framings of madness.[4] I am arguing in favour of a model of care that embraces the relational, three-dimensionality of distress. Artistic practice, of all stripes, has its place in this radical refashioning of care. The works interrogated here, and elsewhere in this volume, ought to be situated within a matrix of voices, as part of an interlocking, interdisciplinary challenge to psychiatric orthodoxy. It is in this network that their force cements. Artistic practice thinks in dimensional, psychosocial manners. It is logical to reason, then, that such forms of thought may offer valuable insight for those who wish to understand treatments and alternatives in these dynamic ways. The examples contained within these pages lay bare the flesh and entrails, the bloody mess of living, and thereby stand in complex contradistinction to the diagnostic system of surface impressions. What follows, then, is an attempt to examine how my examples seek alternatives from within the mainstream. I argue that, taken together, the works expose the political assumptions and values that scaffold historical and contemporary psychiatric treatments. In so doing, together they ask what it has meant, and what it now means, to practice care.

Dredging history

Psychiatry as a distinct discipline really develops in the nineteenth century, emerging in large part out of the asylum movement. One might assume, therefore, that prior to this there were no 'medical' responses to madness, only social, religious, or familial care and custody. However, the history of treatments that have at least a vague perfume of medical or scientific authority is, in fact, long. As Elliot S. Valenstein has noted, 'the earliest records of trepanation have been dated between 1500 and 2000 B.C.' but continued 'throughout the Middle Ages and Renaissance.'[5] Moreover, humoral medicine endured from Hippocrates right through to the late eighteenth century (albeit not in an unbroken fashion) and thus gave rise to all manner of purging, emetics, blistering, cooling and other somatic strategies aimed to restore lost balance within the body. Further, if one turns to the visual history of psychiatric treatments one can witness a startling chronicle of attempts to locate the sources of madness in a physical object to be expunged.[6] Consider, for example, Hieronymus Bosch's *The Cure of Folly* (circa 1480) which depicts the removal of a stone from the afflicted man's head, or, Theodor de Bry's arresting sixteenth-century illustration of a distracted fellow being therapeutically purged of rats and nightmares (Figure 3.1). Curious and barbaric 'cures' in the pursuit of natural equilibrium stud the annals of humoral medicine. As Greg Eghigian charts, 'By the end of the eighteenth century, however, humoral medicine was being challenged by scholars who believed that electricity, not fluids, held the key to the nervous system.'[7]

ARTE MEA CEREBRVM NISI SIT SAPIENTIA TOTVM

FIGURE 3.1 Theodor de Bry, *Distillation*

Such new perspectives led to further 'great and desperate cures' including Joseph Guislain's 'Chinese Temple' (1826) which plunged individuals in and out of water and rotary machines 'designed on the assumption that fast and lengthy rotation would eventually force the trapped fluids in the nerves to move.'[8] Alongside such contraptions were Benjamin Rush's 'Tranquiliser' chair (1811)[9] (Figure 3.2). The nineteenth century gave rise to myriad other interventions from mesmerism to phrenology, to psychoanalysis, to moral treatment, and more. And, as Andrew Scull describes, the twentieth century was no less strident and energetic in its pursuits of cures: 'All across Europe and North America, the 1920s and 1930s witnessed the introduction of a quite remarkable array of somatic treatments designed to root out madness and restore the lunatic to sanity.'[10] David Healy elaborates on these practices and suggests that such interventions can, in part, explain the preference for talking therapies in the post-World War II era:

> There was some grounds for such a bias [towards talking therapies] in the early post war years in that, in the pursuit of a cure for disease, patients had been subjected to a range of psychical assaults, including the removal of tonsils, gonads, stomachs, intestines, spleens, uteri, and teeth; they had had their sinuses and other sites of possible focal sepsis drained; they had had injections of colloidal calcium, inoculations with rat bite fever organisms; they had been rendered comatose with insulin, put to sleep for days, or made hypothermic; and a psychosurgery program was just beginning, which was to lead to 50,000 operations – the majority of which were almost certainly unjustified.[11]

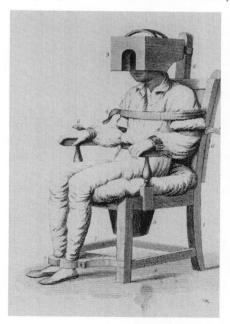

FIGURE 3.2 Benjamin Rush, 'Tranquilizer Chair'

As we skitter through this fleeting and partial history of treatments the purpose is not to offer a comprehensive summary of past healings (some of which we will return to in more depth); rather it is both to glance towards the sheer volume of curative practices and also to pay heed to their varied claims to legitimacy. As Power articulates: 'The history of psychiatry is both absurd and grotesque; with the benefit of hindsight, many of its practices have been cruel and inhumane. Nevertheless, each approach and each treatment was in its time typically based on a proto-scientific theory that led logically to the practices that were extrapolated from it.'[12] Joanna Moncrieff also cautions against the comforts of presentism:

> There is no real demarcation between previous eras' psychiatric treatments, and the theories that justified them, and our own; that the need to believe in a cure for psychiatric conditions that drove and sustained people's faith in insulin coma therapy, ECT, radical surgery, sex hormone therapy and many other bizarre interventions is the strongest impetus behind the use of modern-day psychiatric drugs. I shall suggest that the belief that modern drug treatments represent specific cures for specific illnesses is just as mistaken as the belief that insulin coma treatment was an effective and specific treatment for schizophrenia.[13]

Much of the history of psychiatric treatments is simultaneously a history of a search for origins and causality. However, as the twentieth century progresses, one can witness a decisive move away from causation and towards the alleviation of symptomology in psychiatric practice. This shift, for Darian Leader, not only enacted a movement from depth to surface, but also helped to proliferate 'illness' categories: 'If the drugs affected mood, appetite and sleep patterns, then depression consisted of a problem with mood, appetite and sleep patterns. Depression in other words, was created as much as it was discovered.'[14] Perhaps more opaque, however, is how far this history constitutes an account of what it means to have a valuable life. Indeed, this history asks what qualifies as worthwhile living and who produces and conditions the terms. What standards and values of normalcy are these treatments aiming to restore an individual to? Who decides what consequences or 'side' effects are worth it? What assumptions govern the patrolling of minds in distress? Finally, this history cautions against the assumption that *they* got it wrong, but *we* have finally got it right. This chapter will interrogate how far, and to what end, the artists under discussion have intervened in this pockmarked past.

Hide and seek

Gilman argues, in his study of the visual history of madness, that 'We learn to perceive the world through those cultural artefacts which preserve a society's stereotypes of its environment. We do not see the world, rather we are taught by representations of the world about us to conceive of it in a culturally acceptable manner.'[15] Gilman here suggests that perception is far from spontaneous, natural, or static. Instead, ways of seeing are biased, shifting, and culturally codified. Looking is, then, an act of interpretation. Peggy Phelan's examination of the Abu Ghraib photographs also reminds us that images encode the 'conditions of capture'.[16] The double sense of capture here allows us to understand Phelan's suggestion that what we are able to see via the camera's aperture is far from neutral or random. The images reveal not only the conditions in which detainees are captured but, simultaneously, the ideological conditions that permit and frame the act of photographic capturing (and perceiving). I am concerned, therefore, to consider what conditions of capture are at play in the three portraits of psychiatric treatments under discussion. Both Gilman and Phelan are, of course, discussing documentary photography (and illustration for Gilman's part), and thus questions of gaze are nuanced differently. However, if one pivots flexibly from their starting point of asking what can I see and what conditions my ability to see it, we may be able to strain towards a better understanding of the political density of these populist artistic works. How do these works sustain and disturb diagnostic gaze in their depictions of mad treatments? How do they participate in the long history of displaying the mad? How do these artists treat practices of care? If gaze is core technology in the practice of diagnosis and treatment in the psy disciplines, then it is imperative to understand how these artistic works establish and corrupt logics and regimes of looking.[17]

A cuckoo in the nest

It is unsurprising to observe that for as long as there have been treatments for madness, there have been artistic articulations of such practices. Indeed, as Tiffany Watt-Smith has suggested, the arts and sciences more generally spiral in tandem, as opposed to progressing steadily in hermetically sealed spheres of reference. For example, in her interrogation of the problematic use of mirror neuron theory by humanities scholars, she advances the idea that understanding the 'theatricality of the laboratory reminds us of the deep interdependence of apparently disparate scholarly methods and forms of knowledge.'[18] If we accept this premise, that knowledge is an entangled ecology, then it is not only predictable to find countless examples of cultural works that perform psychiatric treatments, but, moreover, it is worth giving their voices credence and critical attention when analysing the politics of care. A brief survey draws to mind the physician who visits Lady Macbeth but declares her mind's troubles beyond medicine: 'More needs she the divine than the physician',[19] the talking therapies of Georg Wilhelm Pabst's 1926 *Secrets of a Soul* or Christopher Hampton's 2003 *The Talking Cure*, the lobotomising Dr Cukrowicz of Tennessee Williams' 1958 *Suddenly Last Summer*, or the pharmaceutical conspiracy at the heart of Steven Soderbergh's 2013 *Side Effects*, to name but a few. This is to say nothing of the expansive love affair between psychoanalysis and cinema or the multiple depictions of ECT, asylum restraints, or maverick psychiatrists on stage and screen (large and small). Such works, and the many others beyond the scope of listing here, variously lambast, champion, vilify, parody, lament, and probe the practices of psychiatry and the psy disciplines. In this way, they form a compass point in the fraught and incomplete conversation about how to best respond to madness. Perhaps the most iconic, well-known cinematic example of the twentieth century in this regard, however, is the 1975 film version of Kesey's 1962 countercultural novel, *One Flew Over the Cuckoo's Nest* (hereafter *Cuckoo's Nest*). Below I will attempt to discern its role in the matted landscape of the cultural politics of madness.

Filmed over eleven weeks between January and March 1975 at the Oregon State Hospital with the cast and crew living on site on the ward for the duration the film, *Cuckoo's Nest* took a bold step inside 'the combine' of the original novel.[20] In the course of filming, 90 patients and staff were involved in paid roles as crew and extras, including the superintendent of the hospital, Dean Brooks, who plays Dr Spivey in the film. The film opened to critical acclaim and won five Oscars: Best Actor (Jack Nicholson), Best Actress (Louise Fletcher), Best Screenplay (Laurence Hauben and Bo Goldman), Best Director (Miloš Forman), and Best Picture (Saul Zaentz and Michael Douglas).[21] *Cuckoo's Nest* tells the story of R. P. McMurphy's time on a psychiatric ward and depicts the punitive regime of 'treatments' doled out to the men in the name of care. Ken Kesey was infamously critical of the film adaptation (despite claiming never to have seen it) primarily owing to its intention to shift the narrative perspective from Chief to R. P. McMurphy. Indeed, the film differs in numerous marked ways from the novel, notably including a softening of 'Big Nurse' from page to screen. However, the decision to move from the hallucinatory, ambiguous voice of the Chief to a realist mode provoked disdain from Kesey and has been subject to copious critical analysis since.[22] While I would concur that the shift of perspective corrodes the political potency offered by the original text insofar as it contracts the narrative frame to consensus reality thereby jettisoning alterity, I wish to pursue a different line of investigation. Namely, I will analyse how the film employs a visual, comic strategy of 'call back' to expose the fragility of the treatment regime.

First tragedy, then farce

Nurse Ratched runs a tight ship. Days on Ward 23B are a highly orchestrated regime of treatments from medication, to group therapy, to socialising, to visits to the 'Shock Shop' when necessary.[23] While the film does not depict, as the novel does, 'Bromden's constant round of daily tortures' such as violent early morning shaving that 'magnify the sense of anguish and helplessness that pervades the narrative world of *Cuckoo's Nest*', the onscreen ward remains a portrait of punitive rigidity.[24] Indeed, as he is dragged for ECT, Cheswick cries out 'But I didn't do anything wrong.'[25] The legacy of the film has been an enduring condemnation in the popular imagination of the absolute barbarity of ECT and psychosurgery. Notably, psychiatric history books make relatively few remarks regarding art and popular culture. Both the novel and film of *Cuckoo's Nest* however (along with a handful of others such as *The Snake Pit*, *I Never Promised You a Rose Garden* or *The Bell Jar*), are a recurrent stopping point in such historical prose. It is generally acknowledged as a sensationalist but significant work owing to its depiction of somatic treatments (even though these amount to less than five minutes of screen time in a film of two hours). For example, Gerald Grob remarks: 'The characters so graphically portrayed in Ken

Kesey's *One Flew Over the Cuckoo's Nest* are perhaps symbolic of the simplistic perception of psychosurgery that has prevailed in the popular mind.'[26] Joel Braslow similarly describes *Cuckoo's Nest* as the prime example of 'the horrors [of ECT] that have been popularly portrayed.'[27] Andrew Scull too addresses the tenacity of this film: 'Mainstream psychiatrists might continue to protest that electroshock treatment deserved a place in their therapeutic armamentarium for malignant forms of depression that resisted chemical remedies. But in popular culture the verdict was in: ECT was a dangerous and inhumane practice, an intervention that fried people's brains and destroyed memories.'[28] Even the musical *next to normal* references the film during its depiction of ECT: 'Didn't I see this movie/ With McMurphy and the nurse?/ That hospital was heavy/ But this cuckoo's nest is worse./ And isn't this the one where/ In the end the good guys fry?/ Didn't I see this movie/ And didn't I cry?'[29] Nevertheless, while its legacy may be the popularisation of a perception of ECT and lobotomy as brutal, I would like to suggest that there is also a quieter unpicking of therapeutics at play onscreen.

During his initial interview with Dr Spivey, McMurphy sees a framed photo of the superintendent holding a large dead fish on a chain. Spivey comments that it took all his strength to hold it up for the picture, to which McMurphy responds: 'probably that chain didn't help it any either … you didn't weigh the chain did you, doc?'[30] On the one hand, this is an innocuous spot of masculine chit chat. On the other hand, it is hard to miss the extra resonance that shimmers off the photo of an asylum superintendent holding a helpless fish out on a chain as a source of pride. Before one is too tempted to see this as simply heavy-handed symbolism of incarceration, it is important to further contextualise the image in a later moment in the film. McMurphy takes the 'boys' on a deep-sea fishing trip. The activity is tacitly framed as therapeutic insofar as it marks a direct challenge to the treatments of the wards. McMurphy, here, is giving the boys what they *really* need. As they return to shore the audience sees a shot of Dr Spivey waiting on the jetty. The camera cuts back, as if to imply a direct address from the boat to Spivey, to this image of the men (Figure 3.3).

FIGURE 3.3 'Gone fishing', *One Flew Over the Cuckoo's Nest*

One may be tempted to conclude that this visual reversal is merely a contortion of the familiar trope of the lunatics taking over the asylum. And perhaps this is a composite aspect of this frame. However, when taken alongside other moments of therapeutic subversion a deliberate strategy of political critique becomes legible. It is the patients who are now holding the (chain-free) fish. It is a complex image that splices freedom, a blurred occupational therapy, and homosociality and normative masculinity. Here we encounter the splintered logic of the film's critique. In one sense, by denuding Spivey of his privilege and power (albeit temporarily), the film makes plain the sand upon which the house of psychiatry is built. Power is assumed not spontaneous, performed not inherent. In another sense, however, the film relies on a dubious 'natural' masculinity to which the men must return as their route to autonomy (and therefore 'sanity'). This finds further echo in the character of the Chief who figures as a racialised, earthly counterpoint to white men's institutions embodied by Nurse Ratched. As Wilson Kaiser notes, this is not an uncommon trope of the counter cultural sixties: 'The rise of sixties counterculture witnessed an upsurge in interest in Native American culture and traditions, and indigenous customs were frequently figured as a deeper spiritual connection to the environment and a greater sense of personal wholeness.'[31] Perhaps, then, one of the remaining vestiges of Chief's perspective from the novel, in light of this, may be found in the opening and closing shots of the film, which linger on the natural landscape beyond the institutional walls. The bookending of the film thus operates to create a spiritualised myth of natural ways of life. While critiquing orthodox white male authority, it thus comes to reify an alternatively problematic vision of essentialised male sanity.

A second iconic moment from the film is 'medication time'. The men file past the spotless glass of the nurses' station to take their unidentified tablets. McMurphy questions 'what's in the horse pill?' only to be reassured that 'It's just medicine, it's good for you.'[32] Aside from the infantilism of the Nurse's response, which exposes the powerlessness of the men, this scene establishes another visual image of 'care' to be subverted. Towards the film's conclusion, McMurphy – as part of his escape routine – hosts a clandestine party on the ward. The patients once again line up in front of the glass to receive their meds, this time in the form of J&B Whiskey, from the aptly named Candy (Figure 3.4).

FIGURE 3.4 'Medication time', *One Flew Over the Cuckoo's Nest*

This playful sequence of self-medication necessarily calls into question the legitimacy of the drug regime that is imbibed passively. This is not to suggest that the film simplistically proposes booze rather than drugs as the solution; rather, as seen elsewhere such as in Sarah Kane's *4.48 Psychosis*, the juxtaposition of legitimate and illegitimate medicating places both in flux. Consider the following passage from Kane's searing critique of pharmacology and patients' drug charts:

> Venlafaxine, 75mg, increased to 150mg, then 225mg.
> Dizziness, low blood pressure, headaches. No other
> reaction. Discontinued.
> …
> 100 aspirin and one bottle of Bulgarian Cabernet
> Sauvignon, 1986. Patient woke in a pool of vomit and said
> 'Sleep with a dog and rise full of fleas.' Severe stomach
> pain. No other reaction.[33]

What both *Cuckoo's Nest* and *4.48 Psychosis* question, by inverting both the bureaucracy and rituals of treatment, is both the autonomy of the body within psychiatric regimes and the taken-for-granted hope that Drs and nurses know best. If one can be treated against one's will in psychiatric contexts and one's capacity to decide when to, for example, eat or brush one's teeth is pre-determined in hospital, then the hinterlands of the body become sites of contest. McMurphy's parody of treatments thus temporarily reaffirms the sovereignty of the men's bodies. In theatrically usurping the Nurse in this scene, in related ways to Spivey in the fishing episode, the giddy performance of authority exposes its very serious precariousness. In these ways, far from solely and spectacularly portraying the barbarity of lobotomy or the violence of ECT, *Cuckoo's Nest* unbraids the more unremarkable threads of psychiatric power and inequality.

Don't look now

Speaking at the Portland Bagdad Theatre Benefit in December 1975 to celebrate the launch of the film, Michael Douglas praised Dean Brooks for his astute understanding of *Cuckoo's Nest*: 'What was most helpful was that Dr Brooks saw the story for what it really was. It was an allegory about life in an authoritarian structure. It was not an attack on mental institutions.'[34] Brooks himself noted, somewhat elliptically, that: '*Cuckoo's Nest* was not controversial because of the material or because it was set in a mental hospital, but because it has exploded into consciousness the things we have refused to look at.'[35] Moreover, the film credits conclude with the following disclaimer: 'The characters portrayed herein are not intended to depict any existing institution or any real person, living or dead, and any similarity to any existing institution or to any real person is purely coincidental.'[36] Of course, numerous films contain variations of this manner of footnote for legal or other reasons. Nevertheless, it remains striking in this context owing to the use of a real hospital, its real superintendent, and many of its real patients. This does not mean that it is *about* Oregon State Hospital or that the inclusion of 'real' people automatically disqualifies the disclaimer. However, it is useful to situate this within the broader distancing gestures noted above and the tendency to describe the film as sensationalist, as over-the-top. If we accept Douglas's suggestion that it is not an attack on mental institutions, then a curious simulation of cruelty emerges in which psychiatry is only a celluloid metaphor for power. The onscreen hospital facsimile, populated with real figures in their normal environment, are then engaged in acts of hyperbolising their own realities.[37] It is certainly true that madness (and its world) functions, at least in part, as metaphor in *Cuckoo's Nest*. This is ever more apparent in its filmic cult classic status and its repeated re-mounting on stage (replete with star turns in the McMurphy role) which render it akin to a cultural museum piece of 'the bad old days'. I would like to propose here, however, a shift in our cultural-historic perspective and trouble some of the claims of allegory and spectacle by returning, in brief, to the history of lobotomy.

The first medical reports about psychosurgery date from the end of the nineteenth century. However, the lobotomy is generally associated with Egas Moniz, a Portuguese neurologist who pioneered the treatment in 1935 and would go on to win the 1949 Nobel Prize for this work. Today, the lobotomy is, by and large, relegated to a shameful corner of psychiatric history. As Pressman summarises, 'An argument could even be made that it has become our most visible icon for everything that is dangerous and bad about uncontrolled medical science.'[38] However, while one might conclude that lobotomy was barbarous, reducing its practitioners to evil or incompetent individuals is a mistake insofar as it overlooks the structural and epistemic conditions that produced the procedure. In the two decades that psychosurgery was popular, around 20,000 operations were performed in North America and approximately 15,000 in Great Britain. In this period, the lobotomy was not a sideshow or an aberration. As with other somatic interventions, it was a readily embraced new hope for a medical treatment for intractable distress, legitimised through proto-science. Moreover, even at the time its practitioners were not naïve to its efficacy or effects. As Pressman notes, the lobotomy was 'never advertised as a form of medical cure, but as a kind of partial *salvage*, an attempt to make the best of a tragic set of conditions.'[39] While many of the lobotomies were undertaken in the back, refractory wards – and therefore on collections of poor, non-white, and female patients – lobotomies were also regularly performed in 'well-to-do' environments. Indeed, countless hospital case notes and published studies of surgery reveal doctors understood the damage done by the procedure but instead chose to emphasise the resultant functionality and manageability of patients. Walter Freeman, perhaps the most infamous lobotomist, described for example that following surgery, patients 'cannot be serious. They do not dream', but celebrated that: 'Life is enormously simplified by the relatively complete obliteration of the need for introspection.'[40] Discussing a set of patient records, Braslow similarly observes that one woman's loss of memory was deemed far less relevant than her ability to remain attractive and manage her wifely domestic duties competently:

'One could make a further observation that what mattered to these husbands and doctors was that the woman was restored to the abstract category "woman" irrespective of her psychological state.'[41] What is vital to grasp here is that discipline and therapy were not in conflict. Indeed, control of behaviour was in some sense understood to be therapeutic insofar as it restored a patient to a biddable citizen (of the ward or of wider society).

What is hiding in plain sight, of course, in these case histories is a keen sense of what types (in all senses of the term) of lives matter. If we return to *Cuckoo's Nest* and the charge that it is sensationalist, alongside the desire to emphasise the allegorical qualities of the picture, a question of cinematic truth emerges. If we assume that most doctors and nurses were not acting out of wickedness but instead from a (arguably much more pernicious) sense of therapeutic care, then Nurse Ratched becomes a simplistic caricature, and the lobotomy and ECT spectacular cinematic fictions.[42] However, if we juxtapose the psychiatric history, which exposes the use of psychosurgery as a disciplinary strategy to manage 'hopeless' cases, alongside, for example, Rosenhan's 1973 Stanford 'thud' experiment, alongside *Cuckoo's Nest*, alongside another work such as *Titicut Follies* a less allegorical, a less spectacular image spills into view.[43] McMurphy, like countless others in the period, is lobotomised for behaviour that is difficult to manage. Indeed, Chief describes the post-lobotomy McMurphy as a person-less body, abandoned to 'sit in the day room with his name tacked on it for twenty or thirty years so the Big Nurse could use it as an example of what can happen if you buck the system.'[44] While the cinematic story of the attack on Nurse Ratched amplifies the emotional dynamics of treatment and charges the film with a romantic, anti-heroic timbre, the moral logic of lobotomy as managing less valuable lives is violently acute. For example, a clinical conference from Stockton Hospital to discuss the decision to perform a second lobotomy on an 18-year-old patient came to the following conclusion: 'If it does help it does and if it doesn't we are no worse off … We can't do any more harm. It might do some good.'[45] Braslow discusses another patient's case history who was lobotomised five days after this report: 'in view of the fact that he feels there is nothing wrong with him mentally and that he does not need hospitalisation, it is my opinion that he is incompetent at this time.'[46] One cannot simply interchange the convulsing throat of the force-fed man in *Titicut Follies* with McMurphy's ECT spasms and lolling, lobotomised head, or with case notes description of post-operative incontinence *as if they are the same thing*. However, if one places *Cuckoo's Nest*'s vivid populism in dialogue with interlocking cinematic and historical discourses regarding the treatment of the 'insane', then the apparent hyperbole begins to fade to an altogether more familiar, less lurid hue. In this sense the film, echoing Chief's words in the novel, tells the 'truth even if it didn't happen.'[47] Moreover, as Pressman suggests, 'Although the actual use of lobotomy was comparatively moribund in the years that followed, the *story* of what had happened during the heyday of psychosurgery took on a life of its own.'[48] *Cuckoo's Nest* is a central component in that process of cultural storytelling and while it is problematic in numerous ways (from its gender politics to its pantomimic portraits of mad 'tics'), it helps to deconstruct the comfortable authority of psychiatric practices.

You're being hysterical

Sigmund Freud is not what one might call an obscure figure in popular culture. Moreover, his psychoanalytic legacy of talking therapies are similarly well, if not over, represented in diverse art forms. From John Huston's 1962 film *Freud* to Mark St Germain's 2011 play *Freud's Last Session,* to the HBO series *In Treatment,* to Hitchcock's 1945 *Spellbound,* to Philippa Perry's 2010 commix story *Couch Fiction: A Graphic Tale of Psychotherapy,* to Richard Appignanesi's 2012 *The Wolf Man,* even to case histories, books such as Stephen Grosz's 2013 *The Examined Life* or Tanya Byron's 2015 *The Skeleton Cupboard: The Making of a Clinical Psychologist* (to say nothing of Dalí or Woody Allen), there is a vast and varied history of artistic expressions of talking therapies in which Freud appears, at least in the popular imagination, as the original, even mythic, ur-listener. This is without even discussing the influence of Freud and psychoanalysis within the humanities and, in particular, on screen studies in the twentieth century and beyond. The ubiquity of onscreen analysis has led many critics to lament the shoddy imprecision of much of this work. Patricia Gherovici and Jamieson Webster write:

> Most psychoanalysts on film or television are bad psychoanalysts. They bungle the job; they violate boundaries by sleeping with their patients or falling in love with them; they act out aggressively or simply fail to act at all. They often look more troubled than the patient and reverse roles with the patient.[49]

Indeed, there is a body of scholarship which is concerned with, among other questions, the accuracy of cinematic and televisual portraits of analysis and psychotherapeutics more broadly.[50] This is not my concern. Instead, I am interested in the performative nature of psychoanalysis and the politics of its narrative practice. Gilles Deleuze and Félix Guattari remarked that 'no one today can enter an analyst's consulting room without at least being aware that everything has been played out in advance.'[51] Starting from this notion, I will examine Terry Johnson's 1993 play *Hysteria* in order to better understand the performativity of treatment. It is my contention that the amplified theatricality of this piece serves to politically illuminate the gloomier corners of the consulting room. Indeed, as with *Cuckoo's Nest,* I will attempt to decipher the critical voice with the hyperbolic wild play of this Freudian farce.

Hysteria opened on 1 August 1993 at the Royal Court Theatre Downstairs. Directed by Phyllida Lloyd, the play ran for four months to reasonable popular and critical success. Many of the reviews express a preference for the 'funny bits' and observe that the synthesis of farce and incest is dramaturgically challenging, requiring 'some awkward gear changes'.[52] It has recently been revived in the UK in 2013 at the Hampstead Theatre (then touring) with Anthony Sher in the lead, again to a warm critical response. Lyn Gardner described the play as 'not just funny' but 'unexpectedly moving' as it portrays 'the gravitas of the man and his rumbling fear'.[53] The play stages an encounter between Freud, Dalí, and the daughter of a former patient, Jessica Stein. As I have written elsewhere, centrally the play explores the consequences of Freud's renunciation of his 1896 work, *The Aetiology of Hysteria*.[54] Informed by scandals such as the Cleveland Affair and the publication of letters between Freud and Wilhelm Fleiss by Jeffrey Masson, the play takes a serious look at the pervasive denial of child sexual abuse by powerful men. The plot ostensibly concerns Jessica seeking a form of intellectual retribution from Freud for her mother, Miriam, who was 'cured' by Freud only to relapse after he renounced his theory of hysteria. Jessica re-performs her mother's case history of incest abuse as well as revealing her own: 'And please don't suggest that I imagined this. He was no beloved, half-desired father to me. He was a wiry old man who smelt of beer and cheese and would limp to my bed and masturbate on me. Only once was it an unexpected thing.'[55] The play also features Dalí. Yet his character appears to function more as a blast of 'euro' hilarity within the fantasia of pop-Freud that the play revels in: '**Dali** *rubs his nipple exotically*'; '*He* [Dalí] *finds a snail on* **Freud***'s desk. Unsticks it, pulls it from its shell and eats it.*'[56] In another sense, the play stages a nightmare-ish return of the repressed with the discontents of Freud's unconscious strewn across the stage in the form of memories and portents:

> *Sounds of shunting trains compete with music; a drowning cacophony. Grotesque* **Images** *appear, reminiscent of* **Dali***'s work, but relevant to* **Freud***'s doubts, fears, and guilts …* **Old Ladies** *make their way to a gas chamber …* **Dali** *is hit by a swan. Suddenly there appears a huge, crippled, faceless* **Patriarch**.'[57]

Indeed, the play begins and ends in the same moment and thus has the possible sheen of a morphine-filled dream. It is, then, a dense drama that glimpses into Freud's closet to uncover manifold entwined histories. However, for our purposes what is of note is its acute attention to the performative nature of both therapy and psychoanalytic selfhood. In its fevered contortion of treatment, it invites us to interrogate the creation of discourses of care and also the lives lost in the therapeutic fray.

Freudian skits

Rollo May observed that therapists must ask, 'can we be sure that we see a patient as he really is in his own reality rather than as a projection of our own theories.'[58] Sounding a related note, Carl Rogers argued that person-centred therapy ought to aim to adopt the patient's frame of reference and hear the story on her terms as opposed to refracting her experience through the therapist's own. In this sense, Rogers proposed that a therapist ought to attempt to empathetically inhabit the patient's horizon of perception and language. David Pilgrim suggests that such psychotherapeutic principles are what distinguish talking therapies from more somatically minded treatment models: 'The main appeal of talking treatments for those who have been denied them, to date, is their surface validity: they appear to offer precisely what somatic psychiatry does not – personal respect rather than objectification.'[59] Craig Newnes develops the jingle of scepticism in Pilgrim's voice, arguing that: 'Despite the profession-generated myth that clinical psychologists are determinedly anti-psychiatric, many not only ape medical colleagues in the use of diagnosis or so-called treatment but are also silent when it comes to opposing medically defined ills and aid.'[60] In this way, then, talking therapies hold apparent value owing to their attention to the individual, to life history, to the sense that madness is not Other but inherent to the human condition. As Scull describes: 'The same forces that led one to mental invalidism allowed another to produce accomplishments of surpassing cultural importance. Civilisation and its discontents, Freud proclaimed, were inevitably and irretrievably locked in an indissoluble embrace.'[61] The dark shadow of therapy, then, is its capacity to be as prescriptive, coercive, and powerful as its orthodox biological sister. Indeed, Karl Popper hinted at such risks in his conceptualisation of The Oedipus Effect in 1974. David Healy summarises:

> Popper argued patients in therapy present dreams with Jungian themes to a Jungian analyst but dreams with Freudian themes to a psychoanalyst. The hopes of those who go to have their futures read and transmuted into predictions, which are then noticed by the person when they occur. The expectations of the oracle (therapist) condition the behaviour of the person, so that what the oracle predicts is what comes to pass.[62]

Hysteria is alive to the complexities of these debates and supplements them with further moral and political questions. In its Freudian shriek, it exposes how far personhood has been conditioned by Freud, but it also foregrounds how far storytelling becomes a way to survive. In its doubled attention to narratives – both therapeutic and theatrical – it exposes the politics of making sense. Moreover, the play fizzes with meaning and interpretation. From Freud's analytic practice, to Jessica's embodied choreography of hysteric symptoms, to Dalí's evocation of the artistic unconscious *Hysteria* is alive with gestures of communication and acts of interpretation. There is an amplified sense, then, of tales being told.

Hysteria is, in many ways, an onstage closet: stuffed to the gunnels with Freudian clichés. The play begins with Freud asking his daughter Anna what this large 'thing hanging here in front of me' is, 'It's just dangling here. It's got a nob on the end .... Shall I give it a pull?'[63] Surrealism, word association, penis envy, dreams, transference, fantasy, innuendo, jokes, and more populate the stage. It is, in Popper's sense, The Oedipus Effect writ theatrical. A fantasia of Freud is offered, in part one assumes, to render it absurd. Freud operates to a degree as an historical artefact to be mined for hilarity. Indeed, even within the world of the drama, Jessica implies that Freud is something of a relic:

Jessica   I have inverted morbid tendencies,
             I know. And a great deal of free-floating anxiety desperate

for someone to land on. I am mildly dysfunctional, yes.
Freud   You have recently been in analysis.
Jessica   No I have recently been in a library.[64]

As the play concludes, Freud laments: 'I am not so much a man as a museum, and my compassion just another dulled exhibit, so be it. All I have done, what I've become … was necessary. To set the people free.'[65] In another sense, however, in the very availability of Freudianism to exploit, this topsy-turvy play reminds an audience how far Freud (and his distorted legacies) shape common understandings of our interior lives. And perhaps more importantly that such interiority has real value and meaning. Most significantly, though, the play sketches the therapeutic role of narrative. Reflecting on his own imminent death, Freud intimates, elegiacally, that living is an exercise in waiting and organising your bits and pieces so that they are easier to carry:

Freud   Like all the trains I ever caught, this one is
running later. And so I wait. I rearrange the luggage …
I mentally rehearse the panic of boarding,
check my watch with the clock … I prepare and prepare and yet
remain unprepared because when the train arrives there is
never time to button the jacket or check the ticket or even
say a meaningful goodbye. So until my inevitably fraught
departure, all I can do is wait, and rearrange the luggage.[66]

This sense of the centrality of narrative cohesion is echoed in the fate of Freud's former patient, Miriam Stein. Her fatal committal to an asylum was a direct consequence of having the legitimacy of her narrative torn asunder. Freud's recantation of *The Aetiology of Hysteria* abolished the story that Miriam had come to live peacefully with: 'you took back your blessing … You told my mother that her memory of abuse was a fantasy born of desire … You said her father did not seduce her; that is was she who wished to seduce her father.'[67] Here the play most obviously lays a serious charge at Freud's door regarding the enduring and pervasive denial of child sexual abuse. However, also skulking within this condemnation is a keen sense that the value of talking therapies is precisely in their care and attention to helping you rearrange your luggage, so it is easier to bear. In this way, *Hysteria* splices hope with danger: talking treatments are thus relational acts of survival but ones fretted with bias, politics, and power. There is also a key meta-theatrical component to this insofar as the therapeutic act of temporarily holding an Other's story is doubled in the act of spectatorship. In watching the practice of listening (and the failures of listening), an audience is twice present to questions of empathy and tenderness.

Faking it

Patrick Campbell and Adrian Kear describe the relationship between psychoanalysis and performance thus:

If performing is a process in which individuals, physically present on stage, think, speak, and interact in front of other individuals, then that very activity must throw into relief crucial questions about human behaviour. In making the hidden visible, the latent manifest, in laying bare the interior landscape of the mind and its fears and desires through a range of signifying practices, psychoanalytic processes are endemic to the performing arts. Similarly, the logic of performance infuses psychoanalytic thinking, from the 'acting out' of hysteria to the 'family romance' of desire.[68]

In her cultural history of pain, Joanna Bourke also observes that pain is an inter-subjective, social experience: 'Although pain is generally regarded as a subjective phenomenon – it possesses a "mine-ness" [after Paul Ricouer] – "naming" occurs in public realms.'[69] If pain is a public practice, an 'event' as opposed to an object or thing, then can we understand madness as a related process or experience? What are the consequences of understanding mental distress not as a disease category but instead as a felt experience to be encountered and interpreted? Unquestionably, madness is characterised by actual lived phenomena (hearing voices, profound despair, bodily dissociation, heightened sensory perception, and so on). Madness is, in this way, neither conscious choice nor sham. Madness instead ought to be understood as a public, intra-social practice insofar as such experiences, like pain, are felt in and through relationships, environments, languages, naming processes, rituals. Such an understanding, I propose, renders the performative politics of distress more visible. Bourke also points to the degree to which pain is a learned experience: 'people learnt that *this* is being-in-pain while *that* is something else – an itch, a feeling of heaviness, vertigo, or *jouissance*, for instance. Equally, pain becomes recognised by *other people* through the same interactive process.'[70] Crucially, what springs from the page here is a clarion sense that emotion and perception are part of a performative ecology of bodies, environments, discourse, and material existence that is necessarily political. Swivelling our attention away from a biological disease model and towards perceiving the performative qualities of a psychosocial model offers a different way to apprehend the messy, diverse realities of being in the world. *Hysteria*, in its re-performance of an analytic case history, signals precisely this notion – that illness, diagnosis, and treatment have a performative dimension.

Jessica Stein initially tries to pull the wool over Freud's eyes as she recreates her mother's case history: '*She rubs briefly at the top of her breast, as if removing a splash of wine. A hysterical manifestation ... She rubs ... She gags ... She rubs. Shakes her stiff fingers.*'[71] After a time Freud rumbles Jessica, not because her performance was unconvincing but because 'I published the facts of this case thirty years ago.'[72] Indeed, Freud affirms the perspicacity of Jessica's imitation: 'I was very explicit in my descriptions. You were very accurate in your impersonation.'[73] Later in the play, there is a more self-conscious staging of Miriam Stein's case but this time drawn from her personal diaries as opposed to the official published case history. Dalí is enlisted to play Freud:

Jessica	It's a warm day. I had difficulty getting here.
	The cab driver was reluctant to raise the canopy, and I
	cannot travel in an open cab.
Dalí	She knows this; is word-perfect.
Jessica	Shut up. Instead of persuading the cabbie, my
	husband berated me. I have to insist quite firmly, which has
	made me a little anxious.
	She rubs her breast.
	[…]
Jessica	I'm scared of the starlings. I'm frightened
	of the birds.
Dalí	*applauds.*
Jessica	Don't do that.
Dalí	It say this. "There was applause."
Jessica	*takes the journal.*
Jessica	"There was a pause."[74]

The comic undertones, however, begin to dissipate as the threshold between real and theatrical distress begins to distort. The staged therapeutic dialogue becomes triangulated as Jessica's embodiment of her mother's past careens into the present: '*She hits him* [Freud] … *The hysterical symptoms take hold of her, more exaggerated and more frequent. Other physical tics manifest themselves. She returns to the couch in an increasingly distressed state …* **Jessica** *moans loudly, an agonized exhalation that frightens* **Dalí**.'[75] At this point in the drama, Freud replaces Dalí and commences to play himself as he enters the staged history: '*He takes the chair.*'[76] As the theatricalisation of the analysis progresses, live and simulated therapy become hard to distinguish:

	She breaks down. Gags.
Freud	*What is wrong with your mouth?*
Jessica	The taste.
Freud	Describe the taste.
Jessica	The taste of salt. It's salt. Everything tastes of
	salt!! I'm filthy with this shit and all I can taste is salt.
Freud	Associate. The taste of salt.[77]

As the staged encounters conclude, Freud tellingly remarks: 'You have her mouth.'[78] The mouth, the source of telling – both speaking and gagging – becomes shared and the history ingested. This embodied act of ventriloquism thus raises questions about the performativity of symptomology, both at an individual and wider cultural level. One is reminded, here, of Ulrika Maude's account of Charcot's influence on the cultural performance of insanity: 'So pervasive was Charcot's work and so profound its impact on the popular imagination that it rapidly influenced the performance style of the Parisian cabaret and vaudeville "with a new repertoire of movements, grimaces, tics and gestures", which mimicked the comportment and disposition of the Salpêtrière patients.'[79] Jessica's later disclosure that she too was sexually abused like her mother serves to retroactively ghost the performance of distress further disturbing the presumed demarcation between the lived and the learnt. By foregrounding the performative quality of distress and the scripting of anguish, *Hysteria* simultaneously emphasises how far treatment too is a public, politicised practice. Indeed, the play exposes how far distress and treatment are bonded in a dialogue of mutual expectation. In this way, Johnson invites us to imagine an alternative therapeutic conversation about the nature and practice of care.

Is that normal?

Andrew Scull describes the challenging picture for those involved in determining the causes of madness: 'despite the plethora of claims that mental illness is rooted in faulty brain biochemistry, deficiencies or surpluses of this or that neurotransmitter, the product of genetics and one day traceable to biological markers, the aetiology of most mental illness remains obscure, and its treatments are largely symptomatic and generally of dubious efficacy.'[80] He goes on to observe that 'We are decades away, after all, from successfully mapping the brain of the fruit fly, let alone successfully tackling the infinitely more complex task of unravelling the billions upon billions of connections that make up our own brains.'[81] Mark Rapley, Joanna Moncrieff, and Jacqui Dillon concur:

> more than a century of intensive psychiatric research has yet to find *any* form of organic grounding for the overwhelming majority of the 'mental disorders' listed in the *DSM* and psychology likewise has failed to provide any coherent alternative justification for this attempt to catalogue the 'problems of living'.[82]

Moncrieff challenges not only the relationship between correlation and cause and the basis for the varied arguments about faulty brain chemistry, but also the myth that drugs act in specific ways on specific illnesses. Andrew Lakoff describes this phenomenon as 'pharmaceutical reason': 'The term "pharmaceutical reason" refers to the underlying rationale of drugs intervention in the new biomedical psychiatry: that targeted drug treatment will restore the subject to a normal condition of cognition, affect, or volition.'[83] Under this logic, 'illness' becomes 'defined in terms of that to which it responds.'[84] Moncrieff is not arguing that there is no role for pharmacology in managing experiences of madness; rather she is suggesting a paradigmatic shift in approach that advances an understanding that drugs change your brain biochemistry and sometimes this can be helpful – they do not cure or fix it. Furthermore, she suggests, 'The use of drugs to induce temporary states that might bring relief from intense psychological torment is compatible with viewing psychiatric disturbance as an extreme but meaningful response to the world.'[85] Those critical of categorical biological psychiatry frequently note how far the tail wags the dog with respect to drug treatments and diagnosis. David Healy explains that 'drug companies obviously make drugs, but less obviously they make views of illness. They don't do so by minting new ideas in pharmaceutical laboratories, but they selectively reinforce certain possible views.'[86] Alongside funding research trials, ghost writing academic articles, and supporting patient advocacy groups through educational outreach (read: marketing), this reinforcing takes place at the level of PR: 'Their brief is simple – get speakers to talk on the issue of social function-ing generally, and Reboxetine sales will follow. The model worked in the cases of "Xanex + panic disorder" and "Paxil + social phobia."'[87] In light of this complex picture, the final case study of this chapter will examine the political portrait of drugs on stage in the Broadway musical, *next to normal*. I will argue that *next to normal* offers an unusually bold critique of psychiatric treatments but does so, in related ways to *Cuckoo's Nest*, without a reflexive awareness of its own tacit assumptions about what 'normal' really might mean.

next to normal opened off-Broadway at Second Stage Theater on 16 January 2008 to mixed notices. Many reviewers found the hyper-ironic tone problematic.[88] The musical was re-written and ran for just under two months at the Arena Stage, Crystal City, Virginia in late 2008. It then transferred to the Booth Theater on Broadway in Spring 2009 where it ran for 733 performances, finally closing in January 2011. It has been restaged multiple times internationally and won numerous plaudits includ-ing two Tony Awards (Best Musical Score and Best Orchestrations) and the 2010 Pulitzer Prize. It signals its unusual tone in the opening song, 'just another day': 'So my son's a little shit, my husband's boring / And my daughter, though a genius, is a freak.'[89] These lyrics and the rock 'n' roll quality of the musical score place it in a constellation with other contemporary musicals such as Duncan Sheik and Steven Slater's 2006 adaptation of Frank Wedekind's 1906 play *Spring Awakening*, the crea-tors of *South Park*'s 2011 *The Book of Mormon*, or Richard Thomas and Stewart Lee's 2003 *Jerry Springer: The Opera*.[90] The musical glimpses inside a nuclear family's home and theatricalises the discontents contained therein. The two acts tell the story of Diane's experiences of her bipolar diagnosis and resultant treatments from psycho-therapy to pharmacology to ECT. The set, which is part cross-section of a house and part cross-section of a (Diane's?) head, hints at a possible feminist critique of the position of women as 'home' (Figure 3.5).

FIGURE 3.5   *next to normal*, Booth Theater, New York, April 2009. Photo credit: Sara Krulwich/ *New York Times*

One is reminded here in ways of Anne Sexton's 1962 poem 'Housewife':

> Some women marry houses.
> It's another kind of skin; it has a heart,
> a mouth, a liver and bowel movements.
> The walls are permanent and pink.
> See how she sits on her knees all day,
> faithfully washing herself down.
> Men enter by force, drawn back like Jonah
> into their fleshy mothers.
> A woman is her mother.
> That's the main thing.[91]

However, there is little discernible critical dismantling of the set which equates woman with house beyond somewhat glib sardonic dialogue such as 'I keep cave clean. You got out, get fire!'[92] Indeed, while there is a narrative of liberation at stake in this musical, it relies, as I will explore below, on an individualistic tale of self-actualisation that is deeply conservative and tacitly reaffirms a certain model of 'good', 'safe' madness. This is not to imply that the musical has no value, or that only certain types of 'difficult' madness *count*, politically speaking; rather I am simply concerned to excavate the limits of these safe songs of pain.

'Now the drugs don't work'[93]

next to normal rehearses popular perceptions regarding psychiatric treatments. For example, as noted above, infamous works and iconic figures related to invasive surgery and ECT such as *Cuckoo's Nest* or Graeme Clifford's 1982 biopic *Frances Farmer* and Sylvia Plath's *The Bell Jar* are recounted in the song 'didn't I see this movie' as Diane deliberates whether to consent to ECT: 'I'm no Sylvia Plath./ I ain't no Frances Farmer kind of find for you … / So stay out of my brain – / I'm no princess of pain.'[94] At another moment during her psychotherapy, the lyrics conjure a popular perception of talking therapies as a more empathetic, dimensional embrace. During these sessions, Diane sings the repeated refrain 'Catch me I'm falling'. Moreover, during a 'breakthrough' therapeutic moment Diane, Doctor, Husband, Son, and Daughter are all singing overlapping lyrics related to Diane's case history. This harmonising polyphony hums with Bourke's argument that pain can only be understood in three dimensions: 'A pain-event always belongs to the individual's life, it is part of her life story.'[95] The musical does not exonerate psychotherapy as *the* answer. However, *next to normal* certainly stages popular attitudes to treatments which, in broad terms, understand talking therapies as more humane. However, the real strength of the piece is not its gentle echoes of common perceptions. *next to normal* is perhaps most bold in its critique of the warped logic of treatment – if it's not working you must need more – and its attention to the life-robbing effects of drugs. Critiquing North American pharmacological research, Laura D. Hirshbein writes:

Through these studies [drug trials] researchers made explicit assumptions that better research methods would yield better information about medication efficacy. But in the process, investigators changed the focus of the research from patients to medication. Instead of designing interventions around their patient population, researchers selected patients in a way most likely to demonstrate medication effects … Medications dictated diagnosis and patient selection, indeed to the point that medications began to shape how psychiatrists described their patients.[96]

next to normal is particularly astute in this regard through its playful exposure of the circular logic of psychopharmacology. In this sense, it politically theatricalises not only Healy *et al.*'s sense of Big Pharma's tail wagging the dog, but also the vile after-effects of too much wagging. Paradoxically, the saccharine form renders this critique all the more sour owing to the tension between the genre expectation of musical hope and the poisonous reality delivered lyrically.

Discussing the efficacy of anti-depressants, the authors of *Demedicalising Misery* summarise that:

> recent meta-analyses suggest that their [antidepressants] advantage over a placebo is small and possibly clinically meaningless … Contrary to popular belief, it has *not* been demonstrated that depression is associated with an abnormality or imbalance of serotonin, or *any other* brain chemical, or that drugs work by reversing such a problem.[97]

While there is more evidence of the short-term benefits of neuroleptic drugs in comparison to placebo for some patients, it is 'uncertain whether other sedative drugs might not have the same effect.'[98] Furthermore, as Moncrieff argues, 'High rates of non-compliance suggest that many patients decide that they would rather take the risk of relapse than accept a life time of drug-induced disabilities.'[99] Sounding a related note, Healy reasons that:

> cures almost by definition should lead to a fall in drug consumption, and good medical care as defined by Pinel [knowing when *not* to use medicine] should too. But instead we have seen an astonishing and relentless increase in the sale of supposed panaceas that do little or nothing to save lives or significantly improve the quality.[100]

The situation is exacerbated in North America by the role of insurance companies who mandate 'reimbursable' medical diagnoses and pharmacological responses before payment will be released. Darian Leader directs our attention to the fact that 'Mood stabilizing medication is routinely prescribed to adults and children alike, with child prescriptions increasing by 400% and the overall diagnosis by 4000% since the mid-90s.'[101]And, as Scull wryly observes – noting the fact that the majority of members of the *DSM* taskforce have links to Big Pharma – 'drugs that cure are great – for the patient … chronic conditions are chronically profitable.'[102] *next to normal* offers a vivid portrait of the insatiable logic of contemporary drug treatment:

> **Doctor Fine** The pink ones are taken with food but not with the white ones. The white ones are taken with the round yellow ones but not with the triangle yellow ones. The triangle yellow ones are taken with the oblong green ones with food but not with the pink ones. If a train is leaving New York at a hundred and twenty miles an hour and another train is leaving St. Petersburg at the same time but going backwards, which train ….[103]

A sequence in the musical entitled 'who's crazy / my psychopharmacologist and I' captures Lakoff's pharmaceutical reason in a jazz waltz. After reporting that she feels less anxious but now has 'headaches, blurry vision, and I can't feel my toes', Doctor Fine reassures Diane: 'So we'll try again, and eventually we'll get it right.'[104] Seven weeks into treatment both characters chart Diane's progress. Diane relates: 'I don't feel like myself. I mean, I don't feel anything.' The doctor concludes: 'Patient stable.'[105] This is intercut with scenes of Diane's daughter learning to appreciate jazz improvisation thus further underscoring the free-form chaos of pharmaceutical intervention. Later, following her ECT and subsequent memory loss Diane describes feeling little improved. Her current Doctor concludes: 'The treatment is strong / But lasts only so long / It may be your mind's needing more.'[106] Doctor Madden continues and suggests that they can resume the talking therapies, try a new drug regime, schedule more ECT, and try new 'promising therapies. EMDR, for instance or rTMS. Diana'.[107] *next to normal*, here, emotively conveys the image of psychiatry as Ouroboros, eating its own tail. In its cornucopia of staged treatments, the musical renders a fierce critique of psychiatry in an unassuming form. The strength of its critique, in fact, lies precisely in the day-to-day plain-speaking of Diane. Diane's dawning realisation of the incompatibility between problem and response forms the dramatic denouement of her story in a song called 'the break': 'What happens if the medicine / Wasn't really in control? / What happens if the cut, the burn, the break / Was never in my brain or my blood / But in my soul?'[108] An audience is invited to align their perspective with hers in ways that dispense with the possibility of her figuring as medical specimen to be observed and rather as a soul to be explored. As I have argued elsewhere in this volume, the desire to look with, and not at, mad characters marks a decisive political move away from placing a clinical gauze between stage and auditoria. Moreover, Diane's register forms an antidote to the jargon of the Doctors. In so doing, the diagnostic gaze is spun and instead catches psychiatry in its sights. *next to normal* thus delivers a critical prescription for psychiatry under mainstream lights.

That's not political, this is political

One may detect a tacit assumption in this reading of *next to normal* that a Broadway musical is *de facto* a lesser political animal than, for example, a fringe theatre show.

However, as Alan Read has argued, no form has an a priori claim to 'the political'.[109] Rather than suggesting that the musical is apolitical (and putting aside debates as to whether performances can be political or only have political effect), I wish to observe some of the conventions to which this form adheres and how this marks an undoing of some of political thinking that is blasting from the stage in *next to normal*. In particular, I am concerned here with endings. The happy ending of *next to normal* and the terms on which it is predicated expose a number of underlying value systems upon which this musical swivels. The concluding 'big number' is entitled 'light' and its lyrics celebrate fortitude in the face of adversity, urging the characters, and by extension the audience, to be brave in the face of darkness because eventually the dawn will break and 'The light will make it look brand new … So let it shine, shine shine!'[110] On the one hand, there is comforting folk wisdom in this restitution narrative of hard journeys won.[111] On the other hand, the 'heart-wringing' climax drips with privilege, normalcy, and individualism.[112] Indeed, it is positively myopic in its gaze. Governments in both Britain and North America are invested in the biological framing of psychiatry, in part, because faults in brains are less complex political issues to solve than systemic social inequalities. As Moncrieff argues, governments are invested in 'transforming all sorts of problems and dis-affections wrought by social and economic changes into psychiatric deviance.'[113] Chemicals are, in this sense, less volatile material than child abuse, domestic violence, racism, LGBTQ+ oppression, poverty, and so on. *next to normal*'s perspective is also problematically constrained. The musical concludes with ghosts laid to rest, young love triumphing, and adults embarking on journeys of self-acceptance and discovery. In short, everything and everyone is in their 'proper' place. It is not a 'perfect' image but it is, as the play title inadvertently suggests, rather close to normal.

The choice to represent a white, middle-class, heterosexual, able bodied, educated family's struggles is inherently and inescapably marked by a type of conservatism. However, I am more concerned to question how far privilege remains fundamentally unexamined in the musical. Moreover, the traumagenic framing of the madness – Diane is distressed because she lost a child – places the musical squarely in the 'good' madness camp. Again, this is not to say one cannot or should not represent traumagenic experience; rather I simply want to observe that the certainty of 'cause' in this musical, when coupled with the reassertion of dominant images and narratives of hegemonic social values, occupies a politically safe theatrical space. The option to opt out of her marriage in order to self-actualise is simply not available to the majority of women: 'It's time for me to fly ….'[114] At this moment, the musical reaffirms a notion that the capacity to thrive is located within our own psychological resources in ways that wilfully overlook the lived realities for the majority of individuals experiencing mental anguish. In not peering beyond the internal structures of the middle-class household/brain, literalised in the set, *next to normal* fails to engage with the social life of madness. It is the interlocking safety mechanisms that the musical employs (traumagenic causes, conventional narrative arc, values of self-realisation and so on) that render this big show paradoxically small. *next to normal*, in these ways, politely tidies away the complexities of madness in favour of the quick fix of hope. Indeed, in its astringent domestication and blinkered individualist framing of experience, the musical normalises madness and renders it a petty pleasure disguised as politics to be consumed on Broadway. In this way, while, on the one hand, the musical offers an acute critique of psychiatric treatments, on the other hand, it replicates the shallow gaze of orthodox psychiatry.

Reversing roles

David Hillman and Ulrika Maude argue that: 'Authorities (medical and socio-economic and political) have powerfully vested interests in *constructing* bodies in particular ways; literature, throughout the ages, works to remind us of this fact and thereby *deconstruct* these myths, often by reinstating the delirium and the scandalousness of the body.'[115] The three works discussed in this chapter are engaged in this practice of deconstruction from within populist milieus. All three works, in their sticky proximity to highly conventional forms of telling, acquire some predictable and problematic clichés – from *real* masculinity, to hypersexualised psychoanalysis, to neoliberal self-actualisation. Nevertheless, while these mainstream genres lead the artists down some political cul-de-sacs, these three examples all unbraid the values and power structures that are embedded in contemporary and historical practices of care. All three works, in their interrogation of psychiatric treatments, unearth what such activities reveal about whose lives matter. They expose how far treatments tacitly convey a value system about what constitutes a good, worthwhile life. They ask who patrols the body and determines what range of feeling is 'enough'. Whether it is McMurphy's imitative upending of psychiatric power, Jessica's understanding of the disappearance of women inside male-authored theoretical discourses, or Diane's awareness of the incomprehensibility of her call within the current schema of psychiatric responses, all three disassemble the legitimacy of how we practice care. Moreover, they do so by returning us to fleshy, messy, scandalous bodies writ large in hyperbolic three-dimensional form. The examples, therefore, represent depth and dimensionality in direct challenge to the surface and categorical discourse of orthodox psychiatry.

As Moncrieff argues: 'Identifying the interests that have shaped and distorted what passes as knowledge about psychiatric drugs, creates opportunities for "resistance" in Foucault's terms. These opportunities can help to shape a different form of knowledge and activity freed from the constraints of those particular interests.'[116] Artistic practice such as these form one branch in such resistive actions. It is vital to situate such work, however, alongside myriad other interventions from David Healy's critical pharmacology website www.rxisk.org to the development of Open Dialogue therapies in Western Lapland to publications such as Peter Stastny and Peter Lehmann's *Alternatives Beyond Psychiatry*, and many more.[117] In so doing, these activities collectively attempt to shift what Gilman terms the 'root metaphor' of treatments for those experiencing mental distress.[118] Gilman suggests that we begin any project of understanding from a location, and, therefore, this set of coordinates influences how we read subsequent experiences. Gilman here foregrounds how far perception is conditional and interpretive. It is the contention of this chapter that far from weakening the practice of psychiatry and the psy disciplines, a more hospitable and curious embrace of the role of interpretation within care would be a valuable step to more equitable treatment of those in crisis and distress. There is, therefore, a clinical lesson to be learnt from the uncertain practice of humanities scholarship. The artists discussed attempt to explore an ethical practice of care based on difference and not knowing. Rather than assuming that empathy must emerge from imaginative sameness, these artists linger in with the possibility that starting with a radical embrace of difference may in fact be generative. In exploring empathy without sameness, they create more space to explore the multifarious ways that care, therapy, and survival may actually be practised. In this sense, they argue for clinical encounters to emerge not from a sense of what's 'good' for you, but rather from the question: how would you like to be treated? Moreover, all three works discussed in this chapter, like the other examples noted above, argue for a role reversal that would begin with the experts-by-experience and lead to a paradigmatic shift in the root metaphor(s) of psychiatric treatment. In so doing, they argue for nothing less important than treating others the way that they wish to be treated.

Notes

1 Ernest Hemingway, quoted by A. E. Hotchner in *Papa Hemingway: A Personal Memoir* (New York: Random House, 1966), p. 280. Hemingway is reported to have expressed this in direct response to his experience of electroconvulsive therapy.
2 Luke, 6:31, King James Version of Bible.
3 Sander L. Gilman, *Picturing Health and Illness: Images of Identity and Difference* (Baltimore, MD: The Johns Hopkins University Press, 1995), p. 50.
4 Notable figures in this regard include David Pilgrim, Mick Power, Andrew Scull, Dinesh Bhugra, and Richard P. Bentall among many others.
5 Elliot S. Valenstein (ed.), *The Great Psychosurgery Debate: Scientific, Legal, and Ethical Perspectives* (San Francisco: W. H. Freeman and Company, 1980), p. 15.
6 See Sander Gilman's *Seeing the Insane* (Lincoln, NE: University of Nebraska Press, 1982) for a critical account of visual documentations of madness and psychiatry.
7 Greg Eghigian (ed.), *From Madness to Mental Health: Psychiatric Disorder and Its Treatment in Western Civilisation* (New Brunswick, NJ: Rutgers University Press, 2010), p. 9.
8 John Bunyan, quoted in Valenstein, p. 22 and Power, p. 15.
9 See Mary de Young's *Encyclopaedia of Asylum Therapeutics, 1750–1950* (Jefferson, NC: MacFarland, 2015) for further examples.
10 Andrew Scull, *Madness in Civilisation: A Cultural History of Insanity from the Bible to Freud, from the Madhouse to Modern Medicine* (London: Thames & Hudson, 2015), p. 308.
11 David Healy, *The Anti-Depressant Era* (Cambridge, MA: Harvard University Press, 1997), p. 222.
12 Power, p. 1.
13 Joanna Moncrieff, *The Myth of the Chemical Cure: A Critique of Psychiatric Drug Treatment*, rev'd edn (Basingstoke: Palgrave, 2009), pp. 1–2.
14 Darian Leader, *The New Black: Mourning, Melancholia, and Depression* (London: Penguin, 2009), p. 14.
15 Gilman, *Seeing the Insane*, p. xiii.
16 Peggy Phelan, 'Afterword' in Patrick Anderson and Jisha Menon (eds), *Violence Performed* (Basingstoke: Palgrave, 2009), p. 379.

17 'Psy disciplines' here is borrowed from Nikolas Rose's *Inventing Ourselves* in which he clusters 'psychology, psychiatry, and their cognates' under this umbrella term, p. 2.

18 Tiffany Watt-Smith, 'Eating Imaginary Raisin: Theatre's Role in the Making of Mirror Neurons' in *Studies in Theatre and Performance*, 36:1, March 2016, pp. 17–20, p. 20.

19 William Shakespeare, *Macbeth* in Stephen Greenblatt *et al.* (eds), *The Norton Shakespeare* (London: W.W. Norton & Sons, 1997), V:1, p. 2609.

20 In Kesey's novel, the narrator, Chief Bromden, describes the hospital as 'the combine', a huge and fearful all-seeing machine of control.

21 The stage version by Dale Wasserman has also enjoyed enduring success with countless productions and star 'turns' in the R. P. McMurphy role.

22 See, for example, John Zubizarretta, 'The Disparity of Point of View in *One Flew Over the Cuckoo's Nest*' in *Literature/Film Quarterly*, 22:1, January 1994, pp. 62–8 or Marsha McCreadie, '*One Flew Over the Cuckoo's Nest*: Some Reasons for One Happy Adaptation', in *Literature/Film Quarterly*, 5:2, Spring 1977, pp. 125–31.

23 Ken Kesey, *One Flew Over the Cuckoo's Nest* (London: Picador, 1973), p. 58.

24 Wilson Kaiser, 'Disability and Native American Counter Culture in *One Flew Over the Cuckoo's Nest* and *House Made of Dawn*' in *Journal of Literary and Cultural Disability Studies*, 9:2, pp. 189–205, p. 193.

25 *One Flew Over the Cuckoo's Nest*, dir. by Miloš Forman (The Saul Zaentz Company, 1975). Hereafter *Cuckoo's*.

26 Gerald Grob, 'Foreword' to Jack D. Pressman, *Last Resort: Psychosurgery and the Limits of Medicine* (Cambridge: Cambridge University Press, 1998), p. xiv.

27 Joel Braslow, *Mental Ills and Bodily Cures: Psychiatric Treatment in the First Half of the Twentieth Century* (Berkeley, CA: University of California Press, 1997), p. 123.

28 Scull, *Madness in Civilisation*, p. 321.

29 Brian Yorkey, 'Didn't I See This Movie' in *next to normal* (New York: Theatre Communications Group, 2010), p. 56.

30 *Cuckoo's Nest*, 08:49.

31 Kaiser, p. 189.

32 *Cuckoo's Nest*, 27:49.

33 Sarah Kane, '4.48 Psychosis' in *Sarah Kane: Complete Plays* (London: Methuen, 2001), p. 225.

34 Michael Douglas quoted by Ted Mahar in '*Cuckoo's Nest* Cast Praises Oregon Doctor for Help' in *The Oregonian*, 19 December 1975.

35 Dean Brooks, quoted in Diane L. Goeres-Gardner, *Inside Oregon State Hospital: A History of Tragedy and Triumph* (London: The History Press, 2013), p. 223.

36 *Cuckoo's Nest*, 2:14:00.

37 The actual ward used was no longer in use within the hospital but was part of the functioning facility.

38 Pressman, p. 3.

39 Ibid., p. 198.

40 Walter Freeman and J. W. Watts, 'Physiological Psychology' in J. M. Luck and V. E. Hall (eds) *Annual Review of Psychology*, VI, 1944, pp. 517–42, p. 520, p. 522.

41 Braslow, p. 161.

42 I acknowledge here that, particularly in the film version, there is a sense that Nurse Ratched does think that she is delivering care to the men on her ward. However, in the specific case of McMurphy's lobotomy, it is clearly and unambiguously framed as punishment.

43 While the Stanford experiment is not engaged with psychosurgery or ECT, it did aim to interrogate the practice of diagnosis and treatment on psychiatric wards. In 1973 David Rosenhan led an experiment in which eight individuals complained of auditory hallucinations (hearing words 'thud' or 'hollow'). All eight were admitted to psychiatric hospitals where they were detained for between seven and 52 days and between them prescribed a total of 2,100 pills.

44 Kesey, p. 253.
45 Case 59543, 19 February 1951, Stockton Hospital Clinical Conference, quoted by Braslow, p. 145.
46 Braslow, p. 147.
47 Kesey, p. 13.
48 Pressman, p. 401.
49 Patricia Gherovici and Jamieson Webster, 'The Bad Psychoanalyst: Watching the Success of Failure', in Lucy Huskinson and Terrie Waddell (eds), *Eavesdropping: The Psychotherapist in Film and Television* (London: Routledge, 2015), pp. 107–26, p. 107.
50 See, for example, Huskinson and Waddell's *Eavesdropping*, Glen O. Gabbard and Krin Gabbard's *Psychiatry and the Cinema* or David J. Robinson's *Reel Psychiatry: Movie Portrayals of Psychiatric Conditions* (Port Huron, MI: Rapid Psychler, 2003).
51 Gilles Deleuze and Felix Guattari, *Anti-Oedipus: Capitalism and Schizophrenia*, trans by R. Hurley, M. Seem, and H. Lane (New York: Viking Press, 1984), p. 308.
52 Malcolm Rutherford, *Financial Times*, 6 September 1993 and Paul Taylor, *Independent*, 7 September 1993.
53 Lyn Gardner, *The Guardian*, Friday 13 September 2013.
54 See Anna Harpin, 'Unremarkable Violence: Staging Child Sexual Abuse in Recent British Drama' in *Contemporary Theatre Review*, 23:2, May 2013, pp. 166–81.
55 Terry Johnson, 'Hysteria' in *The Methuen Book of Modern Drama: Plays of the 80s and 90s* (London: Methuen, 2001), II, p. 202.
56 Ibid., I:ii, p. 156, p. 138.
57 Ibid., II, p. 199.
58 Rollo May, 'The Origins and Significance of the Existential Movement in Psychology' in R. May, E. Angel and H. Ellenberger (eds), *Existence: A New Dimension in Psychology and Psychiatry* (New York: Basic Books, 1958), p. 3.
59 David Pilgrim, *Psychotherapy and Society* (London: Sage, 1997), p. 139.
60 Craig Newnes, 'Toxic Psychology' in Mark Rapley, Joanna Moncrieff and Jacqui Dillon (eds), *De-Medicalising Misery: Psychiatry, Psychology, and the Human Condition* (Basingstoke: Palgrave, 2011), pp. 211–25.
61 Scull, *Madness in Civilisation*, p. 289.
62 David Healy, *The Anti-Depressant Era*, p. 221.
63 Johnson, I:i, pp. 206–7.
64 Ibid., I:i, pp. 111–12.
65 Ibid., II, p. 202.
66 Ibid., I:i, p. 108.
67 Ibid., II, p. 172.
68 Patrick Campbell and Adrian Kear (eds), 'Introduction' in *Psychoanalysis and Performance* (London: Routledge, 2001), p. 1.
69 Joanna Bourke, *The Story of Pain: From Prayer to Painkillers* (Oxford: Oxford University Press, 2014), p. 6.
70 Ibid., p. 26, emphasis original.
71 Johnson, I:i, p. 118.
72 Ibid., I:i, p. 119.
73 Ibid., I: i, p. 120.
74 Ibid., I:ii, pp. 155–8.
75 Ibid., I:ii, p. 164.
76 Ibid., I:ii, p. 164.
77 Ibid., I:ii, p. 165.
78 Ibid., I:ii, p. 167.
79 Ulrika Maude, 'Literature and Neurology' in David Hillman and Ulrika Maude (eds), *The Body in Literature* (Cambridge: Cambridge University Press, 2015), pp. 197–213, p. 206.
80 Scull, *Madness in Civilisation*, p. 14.
81 Ibid., p. 409.

82 Rapley, Moncrieff, and Dillon, pp. 1–2, emphasis original.
83 Andrew Lakoff, *Pharmaceutical Reason: Knowledge and Value in Global Psychiatry* (Cambridge: Cambridge University Press, 2005), p. 7.
84 Ibid. p., 7.
85 Moncrieff, p. 227.
86 David Healy, *The Anti-Depressant Era*, p. 181.
87 David Healy, *Let Them Eat Prozac* (Toronto: James Lorimer & Company, 2003), p. 174.
88 See, for example, Ben Brantley, *New York Times*, 14 February 2008 or Joe Dziemianowicz, *New York Daily News*, 14 February 2008.
89 Brian Yorkey and Tom Kitt, 'Just Another Day', *next to normal* (New York: Theatre Communications Group, 2010), I, p. 8.
90 The creators of *South Park* and *The Book of Mormon* are Trey Parker, Robert Lopez, and Matt Stone.
91 Anne Sexton, 'Housewife' in *All My Pretty Ones* (Boston, MA: Houghton Mifflin, 1962).
92 Yorkey, I, p. 12.
93 The Verve, 'The Drugs Don't Work' from the album *Urban Hymns*, Hut, 1997.
94 Yorkey, I, p. 57.
95 Bourke, p. 5.
96 Laura D. Hirshbein, *American Melancholy: Constructions of Depression in the Twentieth Century* (New Brunswick, NJ: Rutgers University Press, 2014), p. 32.
97 Rapley, Moncrieff, and Dillon, p. 177, emphasis original.
98 Moncrieff, p. 98.
99 Ibid., p. 230.
100 David Healy, *Pharmageddon* (Berkeley, CA: University of California Press, 2013), p. 10, emphasis original.
101 Darian Leader, *Strictly Bipolar* (London: Penguin, 2013), p. 1.
102 Scull, *Madness in Civilisation*, pp. 401–2.
103 Yorkey, I, p. 16.
104 Ibid., I, p. 18.
105 Ibid., I, p. 22.
106 Ibid., II, p. 90.
107 Ibid., II, p. 91. EMDR is Eye Movement Desensitisation and Reprocessing, a therapy designed to unblock frozen, distressing memories through rapid eye movement. rTMS is Repetitive Transcranial Magnetic Stimulation, a therapy that produces magnetic pulses over the scalp to stimulate brain regions thought to be associated with mood.
108 Yorkey, II, p. 90.
109 See Alan Read, 'Introduction', *Theatre, Intimacy & Engagement: The Last Human Venue* (Basingstoke: Palgrave, 2008), pp. 1–14.
110 Yorkey, II, p. 103.
111 I am borrowing the term 'restitution narrative' from the work of Arthur W. Frank. See, for example, *The Wounded Storyteller: Body, Illness, and Ethics* (Chicago: Chicago University Press, 2005).
112 Ben Brantley's review of *next to normal* described the show thus: 'No show on Broadway right now makes as direct a grab for the heart – or wrings it as thoroughly – as "Next to Normal" does', *New York Times*, 15 April 2009.
113 Moncrieff, p. 136.
114 Yorkey, II, p. 98.
115 Hillman and Maude, p. 5, emphasis original.
116 Moncrieff, p. 244.
117 Peter Stastny and Pete Lehmann (eds), *Alternatives Beyond Psychiatry* (Shrewsbury: Peter Lehmann, 2007).
118 Gilman, *Seeing the Insane*, p. xiii.

PART 2

Experiences: Realities, Bodies, Moods

4

IMAGINING REALITY

Figuring Perceptual Experiences on Stage and Screen

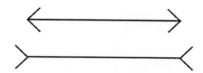

FIGURE 4.1   Two Arrows optical illusion

This well-known optical illusion – in which one line appears to be longer than the other despite them in fact being exactly the same length – allows us to reflect upon the relationship between what we see and what is 'really there', between what we believe to be the case and what materially exists (Figure 4.1). Likewise, we can contemplate the moment that Old Hamlet appears in Gertrude's bed chamber:

> **Hamlet:** Do you see nothing there?
> **Gertrude:** Nothing at all, yet all that is I see.
> **Hamlet:** Nor did you nothing hear?
> **Gertrude:** No, nothing but ourselves.[1]

This is not to equate illusions with hallucinations (or to imply that the ghost in *Hamlet* is an hallucination per se); rather, I am merely drawing our attention to the precariousness and interdependence of perception and reality. It is my contention that reality is a performative, relational, and interpretive practice. Further, following Tia DeNora, I would agree that in place of focussing on what reality *is* we might instead profitably concentrate instead on what it does, by asking *how* it is generated.[2] How can one verify a perception? How do I know that you see what I see, hear what I hear? And does it matter if you don't? In this way, I am concerned with how realities are made and the politics of such meaning making practices. If we accept that some realities are more equal than others – indeed one can be detained and forcibly treated for experiencing certain perceptual phenomena such as hearing voices – then the norms that condition, produce, and constrain reality ought to be considered. If we accept that reality is not simply spontaneous and universal and instead is enculturated, then it becomes important to disassemble the practices that fashion its sights and sounds. In this purview, reality, like truth, has moral and political textures and thus warrants interrogation until the means of production of perceptual legitimacy and authority are more evenly distributed. In related manners to Joanna Bourke's critical understanding pain as an event encountered within a web of stories (personal, biological, social and so on), this chapter proposes that we attempt to think of reality as a relational, always incomplete, encounter.[3] The three artists considered in this chapter – Anthony Neilson, Richard Kelly, debbie tucker green – are all engaged with the contours of realities and collectively illuminate how far reality is neither a place nor a thing, but rather an experience to be explored. In so doing, all three works excavate rich political terrain for a widened understanding of here and now.

Tuning in

Voice hearing and other unusual perceptual phenomenon such as visions have long histories, often twinned in the West with narratives of religious visitation, possession, or ecstasy. As Daniel B. Smith observes, however, the focus shifts from the divine to the pathological following the Enlightenment:

> The divine voice runs like a steady trail through Christian history ... But somewhere around the eighteenth century, the culture's way of thinking and talking about unusual experiences altered markedly. What was once revelation and inspiration became symptom and pathology. What was piety and poetry became science and sanity. In public discourse, voice-hearing became a force of harm and an experience to eradicate.[4]

Yet the uncritical association between voice hearing and mental illness is flawed. As Charles Fernyhough articulates: 'Voice-hearing can be highly distressing and debilitating, but it does not equate to schizophrenia ... In fact, voice-hearing does not even equate to madness.'[5] Fernyhough examines the interrelationships between common experiences, such as inner speech, and less common experiences, such as hearing a voice that feels wholly external to the self, in order to debunk the notion that unusual perceptual phenomena are categorically distinct from quotidian mental life. Furthermore, in his book *Hallucinations*, Oliver Sacks chronicles the extraordinary range of causes and types of unusual perceptual phenomenon that people experience from Charles Bonnet Syndrome to feverish delirium, to drug-induced psychosis, to hypnogogic visions, and more. Moreover, he notes that how we interpret an experience (individually and collectively) is paramount to the nature and quality of that experience. He reasons, for example, that:

children cannot consistently and confidently distinguish fantasy from reality, inner from outer worlds, until the age of seven or so ... children may also be more accepting of their hallucinations, having not yet learned that hallucinations are considered (in our culture) 'abnormal'.[6]

The argument advanced by these authors is not that there is no particularity to unusual perceptual phenomena, nor do they eschew the intersectional conditions that inform lived experience with unusual encounters; their writings pay careful attention to the phenomenal quality of such encounters. However, in advancing continua between common and unusual mental experiences, they attempt to reframe the cultural conversation around voice-hearing and related 'pathological' experiences. For these thinkers, as well as the artists discussed in this chapter, such experiences are meaningful and can offer insight rather than being simply a 'neuro chemical glitch, to which the only proper response is medical, pharmaceutical treatments.'[7] Indeed, rather than understanding experiences such as hearing voices as 'the surplus of what makes sense', these artists and thinkers depart from an a priori sense that such perceptual encounters are creative acts (even if profoundly distressing), and ought to be explored as opposed to being reduced to symptoms to be cured.[8]

The urgency for radically reframing the cultural conversation is plain:

> Analysing data from the 2006 US General Social Survey, a group of researchers found that nearly two-thirds of respondents said that they would be unwilling to work with a person with the diagnosis [schizophrenia], while 60 per cent expected that someone with schizophrenia would be violent towards others. Looking back at the data from ten years earlier, the authors reported little change in attitudes. Although the 2006 respondents were more likely than their 1996 counterparts to attribute schizophrenia to a neuro-biological cause, that shift in understanding seemed to have gone with an increase rather than a decrease in negative attitudes.[9]

While, as noted above, voice hearing and hallucinatory encounters are not unique to schizophrenia (or even mental distress more generally), the point of significance here is that as the master signifier, or what Angela Woods terms the sublime object of psychiatry, schizophrenia functions as something of a cultural metonym and, thereby, reveals a great deal about general cultural attitudes to all forms of mental alterity.[10] If Fernyhough's account above offers a snapshot of systemic attitudes to madness, Eleanor Longden's viral TED talk offers a personal account of the dire consequences of a purely biological approach to experiences such as hearing voices. Longden's talk, filmed in February 2013, has received nearly four million views to date.[11] In her presentation, she describes her early encounters with psychiatry as initiating a 'psychic civil war' that, through the insistence that the voices be eradicated, exacerbated the frequency and tyranny of the voices. On an individual level, Longden underscores the extent to which orthodox psychiatry's refusal to acknowledge the meaning and insight the voices offered encouraged her to occupy an embattled, fearful position against her own voices (as symptom), which created a 'toxic, tormenting sense of hopelessness, humiliation, and despair.'[12] The aggressive position caused the voices to multiply and become increasingly menacing. It was not until much later that, with support, Longden came to understand the voices as wounded parts of herself: 'the voices took the place of this pain and gave words to it … the most hostile and aggressive voices actually represented the parts of me that had been hurt the most profoundly and as such it was those voices that needed to be shown the greatest compassion and care.'[13] This traumagenic understanding of voice-hearing enabled Longden to conceive of the voices as both a survival strategy and a meaningful experience to be explored not destroyed. Similarly, speaking in Conor McCormack's documentary, *In the Real*, all the members of the Bristol Hearing Voices Network pronounced a profound sense of not being listened to. Sardis, for example, implores: 'I'm bleeding man, I'm actually bleeding and no one can hear me.'[14]

What is particularly valuable for the purposes of this chapter is how far the artists discussed are engaged with redirecting the cultural conversation from symptom to experience, from void to meaning, from pathology to person. Furthermore, when situated alongside a rapid expansion in advocacy movements such as the Hearing Voices Networks, one can begin to perceive a wider, growing concern to rethink and reimagine the limits of perceptual horizons.[15] The artists ask us to consider, if unusual perceptual phenomena have value, meaning, and insight, then what does attending in detail to these experiences allow us to see, feel, or hear *differently*? Indeed, they pay acute attention not just to the fact of such perceptual phenomena but to the structure and conditions of both sensory and intellectual reality making practices. Moreover, their works, through an acute attention to form and genre, invite us to consider what the clinical lessons of artistic practice might be, particularly with respect to empathy and the legibility of pain and difference. In short, this chapter will demonstrate how all three artists attempt to expose the constructedness of reality and, thereby, make room to imagine non-normative, legitimate ways of being, feeling, and sensing. More specifically, the works – though distinct – collectively explore questions of cause and effect, mood and atmosphere, haunting, and the temporality of reality in order to shift the coordinates of perceptual understanding on to new ground.

Dirty *Realism*

Theatre provides a peculiarly apt space for examining the politics and philosophy of perception owing to its ready contract with doubled and uncertain vision. Theatre is a place where things are absolutely, and not at all, themselves, real, and true. It has a particular, and unusual, sense-making capacity in this regard. There is almost an hallucinatory quality to the form in its ease with the entangled nature of what is and what is not. Anthony Neilson's 2006 play, *Realism*, offers an especially intriguing example of theatre practice that denudes surface realities in pursuit of expanded horizons of perception. Through an exploration of imagination, truth, and gaze, this chapter will argue that *Realism* playfully explodes the necessary fiction of quotidian reality and, thereby, makes a bit more room for different perceptions of here and now. By messing around with spectacular banality, Neilson muddies the common-sense feeling of how things *must* be. While it may seem contrary, even nonsensical, to begin a chapter on alternative perceptual phenomena with a play that is preoccu-pied with quotidian, almost stridently 'ordinary' experience, it is my hope that in so doing one can begin to ask questions about the coherence and rigidity of 'normal'.

Realism opened at the Royal Lyceum in Edinburgh in 2006 as part of the Edinburgh International Festival and was more recently revived at the Soho Theatre in London in 2011. It is on the one hand, as many of the critics remarked, a play in which very little happens. Susan Irvine described the time frame of the play as one 'apparently uneventful day', while Lyn Gardner summarises the ostensible plot as the day 'Stuart decides not to go out, but instead slob around all day at home in his underpants.'[16] On the other hand, as Dominic Maxwell intimates, '*Realism* is a play in which nothing happens, spectacularly.'[17] The play's ostensibly sluggish frame paradoxically contains a feverish hive of activity: 'stunningly lucid intervention[s]' are made on *Any Questions*, a Black and White Minstrel show tune is performed, elaborate sexual fantasies are enacted, the hero dies (and comes back to life).[18] It is a play, in this sense, which turns both the conventions of theatrical realism and the protagonist's mind inside out. Brian Logan describes:

> he [Neilson] stages 'normality' – i.e. what goes on in the mind of aregular [sic] Joe. The result – a wild cavalcade of fantasies, memories and imaginative non-sequiturs, coming to life around a podgy thirtysomething in his vest and pants – is absurd, outrageous and tender.[19]

As an audience we temporarily cohabit the internal landscape of Stuart's imagina-tion as it variously spills, lurches, and lingers across the stage in the form of carrots, cats, and characters from his life.[20] In effect, instead of watching the duck glide across the water, we are dunked underwater so we can see the flippers frantically paddling beneath.

It is in many ways a companion piece to Neilson's 2004 play *The Wonderful World of Dissocia*, which is also a theatrical portrait of a mind. Indeed, several critics note the synergy between the plays and Neilson confirms their shared ambition in his introduction to the Methuen co-edition: 'Whereas *Dissocia* was partly an attempt to theatrically represent the internal landscape of someone who was mentally ill, *Realism* was an attempt to do the same for someone healthy.'[21] While not disagree-ing with Neilson, I would suggest that there is, in fact, a shared space between these plays that smudges the neat distinction between these apparently 'mentally ill' and 'healthy' protagonists. In this way, there is a union between both plays' politics with respect to non-normative psychological experiences. In his denuding of reality (and theatrical realism) in *Realism*, Neilson simultaneously denudes normalcy in manners that politically echo *Dissocia*. Trish Reid observes that a dominant trope in Neilson's work is to 'make it difficult for the audience to distinguish between fiction and reality' and argues that he 'rejects the more comfortable certainties of dramatic theatre, particularly the laws of cause and effect that typically structure realist narrative, in favour of indeterminacy, poignancy, and atmosphere.'[22] Building on this, I would suggest that both *Dissocia* and *Realism* are engaged in a project of defamiliarising psychological normalcy in ways that have radical implications for the politics of mental health. Indeed, this chapter will argue that by exposing the commonality of unusual psychological phenomena, illuminating the non-finality of truth, and exposing the habits of perception, *Realism* renders the 'ordinary' a much more expansive, hospitable, and exciting place to be.

Did I imagine that?

David Smail thinks most of us are struggling. I would tend to agree. In *Illusion and Reality: The Meaning of Anxiety*, he writes:

> most people keep the way they feel about themselves as a deep and shameful secret. Much of our waking life is spent in a desperate struggle to persuade others that we are not what we fear ourselves to be, or what they may discover us to be if they see through our pretences. Most people, most of the time, have a profound and unhappy awareness of the contrast between what they *are* and what they *ought* to be.[23]

He continues: 'what I want to establish first is that the kind of experience we are so ready to call abnormal is in fact universal.'[24] Stuart, I would suggest, lives in the vale of what Smail describes. Moreover, in *Realism* one witnesses Stuart hearing voices, seeing things, conjuring dead relatives, acting out fantasies, and reliving moments of his past. Neilson is not covertly implying that Stuart is psychotic. Nor do I understand the play to be representing hallucinations or other psychotic phenomena. *Realism*, I think, exists squarely in the realm of imagination. Neilson merely renders the ordinarily invisible practices and experiences of imagination manifest on the stage. However, in so doing, he lowers the drawbridge between the supposedly separate realms of normal and abnormal experience and thereby exposes the busy traffic shuffling interminably between. Neilson's intervention here is not facile: he is not glibly implying 'we are all a bit mad really' (even if we are). In strewing the stage with Stuart's encounters with his psychological discontents, Neilson begins to chill the warm certainty of normalcy.

Lyn Gardner describes *Realism* as a play 'in which the conscious and unconscious mind grate against each other like giant tectonic plates.'[25] Thus, it is that in the course of making a cup of tea, Stuart sings a song, chats to his dead mother, and an old school friend hums to him inside his head:

> *On his way to the fridge,* **Stuart** *looks inside the cup, checking that it's clean. He turns on the electric kettle.*

> **Mother**   Can you see it? There – a castle, look. The tea leaves make a turret, and the tea's like a moat at the bottom.

Stuart	What's a moat?
Mother	It's the water round a castle, to keep the folk from getting in.

Simultaneously, **Mother** *and* **Stuart** *sing a fairly buoyant, very British wartime song – the sort of song a mother used to sing.*
I like a nice cup of tea in the morning
I like a nice cup of tea with my tea …
But **Mother***'s voice fades away, leaving* **Stuart** *groping for the lyrics. A sound arrives, punching into him the realisation of her absence. Mullet takes up the tune, humming to himself. Stuart takes a moment to recover, then puts the cup down. He looks at the jars in front of him.*[26]

I propose that by making an audience grope in the dark for our sure footing about what is 'really happening' and what is 'pretend', the play quietly demonstrates how reality is a house built (quite literally in the original production) on sand.[27] If we return to Smail again, it is possible to discern the radical potential of this for excavating a more open space for the accommodation of alternative mental experiences:

> Those people who opt for a self-deceptive strategy for avoiding this kind of discovery [about the nature of one's predicament] may do so partly out of a dimly sensed anticipation that to acknowledge what in their heart they know to be the case would be to bring about catastrophe. To draw attention to the emperor's nakedness is to initiate the collapse of the entire social system.[28]

Neilson's denuded dramaturgy, in this way, returns us to our own nakedness.

Can you see where I am coming from?

In philosophical studies of perception, the theory of 'realism' conceives of the world as mind-independent. As Fiona MacPherson explains, realism makes the ontological claim that 'there exists a world that is independent from the concepts, thoughts, and beliefs that people do or may have.'[29] 'Idealism', contrarily, understands that 'the world is mind dependent and is simply composed of one's own, and, perhaps others' or God's, perceptual experiences.'[30] For idealists, then, there is no fundamental difference between hallucinations and ordinary ways of seeing in terms of the nature or type of mental experience: this thinking leads to what is termed a 'common kind' understanding of hallucination. A counter argument, loosely termed 'disjunctivist', instead posits that 'when one is hallucinating one's experience lacks phenomenal character altogether.'[31] Here hallucinations are not the same type of mental experience as ordinary perception. While there are vast and complex debates in this field that are beyond the scope of this chapter, for our purposes these rudimentary summaries allow us to rummage a little further inside Neilson's framing of reality and theatrical realism. If, in many ways, *Realism* dispenses with distinctions between real/imagined, past/present, well/unwell, ordinary/extraordinary, then, as noted above, the play expands the horizon of common perception and experience to political ends. In place of insisting on a consensus reality that one must adopt or adapt to, Neilson opens up a more flexible space. However, it also invites an audience to question how far reality is a spatial or conceptual encounter. In this way, Neilson appears, through the doubled quality of theatrical representation, to navigate a curious path betwixt and between the realist and idealist philosophical positions on reality. In his cavalier smashing together of perceptual experiences, Neilson makes real life altogether dirtier. Discussing Mary Douglas's work *Purity and Danger*, DeNora reminds us that, for Douglas, dirt is disorder; it is that which is out of place and thereby disrupting symbolic boundaries.[32] I would like to suggest that *Realism*, by turning things inside out and upside down makes visible how, and what, we have tidied away.

Are you laughing at me?

Realism is a comedy. For example, Stuart is consistently abused by his surly man-sized cat [George] Galloway, who, after Stuart dies, eulogises that 'He was a prick.'[33] One consequence of this is that we are not invited to worry about Stuart. Moreover, we are permitted (or tricked?) to feel less anxious about the ontological unease regarding the nature of reality that is slithering through the play's philosophical territory. This comedic sleight of hand makes the disorientation pleasurable as opposed to alienating. There is an almost childlike quality to the attitude of believing that the play both enacts and demands. The consequence of this register is a clarion feeling that reality is in fact not a place but a practice. Stuart's encounters with his late mother and memories of his childhood friend Mullet offer particularly astute illustrations of this. In her discussion of the interrelationship between the extraordinary and the everyday, DeNora argues that it is erroneous to think of them in spatial terms because, in practice, both the unusual and the quotidian happen in the same place.[34] Instead, she argues for a more intangible mode of thinking:

> If we consider the everyday conceptually, as the process of accomplishing the 'here and now wherever we are', then the everyday is not an enclave … it is the site where experience is made manifest, where it takes shape, where sense is made.[35]

Likewise, in this play reality, fantasy, memory, and so on all take place together, 'here'. In *Realism* here and there, now and then, are simultaneously present in ways that affirm DeNora's approach.

In Act One Mullet chases Stuart around his living room. It is both right now and thirty or so years ago:

> **Mullet** *whoops like a Red Indian and suddenly lots of others appear as if in a playground. He chases them all around and for a moment the stage is full of noise and activity. One by one they claim sanctuary by the walls.*

[…]
Mullet Hop to the carrots, rabbit.
Stuart *hops over to the carrots.*
Mullet Eat one.
Pause. **Stuart** *eats the end of one. He spits it out in disgust.*
Stuart That's fucking awful!
The game's over – **Stuart** *sits on the couch.*[36]

Later Stuart hears his dead mother giving him laundry advice. She is both absolutely present and entirely dead:

He opens the door of the washing machine and starts bundling the clothes in; but, from inside the machine, he hears his **Mother***'s voice.*

Mother *(muffled)*   Have you checked the pockets?
[…]
He drags out a pair of trousers and checks the pockets. He finds something.
Mother   What's that? Is that your bus pass?
[…]
                           – Forget your own head if you didn't –
Stuart   Yes, thank you, Mother.
[…]
He crouches down to look at the settings.
                           What the fuck is a pre-wash? I never do a pre-wash.
                           Maybe I should do a pre-wash?
Pause. He opens the door of the washing machine.
                           Mum – should I do a pre-wash?
A long pause. There is no answer. Of course not. He closes the door and turns the machine on. It trickles into life.[37]

In this way, while not inviting a pathological gaze toward the stage, Neilson evokes a sense of a delusional atmosphere; a mood in which everything is completely ordinary and totally bizarre in the same instance. Karl Jaspers describes a common experience that individuals can experience prior to a psychotic episode, a 'delusional atmosphere', in which 'the environment is somehow different – not to a gross degree – perception is unaltered in itself but there is some change which envelops everything with a subtle, pervasive and strangely uncertain light.'[38] I would argue that *Realism* infuses the theatre with a delusional atmosphere through its disturbance of time signatures and narrative certainty and in so doing shifts the possibilities of exactly what it means to be here and now. Moreover, in his theatrical fusion of temporalities, mind-states, and normative conventions he underscores the conceptual tools we ordinarily employ in the daily labour of reality making. The consequence of this is that if reality is far less fixed than ordinarily assumed, then one's capacity to rearrange the frame to accommodate different types of experience is replenished.

The truth is in here

One could be forgiven for feeling suspicious at this stage that what I am proposing is a rather woolly argument for relativity. To be clear, I see clear value in distinguishing between memory, imagination, fantasy, hallucination, ordinary perception, and so forth. Washing machines exist, mums do die. However, if all ways of seeing are not equal (socially, politically, medically, morally, and so forth) and we can accept that reality is not simply spontaneous or neutral, then it becomes useful to disassemble the structures and conditions through which we, as humans, perceive the world. It is not contentious to suggest that, on balance, the tree in my garden probably is there whether I am looking at it or not. It is contentious for me to say that I talk with the pigeon who lives in the tree and that we have really great chats, whether you can hear them or not. If reality, like truth, is not purely in the eye of the beholder but is socialised, relational and interpretative then it is vital to examine the material practices of truth in order to interrogate the norms of consensus. Further, as Reid argues Neilson's writing frequently foregrounds an audience's awareness of themselves as engaged in a practice of watching and reading the stage. She explains how far Neilson's work 'blurs the boundaries between reality, memory, dream and fantasy in such a way as to confuse audience members thus bringing them into consciousness of themselves as interpreting subjects.'[39] In this sense, one manner in which Neilson spotlights how far reality is a learnt practice is through his acute attention to, and disruption of, habitual perception.

DeNora argues that perception and reality are enculturated:

> Even our most private and personal emotional experience takes shape in relation to cultural media – in music, novels and art, for example, we learn about the shapes, imageries, intensities and temporalities of feeling forms which to greater and lesser extents can be understood to afford emotional subjective experience.[40]

Reality then is neither just *in* us or *out there*; rather, reality is a relational event, which we learn to experience and interpret based on some common coordinates. Moreover, as Maxime Doyon and Thiemo Breyer suggest, our environment is 'a multi-faceted normative space that allows or encourages certain behaviours and practices and disallows and discourages others … In any case, the *style* of perceiving is always shaped by the norms and conventions we have acquired.'[41] D. H. Mellor similarly examines the moral value of truth with respect to perception. He asks why it is that we seem to want true beliefs rather than false ones. Offering the exceptional example of a soldier who kills a man whom he falsely believes has a bomb, Mellor reasons that 'most of our mistakes have no such moral consequences. There's no moral virtue in the truth of most of our true beliefs. But there is a practical truth.'[42] What, then, is the role of truth in *Realism*? It is my contention that in its flirtation with the disallowed, the hidden, the discouraged, Neilson attempts to rearrange the coordinates of reality in order to enable and make valid alternative and idiosyncratic styles of viewing.

Upside down you're turning me

Realism stages a dramaturgical *coup de théâtre*. In related manners to *Dissocia*, *Realism* spectacularly alters an audience's relationship with what is taking place on stage. The move in *Dissocia*, from the underworld of Lisa's mind in Act One to the psychiatric ward in Act Two, fundamentally disturbs our perception of both. The 'reality' of Act Two is disturbed in arresting manners. Likewise, *Realism* returns an audience to the upright position, which has a paradoxically dizzying effect:

Angie	What did you do today?
Stuart	Today?
	Pause.
	Fuck all.
	The lights by now have faded to black.
	[…]
	A box is flown in.
	When the lights come up, it is revealed as a kitchen. The furniture – the washing machine, the cooker, the fridge, etc –is exactly the same as that which was dotted around the set, but is now in its proper place. It looks very real.
	A door opens and **Stuart** *enters. He then proceeds to make himself, in real time and with little fuss, a cup of tea. This done he sits at the kitchen table.*
	Angie *enters, wearing a dressing gown. She takes the washing out of the washing machine (a stray red sock has caused the whites to come out pink).*
	Irritated, she leaves.
	Stuart *sits there.*
	The lights come up. The audience gradually realise they are expected to leave. **Stuart** *continues drinking his tea.*
	Eventually, the theatre empties.[43]

Writing in the *Scotsman*, Joyce McMillan described the play's epilogue in spectral terms:

> they [the audience] will be haunted, as I am, by the show's final naturalistic image of Stuart sitting gazing into space in an ordinary little kitchen; haunted by the richness and squalor of the inner landscape they have seen, and which is now hidden from them once more.[44]

The key here is not that either the main body of the play or the epilogue is straightforwardly 'the truth'. Structurally this reversal does not serve to throw off the blinders so that we can finally see things the way they really are, to do so would just replace one perceptual norm with another. Instead this coup is palimpsestic. The epilogue complicates the relationship between surface and depth, reality and imagination, truth and delusion in striking manners. Through the dramaturgical intervention of the epilogue, an audience sees something at once profoundly routine and utterly unexpected. Moreover, this overlaying of realities shimmers elsewhere in the play-text through Neilson's inclusion of explanatory notes as to what might, at a literal level, be happening in a given scene: '*[***Stuart*** *washes his clothes. He is insulted by a telesales call].*'[45] Both the coup and the notes give lie to the idea that reality is just *out there* happening for one to stumble upon and instead propose an altogether messier encounter between self, other, and world. Reality is made, then, in an extraordinary ecology of intersectional practices. As DeNora observes of the mutuality of the extraordinary and the everyday, so Neilson reveals that reality and imagination are co-constituted, co-located, and equally valid. Furthermore, in the theatrical fusion of realities that takes place in *Realism*, Neilson underscores how far truth is, and always will be, unfinished business.

Extraordinarily normal

Realism is stridently ordinary. Indeed, even Stuart's fantasy life is relatively dull in its predictability (however pleasurable it is to watch). The routineness of the intrusive thoughts and fantasies – from erotic fantasies of sisters to imagining how great everyone will realise you were at your own funeral – is deliberate. If, as I am arguing, a core intervention that *Realism* makes is to attempt to redistribute the means of production of realities to encompass a broader range of experiences, then the unexceptional nature of Stuart's predicament becomes oddly key. The everyman banality paradoxically emphasises the radicality of the play's proposition for expanded perceptual horizons. If someone as ordinary and apparently unremarkable as Stuart has such a vivid and ambiguous perceptual life, then this spectacularly debunks the concept of normalcy. Moreover, the pathos of the quotidian in *Realism* prevents this all from feeling rather vapid. Much of this chapter has focussed on the stage directions and dramaturgy, and it is here one can witness not only the structural interventions but also read the poignancy of feeling that skitters through the language. There is an existential poetic quality to the unremarkable stage directions that curiously bellows with feeling:

> **Stuart** *takes a moment to recover, then puts the cup down. He looks at the jars in front of him*; *A long pause. There is no answer. Of course not. He closes the door and turns the machine on. It trickles into life; The game's over* – **Stuart** *sits on the couch; The audience gradually realise they are expected to leave.* **Stuart** *continues drinking his tea. Eventually, the theatre empties.*[46]

The tone of futility coupled with the vulnerability that is at play in the tender moments reminds an audience why it matters. The play tackles nothing less significant than the bloody mess of living within the realities one has available. DeNora concludes her book with the following question: '*Which* realities, then, deserve virtually to be real?'[47] *Realism*, I propose, concludes in related manners.

In making reality an altogether more dirty and disordered experience, Neilson unmasks practices and hierarchies of knowing and, thereby, practices and hierarchies of being-in-the-world. In so doing, he exposes the absurd fictions we live by in the hope of forging more hospitable and tender realities, both alone and together.

What is *Donnie*?

Richard Kelly's *Donnie Darko* (hereafter *Darko*) is a cult film.[48] It opened on 26 October 2001 to mixed reviews, perhaps in part owing to its somewhat apocalyptic qualities in such proximity to the events of 9/11. While certainly not a critical flop (with some notable exceptions such as Elvis Mitchell's drubbing in the *NY Times*), the press responses were measured in their praise, saluting the ambition, tone, and performance, if frustrated by the film's refusal to be clear. Roger Ebert, for example, found much to praise in how the film creates 'a disturbing atmosphere out of the materials of real life', but lamented that 'the plot wheel revolves one time too many … we don't demand answers but we do want some kind of closure.'[49] Notably his review of the director's cut takes a different stance on the film's ambiguity: 'I ignored logic and responded to tone, and liked it more … I think, after all, I am happier that the film *doesn't* have closure.'[50] Ebert was not alone, however, in his frustration. Writing in *Variety* magazine, Todd McCarthy concludes that 'the narrative chases down so many labyrinthine dark alleys that it finally hits a dead end in the maze of its own making.'[51] Less generously, Sukhdev Sandhu concluded that it is a 'jumbled, rambling, derivative and slightly incoherent mess … [but] has a kind of inarticulate sincerity that is beguiling.'[52] Finally, noting the splicing of genres in the film, Peter Bradshaw wonders aloud: 'Is it a horror film? A black comic parable of generation X angst? A teen drama with a psycho edge? If not, what the hell is it?'[53] As much as critics were mildly (or severely) irked by the film's complexity, most celebrated the fresh new voice and tonal achievements of the film, and *Darko* was nominated for the Grand Jury Prize at Sundance in 2001.

While this partial rundown of critical reception offers something in the way of context for the film analysis below, it also raises a set of questions that I aim to explore with respect to notions of meaning and interpretation more broadly. The reviewers' anxieties about 'solving' *Darko* in some way are striking insofar as they appear to presume that such resolution is both viable and desirable. And, of course, the reviewers are not wrong to do so: the film invites a detective gaze of sorts. *Darko* is puzzling. However, the oft-remarked sense that the film collapses under the weight of its own riddles pivots on an assumption that a cohesive, loosely consensual agreement regarding what the film is *really about* is paramount. But is it? As Martin Crimp's play *Attempts on Her Life* wryly commented on postmodern reflexivity, 'It's surely the point that a search for a point is pointless and that the whole point of the exercise – i.e. these attempts on her own life – *points* to that.'[54] However, what I am arguing is that the question is less *what* does *Darko* mean, but more, *how* does it mean? Through an exploration of form and mood, I would like to examine the ways in which *Darko* not only represents reality but also teaches an audience how to compose it. In so doing, an audience is reminded that if we make it, then we can change it. As with *Realism*, this is partly a question of the relativity of reality, but rather more importantly of its non-finality and its material (and immaterial) everyday composition. I would like to propose that *Darko*'s particular political intervention, with respect to non-normative perceptual experiences, lies precisely in its swerving illumination that the horizons of the thinkable can multiply and bend, and thereby accommodate more expansive realities.

Darko is a story about a boy, the eponymous Donnie Darko, who must save the world in 28 days, 6 hours, 42 minutes, and 12 seconds. Donnie has been advised by his 'imaginary friend', Frank – a six-foot rabbit – that this is his quest (Figure 4.2).[55] At the level of plot, the film enacts a fairly comprehensible temporal reversal. The film begins with Donnie cheating death (a jet engine falls into his bedroom, but he has been lured out sleep-walking by Frank). This death-cheat ruptures the time-space continuum and creates a Tangent universe which will destroy reality (and kill his mother, sister, and girlfriend in the meantime) unless Donnie travels back in time and saves the day. The film concludes with Donnie completing his sacrificial mission, lying in his bed, laughing. During this final sequence, we hear his letter to Grandma Death: 'I hope that when the world comes to an end I can breathe a sigh of relief because there will be so much to look forward to.'[56] In this sense, the film begins and ends in the same moment and Frank, among other elements, comes to form, as Kelly describes, a 'reverse ghost'.[57] Donnie is also in therapy for his psychological distress, which his psychiatrist thinks might be paranoid schizophrenia. Donnie inconsistently takes his medication.

These dual tracks to the ostensible central plot – sci-fi world-saving and psychotic breakdown – have structured many responses to the film. For example, Alex E. Blazer writes: 'it [*Darko*] seems to represent *either* paranoid schizophrenia, a fragmented mind dreading the imminent apocalypse of its own lonely collapse, *or* a sci-fi world in which a young boy must learn to harness time travel to save the world.'[58] Likewise, Bruce Isaacs reasons that, 'If schizophrenic, the spectator contains the strange time travel plot within the all-encompassing delusion of a troubled teenager.

FIGURE 4.2 'Frank', *Donnie Darko*

If not, the spectator engages the film as a hybrid genre, incorporating a teen com-ing-of-age story and speculative science fiction.'[59] Others, such as Bob Graham, are more categorical: 'it [*Darko*] deals with the hallucinations of a paranoid schizo-phrenic.'[60] Elvis Mitchell concurs, 'Donnie *is* a schizophrenic teenager.'[61] However, it is the contention of this chapter that such binary decisions about what *Darko* is about are both flawed and revealing. As noted above, the film, I suggest, is rich in its evocation of questions regarding the nature of reality, personhood, and time as opposed to being primarily a cinematic riddle to be solved.[62] Thus, an approach that sets about unlocking the solution to *Darko* is flawed insofar as it bypasses the pivotal philosophical challenge to narrative truth that the film poses. However, this approach also reveals a tacit division between madness and agency, which is highly problematic. In such binary readings to be schizophrenic is, in effect, to be incapable of time travel. One is either mad or a superhero; to be both is somehow unthinkable. A notable exception to this logic is Emma Radley who argues that the film understands psychosis as a generative space: 'Kelly's film instead presents psychosis as a site of agency, a place of liberation from the restrictions of social real-ity.'[63] I would like to propose, however, that if one dispenses with questions as to whether Donnie is 'really mad', one can begin to perceive the film's more profound questions about how meaning is made. This chapter will thus put aside questions as to how far, or how 'accurately' the film represents schizophrenia (if such a thing were even possible), and instead will sketch a reading that attends to mood, time, and form. I am less concerned, then, with pathologising or de-pathologising an individual character; rather I am preoccupied with how the film adopts a mood of alterity and thereby sheds curious light on the parameters of consensus reality.[64]

Bits and pieces

Alongside the tendency toward 'solving' the film,[65] critics of all stripes are fre-quently at pains to emphasise the intertextuality of the film: John Hughes, David Lynch, Terry Gilliam, *Back to the Future*, *Harvey*, *Ghost World*, *E.T.*, J. D. Salinger, Stephen Hawking, Stephen King, Lewis Carroll, Hunter S. Thompson, M. C. Escher, and so on. Once again, just as the film offers the promise of a solution by establishing a knot, so too does it offer countless clues upon which to base such theorems. However, while one might wish to chase such references down (the rabbit hole) to steady a given interpretative foothold, I suggest instead that there might be two other things critically at play within this hyper-referentiality. Firstly, in its dense, crafted attention to detail the content of the film permits an audience to entangle themselves with a pleasurable web of connections. This ena-bles plural readings of the film based on the cultural, social, political coordinates from which one departs and invites a sense of agency. For example, the religious tones of the film perhaps find support in Jim Cunningham's initials, the bully's name, Seth Devlin, the homage to *The Last Temptation of Christ* and so on. Indeed, Sandhu grumbles that 'Kelly's film is the product of a broadband sensibility, one that's shaped by the mind-boggling range of old facts, images, bits and bytes of culture.'[66] However, Sandhu's complaint might be inadvertently perspicacious.

FIGURE 4.3 'Frank' carving and fridge note

Just as the film invites an entanglement of meaning, likewise, we watch Donnie compose his narrative from the bits and pieces within his frame of reference. From overt coincidences, such as nearly knocking over Grandma Death, to mute ones, such as the Frank imagery that is scattered on the reel, the film plays acute attention to signs (and our willingness to read them) (Figure 4.3). In this way, then, there is an echo between Donnie's act of narration and an audience's own. By returning us to the act of interpretation and composition, an audience is reminded of how far reality, truth, and meaning are culturally located, ontologically unstable, and iteratively produced.

The second aspect to this 'mind boggling range' of connections relates to the relationship between referentiality and cinematic mood in *Darko*. Darian Leader discusses the boundlessness and connectivity often experienced by the manic subject in his work, *Strictly Bipolar*. He writes: 'In a mania, everything seems somehow purposefully connected, as if a vast join-the-dots puzzle had been suddenly completed, to reveal a figure no one had noticed until then.'[67] Discussing Kay Redfield Jamison's memoir of her manic experience – *An Unquiet Mind* – Leader continues and notes that: 'Everything seemed related, and together would contain "some essential key" to the universe as she "wove and wove" her manic web of associations.'[68] The echoes here between such accounts and the imagined world(s) of *Darko* are clarion. The point of significance here, however, is not that Donnie is *actually* bipolar as opposed to schizophrenic; nor is it even that the film is arguing that culture itself is, in some ways, hypomanic. I am proposing instead that *Darko* illuminates how far we compose a sense of reality from language, from images, from objects, and their inter-relationships. In this sense, *Darko* is an amplified illustration of how far reality is not a 'thing', but a sensate, embodied, relational, enmeshed *practice* that is composed and recomposed with infinite nuance. The mood evoked by the hyper-referentiality renders an audience's eyes magnified. This is underscored by the recurrent eye motif that shutters through the film further reminding one of one's own act of critical thinking.[69] Returning an audience to their own agency in meaning-making practices in the context of a filmic exploration of reality, alterity, and alternative futures is a political gesture. In his analysis of Graham Greene's short story, *The Destructors*, Donnie argues that the characters 'just want to see what happens when they tear the world apart. They wanna change things.'[70] While some might argue that such political sentiments of change are naïve, and I would concur that the film's political feeling is denuded of incisive rhetoric at the level of dialogue, in its mood and form the film offers an astute critique of the terms of normalcy, reality, and power. In casting the manic practices of reality-making luminescent, *Darko* implodes stasis and naturalised ways of seeing. In this sense, rather than necessarily representing mad experience, per se, the film creates structures and feelings of alterity in its form and atmosphere in manners that intervene in the politics of mental distress and alterity. In short, it disturbs the way things *must* be.

Do the right thing

Bruce Issacs concludes that 'Kelly's story, characters, and thematic subtext affirm the classical cinematic experience as trauma mastered through heroism and sacrifice.'[71] On the one hand, the logic of this argument is sound. Donnie completes his task, saves his loved ones, and closes the wormhole to restore the 'real' world. On the other, this rests on an assumption of classical narrative resolution: order is restored. Yet this overlooks two aspects of the structuring elements of the film. Firstly, while normalcy is restored, it is haunted. In the closing sequences, Frank touches his eye, Jim Cunningham weeps, Dr Thurman's face is stricken with searching portent, Rose Darko and Gretchen exchange uncanny waves of recognition. One is reminded, here again, of Jaspers' delusional atmosphere, in which the same place is simultaneously unchanged and yet fundamentally altered. Thus, if reality is mastered, as Isaacs implies, it is a fragile, ghostly place. The cinematic reversal, in this sense, evokes a related perceptual shift to that enacted in Neilson's dramaturgical coup. Secondly, the film disturbs the ground between cause and effect to the extent that good/bad, right/wrong are untenable notions. Indeed, a reading of narrative restitution necessarily encompasses the retroactive cover-up of Cunningham's pederasty within the classical 'right' ending. *Darko* disturbs such certitude precisely through its engagement with formal convention and genre expectation. As Peter Mathews notes, 'There are no direct causes, only side-effects: reality is made up of contingencies that project us through our possible lives, and to think otherwise would leave us with the same sense of illusion experienced by Spinoza's stone.'[72] To argue that *Darko* conforms conservatively to narrative convention is, then, to return one to the very binary logic that the film upends. Indeed, the temporality of the film further underscores this feeling. As Claire Perkins intimates, 'the timeline doesn't indicate a beginning and end point but suggests an infinite "middleness".'[73] Likewise the sexualised images of Sparkle Motion invite an audience to consider what is, as well as what is not, a socially acceptable thing to see (and how such norms came to pass). In this way, instability multiplies in *Darko*. For our purposes, what is particularly striking about the structural and conceptual uncertainty of the film is its relation not only to this disturbing of naturalised reality, but also to its interrogation of 'therapy culture'.

Jim Cunningham's therapeutic system 'Controlling Fear' forms a central sub-plot. The programme, taught in Donnie's school, divides the world into two primary categories of feeling and action: 'Fear' and 'Love'. Students are encouraged to choose the path of love and reject the instruments of fear (drugs, alcohol and pre-marital sex). Life, Cunningham proposes, is all about 'attitudinal beliefs' and moral behaviour can be reduced to a spectrum of fear (bad) and love (good) *choices*. The parodic thread is evident in the soft-focus effects of Cunningham's educational VHS tapes, the shoddy production qualities of microphones in shot and cringe-making *mise-en-scène*, Cunningam's coiffure and stage 'bounce'. The therapy-cum-pedagogical intervention is palpably absurd and we are permitted to sardonically observe this scheme (amplified further by the film's historical setting in 1988). Yet, as Donnie suggests, it may not be so funny after all: 'I think you're the fucking anti-christ.'[74] The underlying seriousness lies not only in the multiplication of binary thinking that the film enacts (Bush or Dukakis, for example) but also in how this strand of the film further complicates ideas of fate, tragedy, and individualism. The Cunningham programme is a hyperbolic image of what Frank Furedi has termed 'therapy culture'; a regime under which the self is a neo-liberal project to be managed. In its comic interrogation of therapy thinking, *Darko* probes cultures of well-being to political ends.

Furedi's central thesis is that the rise of 'therapy culture' has created enfeeblement and a 'unique sense of vulnerability', a standardisation of good and bad feelings, and diverted attention from structural and social conditions to self-management.[75] Furedi is less concerned with the patient-therapist relationship than with the culture of therapy. He clarifies thus: 'A culture becomes therapeutic when this form of thinking expands from informing the relationship between the individual and the therapist to shaping public perception about a variety of issues. At that point it ceases to be a clinical technique and becomes an instrument for the management of subjectivity.'[76] Drawing attention to emotional literacy programmes in schools, he argues that such practices of 'therapeutic governance' teach children that there are right and wrong ways of feeling and that one must be vigilant in guarding against bad ones.[77] In this schema, life outcomes become a consequence of successful and unsuccessful self-management and self-realisation as opposed to structural inequality.[78] Published in the year that the director's cut of *Darko* was released, Furedi's book, like Kelly's film, unbraids ideas of well-being, destiny, and the neoliberal subject. Moreover, if we return to Leader and the manic mood of *Darko*, we can witness a further aspect of the film's disturbance of binary thought: 'The hyphen in the term [manic-depression] itself embodies what the condition tries to do: create a separation between two states. Good and bad must be kept apart at all costs.'[79] In exposing the manic institutional efforts towards emotional governance by Cunningham *et al.*, *Darko* muddies the frame: 'you can't just lump everything into two categories and deny everything else.'[80] In this sense, Frank becomes the visual embodiment of ambiguity that resists conclusion. Both rabbit and man, real and imagined, saviour and destroyer, self and other, he encapsulates the simultaneity of *Darko*. The film, like the figure, asks an audience to consider nothing more teenage and nothing less profound than, is this all there is? In permitting an audience to inhabit alterity, *Darko* offers burnished images of alternative visions.

Who do you think you're talking to?

If *Realism* examined the commonality of perceptual experiences and *Darko* illuminated the constructedness of reality, then debbie tucker green's *nut* interrogates intersectional experiences of mental anguish and hearing voices. All three artists are concerned to re-vision the parameters of what is thinkable, feelable, imaginable; however, tucker green is particularly alive to the structural inequalities that produce distress. *nut* sculpts place and environment from language, and renders legible the pain of alterity on bodies, in voices, and in space. As with all of tucker green's work, this is a play that is led by language and voice and is concerned to articulate the unspeakable or unspoken. Indeed, as Deidre Osborne has observed, tucker green is interested in that which resists intelligibility and her use of language seeks to disturb ordinary ways of listening.[81] Sounding a related note, Elaine Aston, in her discussion of tucker green's *Trade*, notes the non-realist strains to tucker green's political voice: 'It is through her use of a poetically brutal but beautiful style of language that tucker green slices through to the social realities and economic disparities of the Caribbean tourist (sex) industry.'[82] In her rejection of the 'naturalising' tendencies of social realism, tucker green's work howls lyrically in stark stage landscapes. As Lynette Goddard summarises, her plays shape realism in new directions by 'having most of the characters on stage throughout and refusing the props and staging that sustain realistic interpretations.'[83] The acoustic quality to tucker green's playwriting resonates in particular ways in *nut*, owing to its exploration of the experiences of distress and voice hearing. It is the contention of this chapter that *nut* renders voice and language spatialised, embodied encounters in ways that amplify the conditions of audibility/inaudibility that structure people's lives. In her theatrical examination of plural vocabularies of pain, intersectionality, and the felt presence of emotions, tucker green invites the audience body to listen in new, less boundaried ways. In short, *nut* dissolves dualisms in favour of radical relationality as a means to ask how, why, and when we can hear other voices.

First performed in the National Theatre's temporary space, The Shed, *nut* opened on 30 October 2013. The central character, Elayne, is struggling. She is searching for some peace and quiet, but it appears that no one is really listening. In some ways, *nut* is related to *Realism* in its ostensible lack of action. Superficially, Elayne chats with her mates about doorbells and funerals; her sister and ex-partner flirt in taut manners; Elayne and her sister discuss Elayne's state of mind. The end. However, the play cumulatively forms a depthless portrait of her environments: familial, emotional, social, sonic. As Rachel Halliburton intimated: 'It's [the doorbell discussion] a beautiful, simple metaphor for Elayne's refusal to engage with the outside world. Yet what's going on with Elayne isn't beautiful and simple at all.'[84] Other critics described it variously; from 'a cry of anguish', 'a world of anguish, a universe of pain' to 'depression with a capital D' and 'remorselessly depressing'.[85] In related manners to *Darko*, several reviewers note the ambiguity that hums through the piece and the centrality of atmosphere. Matt Wolf, for example, notes: 'Debbie Tucker Green [sic] keeps much about the evening deliberately vague, not least the meaning of her titles. What matters more, one gathers, is the mood.'[86] Likewise, Halliburton proposes that the play's mood acts subcutaneously, describing the play as 'intravenous – it seems elliptical, unflashy, until you realise that the characters have slipped under your skin.'[87] Finally, Ian Shuttleworth suggests that 'they [the characters] may be no more than figments. We are left to choose the elements and shading of our own picture of the situation.'[88] What is striking here is the sense that meaning of *nut* is somehow both uncertain and osmotic. In tune with both *Realism* and *Darko*, *nut* uses form to articulate ontological unease. The play employs a dramaturgical reversal to shift an audience's understanding of presence. Moreover, it writes language on the body and in space in manners that demand alternatives modes of embodied, spatialised listening. I propose that, in so doing, *nut* leans purposefully into indeterminacy in order to paradoxically render diverse experiences more visible, legible, felt, and audible.

Bugged out

Discussing Ian Hacking's ideas of looping and feedback, DeNora notes how far this practice shapes social and cultural identity: 'Hacking's concept of looping highlights how we adopt cultural identifications, inserting ourselves into them and shaping ourselves in relation to them, and in ways that in turn modify those identifications iteratively.'[89] Stuart Hall, similarly, acknowledged that representations of identities do not simply reflect us *as we really are*, rather representations themselves produce our self-image.[90] tucker green enacts a form of retroactive looping in *nut* that exposes both how far language produces identities and the ideological refrains at stake within such production. If, as Darian Leader, intimates, 'It is words, ideas and the associations between them that create and shape our realities, and we rely on both the links and the inhibition of links between them to be able to think,'[91] then tucker green's poetics and dramaturgy animate the politics of voice, language, and listening. In related manners to Neilson's coup and Kelly's reverse ghost, the muffling of voices in *nut* – 'AIMEE, DEVON, *and* TREY *are in the room, but unnoticeable to* EX-WIFE' – invites an audience to replay the earlier dialogue for clues as to what was really going on.[92] In this sense, tucker green alters an audience's understanding of presence by asking them to reconsider what exactly it is that they are present to. By changing the coordinates of how one should read a given scene, tucker green exposes the conditions that produce both the original and now current modes of viewing. Crucially, the invitation here is not to reductively read backwards and see Elayne as mad (or to imply singularity in how an audience sees a scene). Representation is disturbed in this sense. By making the voices that we hear in Act One not only embodied, three-dimensional characters, but vitally also funny, tucker green carves out a hospitable encounter with hearing voices: 'Be out buying a bell or something, carrying it back and get mown down … by a bus not even a car – a bendy bus.'[93] Thus, by initially encountering the voices as 'real', an audience's perspective is unmoored from a predictable, pathologising gaze upon 'mad' stages. In related manners, Errol in *In the Real* describes his voices in embodied terms: 'I met several voices.'[94] Returning to the philosophy of perception here, we, the audience, encounter the voices as both simultaneously and necessarily real and unreal, like Zhuangzi's butterfly: 'Zhuangzi dreams of the butterfly, so the dreamer Zhuangzi is real, and the dreamt butterfly is not. But the butterfly also dreams of Zhuangzi who, as being dreamt, should not be real. But nothing can be both real and unreal.'[95] Moreover, by framing an audience's initial encounter with the voices in playful (if also morbid) manners, tucker green emphasises that one's relationship to a perceptual phenomenon is as pivotal as the simple fact of its occurrence. Elayne's sarcasm towards the voices, for example, productively disrupts the cultural narrative of voice hearing as tyrannical affliction: 'She'd have bring-a-dish.'[96]

One of the common ways of describing unwanted thoughts and voices in the global north is 'intrusive'. This language of the psychological interloping of voices, thoughts, and feelings reveals a sense of the dominant conceptualisation of selfhood as boundaried. As opposed to conceiving of the self as a functional, ideological construct, the general perception of personhood is individualised, sovereign, and with clear demarcations between self, world, and other, between inner and outer experience. Moreover, as Sara Ahmed has argued with respect to wilfulness and social order, with bodies (individual and collective) come responsibility: 'To be a thinking member of a body thus requires *you to remember you are part of a body*.'[97] Ahmed goes further and explores the out-of-sync, wanderlust body:

> Normalcy can be understood in terms of function: having a part that can do, and is willing to do what it is assumed as for ("willing and able"). Being willing might be required when one is not able ("willing not able"). Compulsory able-bodiedness could be thought of as a will duty as well as a productive duty: a body that is not whole, that has non-functioning parts, must be willing if not able, or willing to be able.[98]

nut is, in some senses, the wilful subject writ theatrical. In its atomisation of individual character, *nut* explodes the notion of self as singular, instead emphasising the relationality of identity. Elayne is, in root manners, *nut*: 'We're – I am –.'[99] The play does not offer a dramatization of her inner landscape, in a 'it's all in her head' logic for us to glimpse *at*. To do so would seem to reactivate both the inner/outer frameworks and the location of audience as 'sane' onlooker that the play productively retires. Instead, tucker green offers an image of identity that *is* the dialogue between self and other voices:

> EX-WIFE *and* ELAYNE *sit and smoke*
> ELAYNE'*s cigarettes.*
> ELAYNE You're like me.
> EX-WIFE (I'm) not like you.

Beat.

ELAYNE   Smoke like me.

        [...]

EX-WIFE I've given up. This was real wouldn't be
smoking your shit brand.

ELAYNE   I never got them.

EX-WIFE

EX-WIFE You worry me.

ELAYNE   You worry me.[100]

tucker green elaborates this idea further insofar as she underscores how far identity is also spatialised. When EX-WIFE asks 'Elayne, we back here again', the implication is not only that Elayne has returned to a negative psychological space, but one is also invited to reflect upon what and where *here* exactly is for the character.[101] Elayne's experience of identity is marked by class, race, gender, health and thus the experience of 'here' is an intersectional reality. This emphasis on place further agitates ideas of psychological individualism. If emotions, as Sara Ahmed amongst others have argued, are boundary-less, relational, embodied, then it is reductive to locate distress as simply *within* the body (or mind) as opposed to *within* a social reality.[102] 'Here', then, in *nut*, is simultaneously Elayne's landscape of experience and an ideological habitus. In this way, tucker green's theatrical image of selfhood (made manifest in voices who have quite literally breached their boundaries) calls for a radical new understanding of the nature and parameters of you, me, and here: '*There is the sound of knocking from outside the front door. Surprised, they wait listening. Beat. The crackle of the weak bell.*'[103]

Can you believe it?

Matthew Ratcliffe pays critical attention to the act of interpretation with respect to hallucinatory phenomenon and turns to the work of Greg Currie: 'much of what exemplifies the strange and disordered thought of people with schizophrenia would not be remarkable if it were treated by the subject as belonging to the flow of her imaginings.'[104] In this sense, the phenomena of, say, hearing voices is not inherently abnormal let alone pathological. If we accept this premise, then how we conceive of, respond to, and interpret such phenomena is what is at issue. Richard P. Bentall and Filippo Varese similarly trouble commonplace understandings of the nature and origins of apparently abnormal perceptual experiences:

in a recent clinical trial conducted with patients suffering from early schizophrenia in the United Kingdom, 177 out of 255 (69 percent) of patients complained of hearing voices. It is sometimes forgotten that this association occurs not because schizophrenia *causes* hallucinatory voices but because, following [Kurt] Schneider, we define schizophrenia in this way.[105]

Hallucinatory phenomena are commonly eviscerating and distressing experiences. However, it is vital to acknowledge that hallucinatory phenomena, like emotions, are not merely individual but also relational, public practices of sense-making. Moreover, their distressing nature may be significantly ameliorated if one engages with them along altogether more tender, less hostile lines. If this is the case, then tucker green's contribution to the politics of mental alterity comes more keenly into focus.

As Smail notes, many responses to individuals in distress aim to enable them to adjust 'to a world which is taken as *given*, as simply real and there and to be reckoned with, but not altered.'[106] *nut* troubles the principle of adjusting to consensus reality by exploring the relationship between perception, interpretation, and belief systems. The doorbell debate, in this respect, is not only a metaphor for isolation and communication. It is also a reminder that what one believes to be the case is essential to navigating reality:

AIMEE	Knock.
DEVON	Ring the bell, it's a quiet one –
ELAYNE	knock
DEVON	ring it twice just in case – ring it a third time knowing whoever is in is by now pissed off to the highest – you will not die dropping a a knock as well, talk/ sense.
AIMEE	Ring it once – don't get shit – knock twice –
ELAYNE	twice is annoying
AIMEE	thass the code – knock twice just in case the inside person aint heard –
DEVON	confusion.
ELAYNE	Code?
AIMEE	Social code everyone /knows
ELAYNE	Everybody/who?[107]

This is politically urgent in the context of voice-hearing insofar as it underscores the degree to which such perceptual phenomenon can be coping strategies and attempts at self-care. If one understands voices, for example, not as aberrant symptoms to be banished but instead meaningful dialogues that are attempting to negotiate a liveable path, then belief in the reality of the voices is vital, in the root sense of the word. As Rene describes of his Godly voices in *In the Real*: 'if you take away my beliefs then I am just a mad person.'[108] The removal of a belief system by way of psychiatric intervention, thus, becomes a question of ideological authority and power. This underscores the value of assigning value and meaning to the content and nature of unusual experiences. tucker green's dramaturgical positioning of an audience within Elayne's belief system, then, is a radical act of hospitality towards self and others.

It's your look out

Dan Rebellato debunks the argument that theatre is illusion:

> The views of 'dramatic' theatre are wrong; representational theatre is not illusionistic. In illusions we have *mistaken beliefs* about what we are seeing. No sane person watching a play believes that what is being represented before them is actually happening. We know we are watching people representing something else; we are aware of this, never forget it, and rarely get confused.[109]

He argues, instead, that theatrical representation is metaphorical and proposes that 'in metaphor we are, I think, equally as interested in the metaphor as the object it represents.'[110] Herbert Blau also dissects the nature of theatrical gaze: 'deconstruct it as you will – theater is specularity. What's there, not there, you really have to *see* it, in that elision of seeing and knowing, whatever it is that escapes you, which is what keeps us thinking.'[111] Both, then, are concerned with audiences' attitudes of believing. As noted above, tucker green problematises the nature of reality, presence, and perception as a means to return an audience to the politics of mental alterity. Moreover, her work is consistently described as non-realist in form. However, unanswered questions remain in this chapter regarding theatrical vision. What impact does the theatrical nature of the philosophical notions discussed above have upon the claims I am making about the disturbance of ordinary perception? Is it always already flawed to examine the nature of reality in a space of apparently wilful unreality? Or does the virtual (in the root sense of the word) nature of theatrical reality actually render it an exemplary philosophical test site? Finally, if theatre is often contrasted (anecdotally at least) to 'the real world' then where, conceptually speaking, is it? And, thus, what is the status of reality in a non-realist play?

Ratcliffe's exploration of the nature of hallucinatory experiences may offer some further insights for thinking about the nature of stage realities. Following Edmund Husserl, he notes that not only is perceptual experience anticipatory insofar as it involves an awareness of what might come next, but it is also a necessarily rooted encounter: 'It is only insofar as we already "find" ourselves immersed in a world that we are able to encounter things as present or otherwise.'[112] That is to say that in order to experience dislocation one must be, to a degree, located. Moreover, socially, there is a value to classificatory systems of knowing insofar as they create some opportunities for common ground, shared experience. However, returning to Theodor Adorno, DeNora states that 'reality is not reducible to or identical with the concepts by which we seek to know it.'[113] Arguing that practices of categorisation always remainder certain elements that do not fit within the conceptual frame, Adorno encouraged a pursuit of uncertainty as a means to broaden the vocabulary through which we may capture reality. However, I would like to propose that one can see this in operation in *nut*, both at the level of dramaturgy and content but also at a metatheatrical level owing to the nature of theatrical gaze. That is to say that tucker green's dramaturgical interventions that disturb reality within the dramatic world of *nut* (and indeed *Realism*) are especially acute precisely because they are taking place in the here and now of a theatre space. The particular contingency of theatrical gaze heightens its capacity to redistribute the terms and practices of knowledge. In its uncertain sense-making, it offers different opportunities for making and remaking realities. While I recognise that all artistic encounters involve interpretation and are, therefore, unstable, the particularity of the theatre space with respect to questions of reality amplify this feeling. In this way, I wish to consider how far one might think of theatre, conceptually, as a curious boundary object between what is and what is not.

DeNora summarises boundary objects as things which are fixed at an individual level but uncertain at a common level. She offers the example of an unborn foetus, which is both unassailably a collection of cells for some and incontrovertibly a baby for others.[114] I am arguing that theatre forms a type of boundary object insofar it is both real and unreal, fixed and uncertain, simultaneously. I am not disagreeing with Rebellato here. I absolutely concur: I am not confused as to whether David Tenant really *is* Hamlet or worry about how the hell I am now somehow in Elsinore. Yet, with respect to reality and perceptual encounters, something is *happening*, and it is happening with me (emotionally, intellectually, somatically, and so on). In this way, I am curious as to how far it is of a completely different type of mental experience to other 'real' encounters, or how far it is reductive to conceive of theatre as a place apart from 'the real world'. One response here would be that it is distinct and categorically not real insofar as it has no effect or consequence beyond itself. But is that the case? It is here that I would return us to the Jaspers 'delusional atmosphere'. Theatre is not a collective delusion in this sense. We do not have a quasi-hallucination while tucked in a red velvet seat. Oliver Sacks argues that hallucinations enable us to experience and feel things that are beyond the material and everyday.[115] Returning to *nut* and *Realism*, I propose something similar. Ratcliffe's account of delusional atmosphere is striking in relation to the staging of both plays:

> Everything looks just as it was, but also radically different. Hence, delusional atmosphere is not a change in any number of perceived properties. In principle, the person could offer a comprehensive list of everything he perceives and it would be no different from a list he might have offered before – the chair is still red; the clock still ticks; the sofa is still in the same position. Nothing has changed and everything has changed.[116]

I am reminded here of the transformation at the heart of Tim Crouch's *An Oak Tree* in which a tree by the side of the road *is* Andy's dead daughter, Claire.[117] Perhaps, then, what theatrical gaze in general, and in relation to these plays in particular offers to psychiatry, is a way to differently sense and understand what might be really happening.

'the centre cannot hold'[118]

Hearing voices and other interesting perceptual experiences are as diverse as they are meaningful. Thus, what has preceded is neither exhaustive nor are the works examined offered up as in some way exemplary of the broad phenomenon. Indeed, in many ways they move productively away from straightforwardly representational practices and instead engage form to evoke atmospheres, create audience encounters with altered perceptions, and foster curious hospitality towards difference. The spirit of this chapter, as with the second half of the book, more broadly, is to take a decisive step away from diagnostic frameworks in favour of experience-led models. This lunge is concerned with the synergies between art and lived experience in order to search for different ways of thinking about mad subjectivity. While the three works discussed tackle the subject in markedly different ways and lay emphasis on different facets of perceptual experience and political life (from commonality to the constructedness of reality to the intersectionality of experience), all three are concerned to invite reconsideration of naturalised ways of thinking about self, other, and reality. Moreover, all three works make the hierarchies of legitimate and illegitimate realities newly legible and felt in plural manners. Radically, all three accept as a starting point the inherent value of perceptual phenomena, such as visions and voices, as experiences to be explored, not blank signals of psychological disarray. At the screening of *In the Real* in June 2016, a clarion note was sounded from the post-screening panel comprised of mainly voice-hearers: listen.[119] These three works demand the same. Through formal experiment and acute attention to questions of gaze, temporality, and language, all three return audiences to the ideological shape of interpretation. In exposing the social, material, psychological practices of reality, truth, and value, *Realism*, *Darko*, and *nut* insist on a widened aperture of looking and embodied acts of listening. In so doing, the three artists suggest that the centre cannot, and should not, hold.

Notes

1 William Shakespeare, *Hamlet* in *The Norton Shakespeare*, Stephen Greenblatt *et al.* (eds) (London: W.W. Norton & Company, 1997), 3.4, pp. 123–6.
2 Tia DeNora, *Making Sense of Reality: Culture and Perception in Everyday Life* (London: Sage, 2014), p. xx.
3 Joanna Bourke, *The Story of Pain: From Prayer to Painkillers* (Oxford: Oxford University Press, 2014).
4 Daniel B. Smith, *Muses, Madmen, and Prophets: Hearing Voices and the Borders of Sanity* (London: Penguin, 2007), pp. 13–14.
5 Charles Fernyhough, *The Voices Within: The History and Science of How We Talk to Ourselves* (London: Profile Books, 2016), p. 129.
6 Oliver Sacks, *Hallucinations* (London: Picador, 2012), p. 252.
7 Smith, p. 12.
8 Conor McCormack, speaking at Psychosis on Screen: *In The Real* at the Watershed Cinema, Bristol, 27 June 2016. McCormack was commenting here on the dominant perception of voice hearing. His film, *In The Real* is a documentary shot with Bristol Hearing Voices Network and explores the politics and life histories of voice-hearers in the city.

9 Fernyhough, p. 126.
10 Angela Woods, *The Sublime Object of Psychiatry: Schizophrenia in Clinical and Cultural Theory* (London: Routledge, 2011).
11 See www.ted.com/talks/eleanor_longden_the_voices_in_my_head?language=en (last accessed 11 April 2017).
12 Ibid.
13 Ibid.
14 Sardis, in Conor McCormack (dir.), *In the Real.* 2014. www.inthereal.org, 23:40.
15 According to Fernyhough there are Hearing Voices Networks in twenty-three countries and over 180 voice groups in the UK, pp. 204–5.
16 Susan Irvine, *The Sunday Telegraph*, 20 August 2006 and Lyn Gardener, *The Guardian*, 17 August 2006.
17 Dominic Maxwell, *The Times*, 17 June 2006.
18 Anthony Neilson, 'Realism' in *The Wonderful World of Dissocia* and *Realism* (London: Methuen, 2007), 1.3, p. 112.
19 Brian Logan, *The Guardian*, 17 June 2011.
20 The central character is always called the same name as the actor portraying him. In the original production, this was Stuart McQuarrie. In the Soho production, it was Tim Treloar. I shall refer to the original production throughout.
21 Neilson, 'Foreword'.
22 Trish Reid (ed.), *Contemporary Scottish Plays* (London: Methuen, 2014), pp. xvi and xvii.
23 David Smail, *Illusion and Reality: The Meaning of Anxiety* (London: Karnac, 2015), p. 4.
24 Ibid., p. 7.
25 Gardner, np.
26 Neilson, 1.2, p. 100.
27 The original set design by Miriam Buether sunk an ordinary domestic scene (sofa, bed, washing machine and so on) in several tonnes of white sand. The result was a traditional 'kitchen sink' scene submerged with appliances and furniture protruding out at irregular angles.
28 Smail, p. 159.
29 Fiona MacPherson, 'The Philosophy and Psychology of Hallucination: An Introduction', in Fiona Macpherson and Dimitris Platchias (eds), *Hallucination: Philosophy and Psychology* (Cambridge, MA: MIT Press, 2013), pp. 1–38, pp. 3–4.
30 Ibid., p. 4.
31 Ibid., p. 21.
32 DeNora, p. 57.
33 Neilson, 3.1, p. 151. Part of the 'joke' here is that Neilson, by calling the cat Galloway, is referencing an embarrassing moment on reality TV in 2006. The then Respect Party politician George Galloway pretended to be Princess Runa Lenska's cat on *Celebrity Big Brother* by purring, crawling around on all fours and lapping imaginary cream from her cupped hands.
34 DeNora, p. xx.
35 Ibid., p. xx.
36 Neilson, 1.2, pp. 106–7.
37 Ibid., 2.1, pp. 123–4.
38 Karl Jaspers, *General Psychopathology*, trans. by J. Hoenig and M. W. Hamilton (Manchester: Manchester University Press, 1963), p. 98.
39 Trish Reid, '"Deformities of the Frame": The Theatre of Anthony Neilson', *Contemporary Theatre Review*, 17:4, pp. 487–98, pp. 489–90.
40 DeNora, p. 38.
41 Maxime Doyon and Thiemo Breyer, 'Introduction', Maxime Doyon and Thiemo Brewer (eds), *Normativity in Perception*, (London: Palgrave, 2015), pp. 1–13, p. 4, emphasis original.
42 D. H. Mellor, *Mind, Meaning, and Reality: Essays in Philosophy* (Oxford: Oxford University Press, 2012), p. 48.

43 Neilson, 3.1, pp. 155–6.
44 Joyce McMillan, *Scotsman*, 16 August 2006.
45 Neilson, 2.1, p. 123.
46 Ibid., p. 100, p. 107, p. 124, p. 156, emphasis added.
47 DeNora, p. 149.
48 In 2004 Kelly released a director's cut of the film. This version involves new visual motifs, new sound material, and deleted scenes. It offers a somewhat more coherent and explanatory version of the film. This chapter will focus on the original theatrical release. For an interesting discussion of the two versions of the film, however, please see Randolph Jordan, 'The Visible Acousmêtre: Voice, Body, and Space Across the Two Versions of *Donnie Darko*' in *Music, Sound, and the Moving Image*, 13:1, Spring 2009, pp. 47–71.
49 Roger Ebert, www.rogerebert.com (last accessed 20 June 2016).
50 Ibid. (last accessed 20 June 2016), emphasis original.
51 Todd McCarthy, *Variety*, 21 January 2002.
52 Sukhder Sandhu, *The Telegraph*, 25 October 2002.
53 Peter Bradshaw, *The Guardian*, 25 October 2002.
54 Martin Crimp, *Attempts on Her Life* (London: Faber and Faber, 1997), 11, pp. 46–7, emphasis original.
55 It is highly debatable as to what Frank *is*. In referring to him here as an 'imaginary friend', I am directly quoting Donnie's description of Frank to his therapist in the film.
56 Richard Kelly (dir.). *Donnie Darko.* Pandora Cinema. 2001.
57 Kelly quoted in Jordan, p. 66.
58 Alex E. Blazer, 'A Phenomenological Approach to *Donnie Darko*' in *Film Philosophy*, 19, 2015, pp. 208–20, p. 213, emphasis original.
59 Bruce Isaacs, 'The Image of Time in Post-Classical Hollywood: *Donnie Darko* and *Southland Tales*' in Warren Buckland (ed.) *Hollywood Puzzle Films* (London: Routledge, 2014), pp. 198–213, p. 204.
60 Bob Graham, *San Francisco Chronicle*, 26 October 2001.
61 Elvis Mitchell, *New York Times*, 26 October 2001, emphasis added.
62 The extraordinary number of websites, YouTube videos, and publications dedicated to 'explaining' *Donnie Darko* bears witness to the intense desire to 'get it'.
63 Emma Radley, 'Where's Donnie? Psychosis and Agency in Richard Kelly's *Donnie Darko*' in *Psychoanalysis, Culture & Society*, 17:4, 2012, pp. 392–409, p. 393.
64 I recognise that there is a larger political conversation to be had regarding the politics of sci-fi with respect to the depiction of madness. Indeed, the psychiatrist is a recurrent figure in sci-fi films (from *Invasion of the Body Snatchers* to *Terminator II: Judgment Day*). An obvious concern is that the form renders alterity quite literally the stuff of science fiction. While I would concur with this in many cases, with respect to *Darko*, I would suggest that its highly ambiguous relationship to representation and psychological realism complicates this in productive manners. I do not, however, offer the film as exemplary or flawless in this discussion.
65 I am aware that I am also offering a further reading of the film, which could be classed as an attempt to solve the film. However, I would counter that the chapter maintains a deliberate position of non-finality. This is not offered as the sole, right, or last word on *Darko*. I aim simply to prise it away from typical approaches to its subject matter.
66 Sandhu, np.
67 Darian Leader, *Strictly Bipolar* (London: Penguin, 2013), p. 16.
68 Leader, p. 16. See also, Kay Redfield Jamison, *An Unquiet Mind: A Memoir of Moods and Madness* (New York: Knopf, 1995).
69 The visual eye motif is further emphasised in the director's cut.
70 *Darko*, 19:04. See also, Graham Greene, 'The Destructors' in *Twenty-One Stories* (London: Penguin, 1992).
71 Isaacs, p. 208.
72 Peter Mathews, 'Spinoza's Stone: The Logic of *Donnie Darko*' in *PostScript*, Fall 2005, 25:1, pp. 38–48, p. 48.

73 Claire Perkins, 'Becoming-Democratic: *Donnie Darko* and Other Recent Suburban Utopias' in *Rhizomes*, Summer 2008, 16, np.

74 *Darko*, 57:16.

75 Frank Furedi, *Therapy Culture: Cultivating Vulnerability in an Uncertain Age* (London: Routledge, 2004), p. 21.

76 Ibid., p. 22.

77 Ibid., p. 62.

78 Ibid., p. 65.

79 Leader, *Strictly Bipolar,* p. 43.

80 *Darko*, 40:00.

81 For a discussion of intelligibility see 'Resisting the Standard and Displaying Her Colours: debbie tucker green at British Drama's Vanguard' in Mary F. Brewer, Lynette Goddard, and Deidre Osborne (eds), *Modern and Contemporary Black British Drama* (London: Routledge, 2015), pp. 161–77, and also for issues of listening see 'How Do We Get the Whole Story: Contradictions and Counter-Narratives in debbie tucker green's Dramatic Poetics' in Merle Tönnies and Christina Flotmann (eds), *Contemporary Drama in English: Narratives in Drama*, 18, pp. 181–206.

82 Elaine Aston, 'A Fair Trade? Staging Female Sex Tourism in *Sugar Mummies* and *Trade*' in *Contemporary Theatre Review*, 18:2, pp. 180–92.

83 Lynette Goddard, *Staging Black Feminisms: Identity, Politics, Performance* (Basingstoke: Palgrave, 2007), p. 52.

84 Rachel Halliburton, *Time Out*, 6 November 2013.

85 Michael Billington, *The Guardian*, 6 November 2013; Aleks Sierz, www.theartsdesk. com, 6 November 2013; Matt Wolf, *New York Times*, 13 November 2013; Charles Spencer, *The Telegraph*, 6 November 2013. Notably both Wolf and Spencer make angry reference to tucker green's use of non-capitals, apparently baffled by the possible rationale, and thus Wolf's use of capital D here is a deliberate, petty swipe.

86 Wolf, np.

87 Halliburton, np.

88 Ian Shuttleworth, *Financial Times*, 6 November 2013.

89 DeNora, p. 50.

90 See, for example, Stuart Hall, 'The Work of Representation' in Stuart Hall (ed.), *Representation: Cultural Representations and Signifying Practices* (London: Sage, 1997), pp. 13–74.

91 Leader, Strictly Bipolar, p. 17.

92 debbie tucker green, *nut* (London: Nick Hern Books, 2013), III:ii, p. 64.

93 Ibid., I:iii, p. 27.

94 Errol in McCormack, *In the Real*, 04:06.

95 Jan Westerhoff, *Reality: A Very Short Introduction* (Oxford: Oxford University Press, 2011), p. 28.

96 tucker green, I:iii, p. 25.

97 Sara Ahmed, 'The General Will' in *Wilful Subjects* (Durham, NC: Duke University Press, 2014), pp. 97–132, p. 100.

98 Ahmed, *Wilful,* pp. 109–10.

99 tucker green, III:ii, p. 70.

100 Ibid., III:iii, p. 71.

101 Ibid., III:ii, p. 69.

102 See Ahmed, *The Cultural Politics of Emotion*, 2nd edn (Edinburgh: Edinburgh University Press, 2014).

103 tucker green, I:iii, p. 35.

104 Currie quoted in Matthew Ratcliffe, 'How Is Perceptual Experience Possible? The Phenomenology of Presence and the Nature of Hallucination', Maxime Doyon and Thiemo Brewer (eds), *Normativity in Perception* (London: Palgrave, 2015), pp. 91–113, p. 106.

105 Richard P. Bentall and Filippo Varese, 'Psychotic Hallucinations' in Fiona Macpherson and Dimitris Platchias (eds), *Hallucination: Philosophy and Psychology* (Cambridge, MA: MIT Press, 2013), pp. 65–86, p. 65, emphasis original.

106 Smail, p. 2, emphasis original.
107 tucker green, I:ii, p. 16.
108 Rene in McCormack, *In the Real*, 47:36.
109 Dan Rebellato, 'When We Talk of Horses: Or, What Do We See When We See a Play?' in *Contemporary Theatre Review*, 14:1, 2009, pp. 17–28, p. 18, emphasis original.
110 Rebellato, p. 26.
111 Herbert Blau, *Reality Principles: From the Absurd to the Virtual* (Ann Arbor, MI: University of Michigan Press, 2011), p. 12, emphasis original.
112 Ratcliffe, p. 97.
113 DeNora, p. 8.
114 Ibid., p. 90.
115 Oliver Sacks, *Hallucinations* (London: Picador, 2012), p. xii.
116 Ratcliffe, p. 96.
117 Tim Crouch, *An Oak Tree* (London: Oberon, 2005).
118 W.B. Yeats, 'The Second Coming' in *W.B. Yeats* (London: Faber and Faber, 2009).
119 The panel discussion was chaired by Angela Woods (Hearing the Voice) and included Rene, Don, Errol, and Aaron from Bristol Hearing Voices Network, as well as the film-maker Conor McCormack on 27 June 2016 at Watershed, Bristol.

5

'I WATCH MYSELF DISAPPEAR IN THEIR EYES, IN THEIR TESSES, I TALK LOUD BUT STILL I DON'T EXIST'[1]

Women's Bodies and Psychopathology

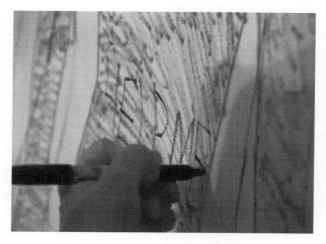

FIGURE 5.1 Therapeutic body image exercise from Lauren Greenfield's 2006 documentary *Thin*

Women and girls learn quickly. We learn from an early age that our body is the most important thing about us. We learn to be the observed sex. We learn that there are visual and behavioural parameters of acceptable being-in-the-worldness that are particular to our gendered flesh.[2] Susie Orbach reasons, therefore, that: 'As long as bodies are by proxy the standard for women's self-evaluation and the evaluation of others, women will have difficulty with their food and with their body image.'[3] It is logical, then, that women's political conflicts are commonly written on and through the body: 'If a woman's body is the site of her protest, then equally, the body is the ground on which the attempts for control is fought'.[4] Sounding a related note, Kim Chernin observes that 'a troubled relation to food is one of the principal ways the problems of female being come to expression in women's lives'.[5] One might add other somatic articulations of distress and conflict to this assertion, from self-harm to plastic surgery. However, the focus of this chapter is less on a given set of observable behaviours – self-starvation, body augmentation, bingeing, extreme exercise and so on – and more with what those bodies and behaviours might be attempting to communicate. That is to say that the chapter departs from an a priori sense that the surface manifestations of 'disorder' (for example, drinking too much, eating too little, cleaning too often) should not be understood as pathological in and of themselves. Rather, I argue that such activities may well be survival strategies and modes of managing pain, distress, and excitation. These are, thus, bodily coping mechanisms and not disease entities. I follow here Darian Leader's concern regarding the tendency to collapse surface and depth in contemporary biomedical psychiatry.[6] Moreover, I propose that it is imperative that we begin listening to the plural, ambiguous languages of the body in pain, and listen in new, more tender ways. By rejecting a model that understands and frames women's bodies and behaviours as 'the problem', one can open up a space in which to rummage around for more complex engagements with biopsychosocial subjectivity and embodiment. This is not a new debate, yet it remains an urgent one (Figure 5.1).

In her seminal work, *Unbearable Weight: Feminism, Western Culture, and the Body*, Susan Bordo writes: 'I take the psychopathologies that develop within a culture, far from being anomalies or aberrations, to be characteristic expressions of that culture; to be, indeed, the crystallization of much that is wrong with it.'[7] Building on Bordo's formulation, that finds acute sociocultural critique in women's apparently pathological behaviours, I offer examples of artistic practices that are attempting to interrogate biomedical, individualised understandings of 'disordered' behaviours (and by extension their solutions). If Chapter 4 examined the limits and tyrannies of consensus reality, then this chapter seeks to reconsider cultures of thinking around mad women's bodies. Psychiatry, of course, already pays heed to biography and social context. And neuroscience is casting new light in this field. However, in its preoccupation with identifying and correcting symptomology, conceptual complexity is necessarily partially lost in current psychiatric models of diagnosis and recovery. As one survivor of self-starvation, Fiona, describes it: 'What really surprised and shocked me was the fact that the focus was on feeding me up to produce a change in my body, but never once did they take my mind into consideration.'[8] Moreover, disease models of starvation, obesity, addiction, and so forth frequently locate the 'fault' or origin of the distress within the individual in a way which is both reductive and punitive. As Devine describes:

> I was put on complete bedrest; all my possessions were taken away on a punishment/reward system where if you did something "good", such as eat a meal, you were rewarded by being given back one of your possessions. If you did something "bad" it was taken away again. I put on four stone in eight weeks under that regime. I then returned home to lose it all again.[9]

Artistic practice wilfully returns to complexity in its inclination to dwell in uncertain, incomplete, and contingent understandings of unusual or extreme behaviours and experiences.

If we repurpose Sara Ahmed's thinking around the feminist killjoy perhaps a clearer articulation of this approach may emerge. Ahmed observes that, too often, the naming of a given problem (institutional sexism, for example) becomes identified as the problem itself. She writes that 'the feminist is usually the one who is viewed as "causing the argument", who is disturbing the fragility of peace' and 'at odds with the performance of good feeling'.[10] Thus, she suggests, 'The exposure of violence becomes the origin of violence.'[11] If we extend this analogy to women's psychopathologies, then under this scheme of thinking, we can see that women's violent or turbulent behaviours are likewise misapprehended as the source of disorder itself. One cannot simply replace this individualised, pathologised understanding of distress in favour of one that straightforwardly indicts culture as *the* problem. It is unhelpful, I propose, to rehash a causal line of thought that argues the media *makes us* ill. I am also not suggesting that the behaviours are incidental or insignificant. I am, however, proposing that a more complex, *dimensional* engagement with precisely how and why the body speaks to self, other, and world is paramount. Indeed, as Becky Thompson argues in relation to eating issues, these questions are, at root, ones of political freedom: 'Ultimately, the prevention of eating problems depends on women's access to economic, cultural, racial, political, social, and sexual justice.'[12] If distress is personal, social, relational, and biological then artistic practice offers a valuable intervention in critical thinking around fundamental questions about how to live. In its attention to depth, contradiction, and multiplicity artistic practice returns questions of power, culture, and politics from periphery to centre. The examples of this chapter certainly do disturb the peace of psychopathological understandings of women's bodies and behaviours. However, they do so, I suggest, in a bid to ensure that the distressed languages of women's bodies are re-understood as meaningful, articulate, and audible. Women's bodily 'pathologies' are thus *heard again* as relational, embodied dialogues of anguish and not simply involuntary confessions of disease.

The three works discussed in this chapter are Mike Leigh's 1990 film *Life Is Sweet*, Lee Daniels's 2009 film adaptation of Sapphire's 1996 novel *Push*, entitled *Precious*, and Duncan Macmillan's 2015 play *People, Places, and Things*. These works are markedly different with respect to form, tone, social context, and plot. However, all three feature young women in violent dialogue with their own bodies. Nicola, Precious, and Emma are, in varied ways, in revolt against themselves and their environments.[13] Further, all three women are suspended in a highly gendered paradox of simultaneous invisibility and hypervisibility. The three works all explore the fractured and faltering attempts at communication that these women make through, with, and against their bodies. In their diverse ways, these works are preoccupied with failed and failing acts of communication. Paradoxically, however, it is precisely in the incomplete acts of dialogue that the works attain their critical intervention in this subject matter. Nicola's silences, Precious's illiteracy, and Emma's verbosity collectively speak of the limits of what can be spoken, what can be heard, by whom, and how. Furthermore, in lingering in the cruel mundanities of everyday living, all three posit fundamental questions about the values of normative aspiration and success for women. In short, all three works examine what lives, stories, and appearances are available and permissible to them as women. Eschewing causality and biomedicine, all three examples set up camp on more ambiguous ground. Anorexia, pathologically marked obesity, and addiction are disassembled as the outward markers of inner dismay. Instead, all three works sit within a range of vivid lived experiences in order to offer a constellated image of distress, hope, and survival. By redistributing languages of pain and optimism across a breadth of lived encounters, these three works insistently reject a neat bifurcation of illness and wellness. In its place, they proffer an expanded landscape of experience in which bodies like theirs can be seen, heard, and actually exist.

Threads

The history of women's bodies as medical and psychiatric specimens and curiosities is not brief. Even if one limits oneself to the twentieth century and psychopathology in particular, the medical history is abundant. From *fin de siècle* hysteria to binge drinking at the other end of the century, women's physical behaviours have been subject to scrutiny. Likewise, cultural artefacts that capture women's relationships with their apparently deviant bodies are in ready supply. From Charlotte Perkins Gilman's 1892 *The Yellow Wallpaper* to Rae Earl's *My Fat Mad Teenage Diary* in 2007 women have voiced their bodies. At the root of many of the pathological narratives around women's bodies is an attempt to locate the source of deviance in a material object – the womb, the tonsils, the brain.[14] However, such endeavours frequently founder owing to the circumscription of their gaze. As Nikolas Rose and Joelle M. Abi-Rached note in relation to the rapid expansion of the 'neuro' disciplines:

> At root, the neurobiological project in psychiatry finds its limit in the simple and often repeated fact: mental disorders are problems of persons, not of brains. Mental disorders are not problems of brains in labs, but of human beings in time, space, culture, and history. And indeed, so is diagnosis; however well-trained and stabilized the gaze of the doctor, however regulated by criteria and augmented by neuromolecular indicators, diagnosis is a practice governed by its own rules – rules that are different in epidemiology, in cohort studies, in research, in the clinic, and in life.[15]

Expressed more directly, Ann Cvetkovich argues, in relation to the depression 'epidemic' sweeping the Global North: 'We don't need scientific research to explain what's going on; we need better ways of talking about ordinary life, including the dull feelings of just getting by.'[16] In both cases, what is foregrounded is an entangled understanding of distress and subjectivity that is located in time, space, and bodies.

It is thus the coordinates of such collisions that need attending to as opposed to the physical phenomena in isolation. As Bordo suggests:

> like hysteria in the nineteenth century, the incidence of eating disorders has always been disproportionately high among females: approximately 90 percent of sufferers are girls or women. Second, and again like hysteria, eating disorders are culturally and historically situated, in advanced societies within roughly the past hundred years.[17]

She continues: 'Looking to biology to explain the low prevalence of eating disorders among men is like looking to genetics to explain why non-smokers do not get lung cancer as often as smokers.'[18] In this sense, both symptom and classification are ideologically, culturally, socially, historically fretted. As one nurse described:

> The smallest one that I've seen wasn't actually an anorexia patient anyway. He was supposed to be schizophrenic and he was, like, 5ft 3 inches and 4 stones, but he wasn't, again he wasn't classed as anorexic. He was classed as schizophrenic.[19]

Ways of seeing, then, as I explored in Chapter 4, are neither neutral nor spontaneous but embodied, encultured, and relational. The case studies in this chapter, via their respective engagements with realism and embodiment, remind us of the fact of looking in deliberate manners.

If we accept, then, that brains are not abstracted from, for example, geography, then a more textured picture of embodied mental anguish emerges. Taking racial violence as an example, Cvetkovich observes:

> The legacy [of racialized histories] continues to pervade everyday experience – we are all living in an environment steeped with racialized violence: the land we walk on is stolen, the labor that produced the things we use is underpaid and exploited; the neighbourhoods we live in are either segregated or gentrifying.[20]

In this sense, the threads that tangle up histories of hysteria with histories of anorexia are not signalling a simple continuity of 'women's problems'; rather the knots indicate the continuity of inequality, violence, discrimination, oppression, and women's attempts to manage these conditions. It is, then, the multidirectional interactions between bodies, brains, and environments that produce distress and attendant modes of coping. In this sense, I echo Cvetkovich's call for attention towards a reconsideration of how to live and get by. It is here that artistic practice offers a critical intervention in the politics of health and survival. *Life Is Sweet*, *Precious*, and *People, Places, and Things* offer portraits of women's bodies under siege. They examine the ordinary violence of women's experiences and seek alternatives within the gloom (as opposed to transcending their bodies and worlds). In this sense, these works take strides towards Cvetkovich's call for a radical reimaging of the politics of despair: 'The goal is to depathologize negative feelings so that they can be seen as a possible resource for political action rather than as its antithesis.'[21] I argue that, through their respective animations of proximity to death and morbidity, these works get under the skin of what makes life worth living.

Grounded

Condemned in some quarters as sneering and celebrated elsewhere as an innovative auteur of British working-class realism, Mike Leigh is a cinematic voice of ordinary lives. While commonly associated with directors such as Jean Renoir, Yasujirō Ozu, and Satyajit Ray, Leigh's work retains a distinctly British sensibility. Richard Porton describes his work as exercises in mundanity: 'Leigh's modernist realism infuses films featuring detailed portraits of eccentrics, observers, curmudgeons, and madmen ⊤ characters who sometimes win, but more often lose, a constant battle against monotony.'[22] However, writing in the *Sunday Times* in 1977, Dennis Potter lambasted Leigh's then recently aired TV adaptation of his stage play *Abigail's Party* as 'nothing more edifying than rancid disdain, for it was a prolonged jeer, twitching with genuine hatred, about the dreadful suburban tastes of the dreadful lower-middle classes.'[23] His particular working methods, political controversy, and thematic preoccupations are, however, well documented and thus will not be rehearsed at length here.[24] Instead what is of note for our purposes is his film from 1990, *Life Is Sweet* and specifically his cinematic framing of the character, Nicola – a young woman who starves, binges, and is profoundly sad. In Leigh's words, *Life Is Sweet* is 'a film about a girl coming out of a nightmare, about connections being made through things going wrong.'[25] Nevertheless, it is perhaps misleading to suggest that the film is *about* Nicola. Leigh dispatches singular, character-focussed narrative arcs in favour of a more diffuse, incremental style of visual storytelling. As Edward Trostle Jones suggests: 'He encourages an unmediated perspective on his characters that we understand principally through their social relationships and their being in a particular context, not from audience identification with their consciousness or internal states of mind via frequent point-of-view shots.'[26] It is precisely this socialised approach to psychological realism and pathology that forms the focus of what follows. It is my contention that through his use of language, form, and narrative uncertainty, Leigh redirects our gaze from individual pathology to the politics of womanhood in Thatcherite Britain.

Life Is Sweet ostensibly tells the tale of a relatively uneventful few days in the lives of one family – Wendy (Alison Steadman), Andy (Jim Broadbent), and the twins Natalie (Claire Skinner) and Nicola (Jane Horrocks). Andy buys a rusty snack van from his mate Patsy (Stephen Rea) and breaks his ankle at work. Wendy helps a family friend, Aubrey (Timothy Spall), at his new restaurant, 'The Regret Rien'. Natalie books a holiday to New York. Nicola eventually admits she is struggling. The film proceeds in an almost collage form: meaning and mood seem to accumulate in the patching of scenes on top, beside, and underneath one another. Yet work and food provide a clear scaffold for this film. As Trostle Jones notes, 'Besides Nicola's eating disorder, food, its preparation and consumption becomes a major theme in *Life Is Sweet*.'[27] From Aubrey's outlandish recipes such as pork cyst to the family meals of roast lamb and cheese toasties to the chocolate spread that is licked off Nicola's breasts by her boyfriend, food communicates, organises, and dominates the frame. Work, likewise, forms a structure around which the action turns, enacting a dramaturgy of social utility. Nicola's lack of employment is set deliberately against the grinding slog of Andy's loathed job in a commercial kitchen, Natalie's plumbing, and Wendy's dance class and clothes shop roles. When taken together food and work invest the film with a temporal dynamic that is marked with political signature. How one chooses (or in Nicola's case is unable to choose) to spend one's leisure time, one's money, one's life is sutured to questions of capitalism and consumption. Holidays, pints, chocolate, and clothes are the apparent pleasures afforded by gainful employment. Nicola's self-exclusion from both food and occupation thus positions her interestingly in relation to these economies of worth and values. It is here, and elsewhere, that one can begin to witness Leigh's attempt to sketch the political interrelations between class, gender, and the pathologised female body.

In *The Politics of the Body* Alison Phipps argues that, in post-Fordist capitalism, 'Identity no longer derives automatically from one's position in the matrix of production, leading to a greater emphasis on the body which is shaped to a great extent by consumer culture.'[28] She proposes that, within the architecture of neoliberalism, 'political and social problems are converted into market terms, becoming individual issues with consumption-based solutions' and thus 'success is measured by individuals' capacity for self-care via the market, and those who do not achieve their potential are viewed as failures rather than as victims of oppressive social structures.'[29]

Elizabeth Grosz similarly argues that:

> Food, dieting, exercise, and movement provide meanings, values, norms, and ideals that the subject actively ingests, incorporating social categories into the physiological interior. Bodies speak, without necessarily talking, because they become coded with and as signs. They speak social codes. They become intextuated, narrativized; simultaneously, social codes, laws, norms and ideals become incarnated.[30]

What is luminously clear in both of these analyses is not only the degree to which politics are written on and enacted by the body, but also the extent to which productive self-management is culturally valorised. Nicola, however, is not managing or succeeding. Indeed, she insistently questions and resists the normative aspirations of marriage, babies, and career ascribed to her – both culturally and within the domestic sphere. For example, Wendy laments her lost hope of the twins 'going to discos and bringing their boyfriends home' and Nicola says she doesn't want kids because she does not want to 'look like a tank for nine months'.[31] Moreover, Nicola has economically partially opted out of a system of capitalist consumption. While she binges on confectionary and smokes and thus is not represented as being *outside* capitalism (if such a thing were even possible), she does not work and is not preoccupied with a broad range of 'consumption-based solutions' towards social success. In its place, she is house-bound, occupying a hinterland of dislocated longing. She is framed as awkwardly and persistently out-of-sync with the rules and rituals of everyday life and citizenship in a capitalist economy. This is witnessed primarily through Leigh's quiet emphasis on work and food as codes of valuable living from which she is persistently set apart – both visually and narratively. Instead she is grounded in a space of hunger. Through her eating, starvation, and domestic isolation, one witnesses both a crystallisation of, and attempt to resolve the socio-political bind with which she is in violent conflict. As Bordo argues: 'we find ourselves continually besieged by temptation, while socially condemned for overindulgence.'[32] In one sense, Nicola's denial makes her, curiously, the neoliberal subject par excellence as the ravaged embodiment of desire and denial. However, as Cecilia Hartley notes (drawing on Sandra Bartky), 'cultural expectations have progressively shifted away from what a woman is allowed to *do* onto what a woman is allowed to *look like*.'[33] Nicola, it would seem, at the moments of her bingeing and denial is at war with the lives, appearances, and aspirations available to her as a working-class woman in 1990s Britain. Her body thus performs a distorted sketch of the feminine ideals of being slender and domestic.

Her simultaneous persistence in hunger also marks a broader conflict with respect to need and desire. As Colette Conroy describes: 'Bodily desires such as the need for food, material comfort and sex are seen as the factors that chain us to the physical world. The transcendence of bodily desires is regarded as a perpetual and necessary struggle.'[34] It is notable that agoraphobia, in its root sense, means fear of the market. This etymology yields further insight regarding Nicola's steadfast refusal to go out of the home: to leave the house is to consume, to be a consumer. Nicola's self-denial, thus, can be partly understood as an attempt to expose and escape the cult of thinness that has ensnared her. In his study of hunger artists, Patrick Anderson, following Freud, proposes that 'hunger describes the primordial experience of being' and thus 'it is also the paradigm for all somatic, psychic, and social need. Hunger models and rehearses desire in all of its forms: the unfulfilled in dreams, the *objet-a* of love, the utopia of hope.'[35] It is possible, therefore, to understand Nicola's self-starvation as a distorted utopic gesture. That is to say, without stripping her extreme denial of its felt despair, one is still able to perceive an act of protest that is paradoxically politically hopeful. While the gesture has turned both inwards and violent, if one shutters a pathological gaze, it becomes possible to understand both her starvation and her consumption as articulate howls against the gendered strictures of consumer capitalism. The challenge thus becomes not how to make Nicola eat but how to create conditions in which eating is not the terrain on which her battle is fought. One ought, of course, to treat with suspicion attempts to romanticise either Nicola's pain or her mannered, and at times almost indiscriminate, non-conformity. The risk of wresting her body away from psycho-pathology only to co-opt it at the service of an alternative political discourse is plain. It is also problematic to suggest that self-starvation is simply and always a conscious and direct act of protest. Nonetheless, it is here that one returns to the challenge that this chapter proposes of listening to the body and the complexity that artistic practice insists upon. In this scheme, one can simultaneously hear the voice of someone in profound, private distress and also hear the indictment of a destructive culture for young women. If one listens to both cries, one can begin to discern the vital pursuit of political hope in an encounter with death.

'Bollocks'[36]

The double bind of Nicola's self-starvation finds productive echo in her vocal skit-tering as she moves between expletive venom and floundering silence. She darts from invective ('capitalist', 'racist', 'all men are bastards'[37]) to silence in marked man-ners (...[38]). Notably, the reviews are often unkind about Nicola, especially with respect to her sadness and her rage. Hal Hinson describes her as a 'flat-out disaster' who is 'tantruming' under her own self-imposed 'thundercloud', while Jay Boyar summarises her as 'a bulimic with an especially bad attitude. Nicola is a total mess ... with her angry-young-woman-bile.'[39] The flippancy and misogyny of these comments is striking and finds curious echo in other apparently inconsequential remarks within other press clippings. For example, Vincent Canby, writing in the *New York Times*, relates that Wendy is 'an enthusiastic aerobics instructor to a class of *tubby little girls*'.[40] If we linger over the opening sequence to which he is referring, we actually encounter a room of average-sized children who are around 6 and 7 years old (Figure 5.2).

FIGURE 5.2   'Dancing with everyone watching', *Life Is Sweet*

The issue of reviewers' unthinking violence towards women and girl's bodies when critiquing a film that is expressly concerned with the politics of the body will recur in the discussion of *Precious*. However, its point of significance here is precisely the unremarkability of the sexist dismissal of Nicola. To be sure, she is not a master of rhetoric and her fury appears scattergun. However, to diminish her voice entirely as irrelevant – as pure 'woman-bile' – is to replicate the social tyranny that has pro-pelled her towards conditions of abject hunger. If, on the other hand, we suggest that Nicola's voice and her silence are in fact meaningful, one can discern a clarion articulation of gendered disenfranchisement.

Wearing a 'Bollocks to the Poll Tax' T-shirt, Nicola calls out racism and sexism, states that reading has taught her that she is a feminist, and proclaims that she is writing a novel: 'I haven't started it yet.'[41] In these moments her voice is strident. Elsewhere she is lost in silence. For example, in the second encounter with her lover, played by David Thewlis, he bullies her, asking if she is actually capable of intelligent conversation (and not just sex). Knocked into silence, she eventually retorts defensively: 'I am intelligent. Are you coming upstairs?'[42] Unable to speak, she returns to the body as her site of communication. These moments are multiplied across the film. Silence bellows from Nicola whenever she is confronted with her own identity and desires. In another example, she remains sat impassively, Godot-like, in the front room having claimed to want to leave. Natalie observes: 'You can't go, can you? … See you wanna be with us, so why don't you just act normal?'[43] It is my contention that it is the specificities of Nicola's clichéd voice, counter-posed with her raging silences that reveal a hoped-for legitimacy for her own distress. It is not incidental that her anger is funnelled through familiar, almost-glib political refrains, or that she is writing a novel and reading feminist theory. It is precisely the stereotypical quality of the discourses she is attempting to situate herself among that signal their import. She grasps towards the recognisable language of dissent precisely because there is no adequate or legitimate language available personally or politically to articulate her own violent despair. In this way, if we strain past the holler and read across the plural languages she employs, Nicola articulates the rav-ages and double binds of neoliberalism on the young, female, working-class body.

Restricted view

A related intervention that Leigh enacts alongside his challenge to modes of listen-ing is the use of form to foreground the relational elements of survival and recovery. Critical commentary on Leigh's work often comments on his extensive use of the fixed long shot. For example, Sean O'Sullivan notes that: 'Leigh's unbroken shots, produced for much of his career by a fixed camera, often do not draw attention to themselves as cinematic material; we may be in them for a long time without real-izing we are in them.'[44] Ray Carney and Leonard Quart also note that character arcs do not conform to standard Hollywood cinematic models in Leigh's oeuvre: 'His greatest characters triumph, not by rising above social contexts and forms of expression (in the visionary/romantic/idealistic mode), but by plunging into and mastering them.'[45] *Life Is Sweet*, then, is not a picture of overcoming. Nor is it a picture with overt social politics. Indeed, there is a deliberate and curious lack of context. While an audience glimpses the wider world of Andy's kitchen, Aubrey's restaurant, or Wendy's shop these elements largely remain at the level of visual background noise. They loosely indicate social class, period, and geography but are overall peripheral to the focus on people and relationships. Carney and Quart distinguish him from other filmmakers, such as Ken Loach, on this basis: 'Leigh's work was shaped by his political perspective; yet despite his antipathy his films carry no political agendas, nor do they offer political alternatives or solutions in the Ken Loach mode.'[46] However, to suggest his work carries 'no political agendas' is problematic. I would propose that rather than the films occupying a curious apolitical landscape, instead they advance simply on different political terms than, say, Loach. Indeed, I argue that his formal use of long shots, images of character juxtaposition, lack of point-of-view shots, absence of leading characters, and lack of narrative resolution enact the politics of his cinema. Crucially, taken together these elements ensure that an audience look deliberately *at* and not *with* these characters. This runs contrary to much contemporary understanding of the centrality of empathy to a politicised cinematic gaze. However, I propose that it is the half-formed, incomplete view an audience is afforded that speaks to the political energy of *Life Is Sweet*.

Carney and Quart suggest that: 'In *Life Is Sweet*, we learn things in bits and pieces, with continuous slight adjustments of view and revisions of understanding.'[47] Muddying the purity of Hollywood emotional sentiment, they reason that 'Leigh returns us to the real world, where intentions, feelings, and ideas are compromised, mixed, and impure.'[48] Alongside its contribution to realist aesthetics, however, this form of composition is political. The politics of this uncertain and partial cinematic view lie in its deliberate contradistinction to a more certain pathological gaze. Put simply, if diagnosis claims to produce knowing, Leigh returns us to productively not knowing. Moreover, by flattening the screen somewhat through the rejection of individualised, psychological realism and identification, Leigh maintains a critical distance between audience and meaning. While much criticism around his canon emphasises the dissolving of artifice and thus argues that the mechanics of looking are rendered less present, it is possible to read his realism contrarily. An audience is invited to sit temporarily within this world but without concomitant access to a supposed truth or interiority. We watch Nicola vomit without being able to flatter ourselves that this affords clear understanding of her lived reality. Instead, we intimate, speculate, and interpret. Of course, all artistic encounters involve interpretation, so I am not proposing Leigh is unique; rather I simply wish to linger on the manner of his invitation and the specific consequences of this for the politics of pathologised women's bodies.

If self-starvation is a spectacular performance in some ways and if, like the disabled body, it appears to mandate the stare, then the ways in which one is positioned as viewer of such bodies is paramount. I argue that it is precisely Leigh's dulling of the possibility of special knowledge about Nicola that marks his attempt to deprivilege the dominant narrative of understanding Nicola as just an anorexic. Indeed, it is notable that the word is never used throughout the film. Discussing the 'fat' female body with Eve Kosofsky-Sedgwick, Michael Moon argues:

> Incredibly, in this society, everyone who sees a fat woman feels they know something about her that she doesn't herself know. If what they think they know is something as simple as that she eats a lot, it is medicine that lends this notionally self-evident (though as recent research demonstrates, usually erroneous) reflection the excitement of inside information; it is medicine that, as with homosexuality, transforming difference into etiology, confers on this rudimentary *behavioural* hypothesis the prestige of a privileged narrative understanding of her *will* (she's addicted), her *history* (she's frustrated), her *perception* (she can't see herself as she really looks), her *prognosis* (she's killing herself) – the fat body "outs" itself.[49]

While there are keen distinctions to be drawn between the cultural readings of 'fat' and 'thin' bodies it is possible to replace corpulent with wasted bodies in the above extract and reach related conclusions regarding the hypervisibility of the confessional starving body. This is not to fetishise self-starvation as fundamentally unknowable; rather it is simply to observe the ways in which *Life Is Sweet* debunks authoritative capacities and strategies to *know* women's bodies. Indeed, Leigh's portrayal of Nicola's intimate self-alienation from her own form ('I'm too fat') emphasises the lack of an objective correlative between what exists and what is seen – both personally and culturally.

'Mums don't eat'[50]

In his 2003 stand-up show, Peter Kay joked that 'mums don't eat'. Impersonating his Mum feeding the whole family but denying herself, he jokes (as her), 'I had a crackerbread yesterday.'[51] Unsurprisingly, there is a great deal written in the literature on anorexia specifically, and eating disorders more generally, about the role of mothers in the development of difficulties around food, eating, and body image. It is notable that in all three examples analysed in this chapter, mothers loom large, for good and ill. Chernin, informed by a Kleinian psychoanalytic model, in particular emphasises mother-daughter relationships as central. Likewise, Orbach summarises that: 'Throughout history women have occupied this dual role of feeding others while needing to deny themselves.'[52] However, even in more broad-based discussions about women's eating, mums figure. For example, in Gaye Poole's study of food on screen she writes: 'Even when alone, daughters never eat alone, they eat with their mothers: accompanied by the preferences, lessons, economies, wisdoms, and anxieties their mothers, however inadvertently taught them.'[53] While there is a great deal to say about Wendy's attitudes to Nicola's eating, or lack thereof, as well as about her own apparently uncomplicated relationship to food and her body, I would like to focus in particular on just one aspect of their bond: that is the dynamic of female collectivity that shapes the film's survival narrative around Nicola.

Mums exist in a shared ideological space with their daughters: 'The mother-daughter relationship is inevitably an ambivalent one, for the mother who herself lives a circumscribed life in patriarchy, has the unenviable task of directing her daughter to take up the very same position that she has occupied.'[54] Wendy hoped for boyfriends, babies, and suitable (read: feminine) careers for Natalie and Nicola. Her hopes are long since dashed. However, in the film's somewhat climactically charged emotional scene between mother and daughter, Wendy declares: 'I wouldn't care what blummin' job you did, I wouldn't care how scruffy you looked, as long as you were happy. But you're not, something inside you has died.'[55] It is a tender and humane moment: 'If one day I could just walk through that door and you could look at me and say "look mum, help me, please, I don't know what I'm doing, I don't know where I'm going". And I'd say great because now we can be honest with each other, now we can start talking.'[56] However, Wendy also trades in some pernicious neoliberal values of individuals facing adversity with inner resilience. This narrative of individual fortitude, in certain ways, implies that victimhood is primarily connected to choice and inner resources as opposed to social and structural power and opportunity. Yet, also nested within this rhetoric of self-determination is a contrasting sense that survival, for women in particular, is a collective activity, a shared endeavour. We survive, the film suggests, together. Similarly, the film concludes with the sisters communing about Nicola's purging. Natalie expresses understanding that Nicola 'can't help it' but that '*we* should do something about it'.[57] Nicola responds to this by asking 'who's we?' to which Natalie replies 'you and me'.[58] The combination of the irresolution of the narrative (Nicola isn't 'fixed') and the collectivity of the endeavour marks a rejection of the expectation of the neoliberal subject to overcome through self-will, self-actualisation, and self-management. *Life Is Sweet* proposes that the art of living and getting by is a far more conflicted and collective affair. Indeed, the first time Nicola expresses an unambiguous desire, it is to be heard by Wendy: 'I just wanna talk to you.'[59] In *Life Is Sweet*, then, Leigh returns us to the urgency and paucity of collectivity and relationality. Here, as with respect to Leigh's broader attention to listening and looking in different manners, one can witness a careful attempt to reimagine the pathologised female body in relational, encultured terms.

Black lenses, white dreams

In *Black Skin, White Masks*, Frantz Fanon offered a striking critique of the alienating and divisive impact of colonialism on the colonised subject's self-perception.[60] In the famous 'Look, a Negro' section of the book, Fanon critically examines how he is interpellated within a white gaze. The first words an audience hears in Lee Daniels's film adaptation, *Precious*, are: 'My name is Claireece Precious Jones. I wish I had a light-skinned boyfriend.'[61] Elsewhere in the film we see Precious look in the mirror and perceive a white reflection (Figure 5.3) and hear her fantasise about marrying her white maths teacher, Mr Wicher, and living in 'Weschesser, wherever that is.'[62]

FIGURE 5.3   'White mirror', *Precious*

Discussing the apparent dysmorphia of anorexic self-image, Bordo corrects that, in fact, 'the anorectic does not "misperceive" her body, rather, she has learned all too well the dominant cultural standards of *how* to perceive.'[63] In related manners, Precious has learnt to accurately self-perceive in accordance with dominant frames of beauty. Her self-image is thus always already in dire deficit in its dialogue with both thinness and whiteness. Indeed, as Michael Bennett and Vanessa D. Dickerson argue:

> historically and socially, the black female body tends to be defined and viewed as the antithesis of the good, the true, and the beautiful. Demonized, debased, raped, dismissed – no other body in the United States has been so materially and discursively hobbled.[64]

The mirror scene thus renders visual, the issue of how far to discuss race is to simultaneously and necessarily to discuss white hegemony. Moreover, as Toni Morrison reminds us, in *Playing in the Dark: Whiteness and the Literary Imagination*, the subject of the dream is the dreamer.[65] This is to say that white writers' portraits of black characters depict white anxieties around race as opposed to revealing truths of black realities and consciousness. While directed by an African American, the film illuminates an internalised white gaze through Precious's fantasies that reveal the neo-colonial occupation of her imagination by white racist ideology. In this sense, *Precious* is caught in a fraught filmic suspension between black lenses and white dreams. However, what I hope to demonstrate below is that while it is a problematic film, it nonetheless offers some key critical interventions with respect to the pathologised fat, black, female body. In particular, I will argue that through its engagement with race, institutional bureaucracy, weight, and happiness, *Precious* poses a challenge to the apparent ready legibility of poor black women's bodies.

   Precious opened in 2009 to mixed notices and political controversy, in particular in relation to the film's alleged colourism. Adapted from Sapphire's novel *Push*, based on her experiences working in social care in New York, the film is broadly faithful to the novel with respect to plot.[66] Concerned with the plight of a 16-year-old girl who has been systematically physically and sexually abused from the age of three by both of her parents, *Precious* is a relentless tale of suffering and hopelessness. In the face of such degradation, many reviewers resorted to simply listing the identity classifications (or 'social facts', to borrow from Stuart Hall) of the protagonist: poor, obese, illiterate, HIV positive, black, girl. There is an almost sceptical tone in a handful of reviews, as though the accumulating despair is somehow ludicrous, as though all of this surely could not (and therefore does not) happen to one body. I will return in detail to the *timbre* of the press responses but suffice to say that such disbelief betrays a lack of understanding of the intersectional nature of violence and inequality.

The film, like *Life Is Sweet*, does not overtly diagnose Precious as mentally ill within its framing; nevertheless, it remains a portrait of profound despair. Describing her weariness with the desolation of her life, Precious says: 'Love ain't done nothing for me; love beat me, raped me, called me a [sic] animal, make me feel worthless, make me sick.'[67] The film in this way disbands a biomedical frame in favour of an emotional register of stark, melancholic alienation. Love, for Precious, is a past tense. Hope lies elsewhere, ahead, in the future tense of education. Indeed, speaking of how talking in class for the first time at her alternative school makes her feel, she relates: 'Here. It makes me feel here.'[68] What follows then will examine three primary areas in relation to *Precious*'s visual politics of psychopathology. Firstly, I will critique the racial politics of both the film and its popular and academic reception in order to chart the complex and, at times, contradictory positions the film occupies. Secondly, I will consider the narrative framing of Precious's weight and its relationship to racialised understandings of the 'civilised' body. Finally, I will address the film's narrative of resilience and the politics of invulnerability. Here I will turn to the conflicting politics of self-actualisation and happiness in dialogue with the film's attention to systemic inequality. The chapter will argue that, though uneven, *Precious* makes critical strides in troubling the dominant cinematic gaze on abjected female bodies. In so doing, the film raises thoughtful questions that disrupt the ordinary cultural traffic between mad minds and mad bodies.

White lines

One of the central accusations levelled at *Precious* is that, in casting light-skinned actors in the caring roles, the film reasserts racist stereotypes that associate darkness with 'badness'. Sukhdev Sandhu, for example, argued that 'pretty much all the good ethnics in this film … are less than dark-skinned. Blackness is ugliness, a social pathology.'[69] This critique, along with an objection that the film reifies the image of 'black man as sexual predator', is echoed by other writers such as Ishmael Reed and Ed Gonzalez, who likewise vilified the film, its director, and its high-profile producers – Oprah Winfrey and Tyler Perry.[70] Reed goes as far as to label the film a hate crime. Perhaps the most vitriolic critique came however, perhaps unsurprisingly, from polemical Armond White. White described it as a 'sociological horror show' that the Ku Klux Klan would adore: 'Not since *The Birth of a Nation* has a mainstream movie demeaned the idea of black American life as much as *Precious*.'[71] One is reminded here not only of the related critical debates surrounding Steven Spielberg's adaption of Alice Walker's *The Color Purple* (1985), but also the narrator of Ralph Ellison's *The Invisible Man* (1952), who frets about Trueblood's telling of his incest tale to white folks: 'How can he tell this to white men, I thought, when he knows they'll say that all Negroes do such things.'[72]

One cannot and ought not dismiss such concerns, particularly in relation to both the broad context of American racial history and, more specifically, the political narratives that have persistently sought to racialise poverty and thereby demonise black families. Whether one examines the Moynihan Report of 1965 or the rhetoric of Reaganomics, one can witness a deliberate attempt by successive white governments to portray black families as a social ill. As Patricia Hill Collins has argued:

> the Reagan/Bush administrations also realized that racializing welfare by painting it as a program that unfairly benefited Blacks was a sure-fire way to win white votes. This context created the controlling image of the "welfare queen", primarily to garner support for refusing state support for poor and working-class Black mothers and children.[73]

These are, thus, far from abstract or inconsequential concerns. Furthermore, as Mia Mask suggests, 'For some progressive thinkers, there are simply too few cinematic representations of African Americans to accommodate a motion picture as negative in its depiction of black inner city life as *Precious*.'[74] This wide-ranging concern is amplified in a film such as *Precious*, perhaps paradoxically, owing to the lack of white characters and white constructions. Indeed, as James Snead suggests, in relation to a broader history of black cinema such as *Hallelujah* (1929) and *The Color Purple*, black characters' 'behaviour is being portrayed as something static, enduring, and unchangeable, unrelated to the history that whites have trapped them in. Blacks are seen as ahistorical.'[75] However, I argue that there is an alternative way of reading the racial politics of *Precious* that challenges the critical perception that the film simply valorises whiteness and demeans blackness. Without question, there are problematic politics at play within the casting. Nevertheless, I propose that it is imperative to also attend to the critique that is at play within the film's racial logic as well as interrogating the misogyny in operation within voices such as Reed and White.

Armond White describes Precious as 'the hippopotamus-like teenager'.[76] Sandhu, in the course of a short review, describes her as 'mortifyingly fat' and jokes that 'Those chaps on the World's Strongest Man who tug trucks behind them move quicker than she does.'[77] His praise for the actor Gabourey Sidibe amounts to: 'Sidibe, a first-time actress, doesn't disgrace herself here. She does have a certain Easter Island stature.'[78] Bob Mondello, reviewing the film on NPR, similarly asserts that:

> Sidibe, quietly monumental as Precious, is more acted upon than active for much of the picture, her face is so full it seems incapable of expression …

Once in motion, though, she's formidable enough that only an immovable object could oppose her.[79]

Moreover, other press reviews are littered with language such as 'monumental', 'towering', 'substantial' and so forth that emphasise, first and foremost, Sidibe's weight. It is precisely the confluence of a critical fury regarding the portrayal of black men in this film with the cruel, misogynistic tone and content of the reviews that expose both the critical blind spots and the lack of depth at work in voices like White's. As David Ikard illuminates:

> They [Reed and White] also get a cultural pass, so to speak, for assaulting black women [in their writings] because the discourse of black men in crisis prioritizes black men's suffering to such a degree that competing narratives of gendered black pain register as emasculating and anti-black.[80]

Ikard cites the high prevalence of obesity, depression, and HIV-related death in African American women as compared to their white counterparts as a further means to privilege the reality, as well as the urgency, of telling a tale like *Precious*. The disavowal of the (gendered) reality of Precious's story in the reviews points to a problematic desire for 'positive' imagery as a counter to the controlling images of blackness. The issue here is that to censor works like *Precious* in this way marks a failure to attend to the structural inequality that produces lives blighted by such violence. Instead, I propose that if one considers two key aspects of the film, one can begin to discern a dynamic critique of whiteness that runs counter to the argument that to portray racism is to tacitly endorse racism: bureaucracy and fantasy.

In the film's narrative, the character Precious is made visible in white systems and structures (from welfare to school to shelters). Many objected to the fact that the institutional characters who come to Precious's aid – Ms Rain, Nurse John, Ms Weiss – are light-skinned. This is particularly noted in relation to Ms Rain who is described as dark-skinned in the original novel. However, given the centrality of colourism within both the film and the novel, it seems unlikely that this is an unthinking aspect of Daniels's overall political intervention. Indeed, there is a logic in the casting insofar as it underscores white privilege. It is precisely the logic of colourism that the film employs that serves to expose the inequity that more advantages are bestowed upon those whose skin is closer to the dominant norms of a white hegemony. On its own, this reading may be on somewhat shaky and speculative ground. However, if taken together with the film's tacit critique of white bureaucratic gaze, the critical illumination of whiteness within *Precious* becomes steadier and more glaring.

Precious is captured in paper. To begin her course at the alternative school, she requires discharge papers, utility bills, and copies of her mother's budget. She is then subject to tests to ascertain her literacy levels. Her response offers an astute critique of the ideological strains that are encrypted within such metrics:

There's always something wrong with the tesses. These tesses paint a picture of me with no brain. These tesses paint a picture of me and my mother, my whole family as less than dumb, just ugly black grease to be wiped away.[81]

Later, in the Social Services Department, Precious is advised that she will have to disclose her private life in order to receive state support: 'You're gonna have to talk to someone if you want your cheques, sweetie.'[82] Furthermore, upon stealing her case file, Precious discovers that the state sees her education at the alternative school as a waste of resources and thus is seeking to place her in a workfare programme. Cumulatively, the bureaucratic imagination of the film points to the public availability and narratability of poor women's bodies, and in particular black women's bodies. As Vivyan C. Adair writes, this has the consequence of rendering such bodies as confessional evidence:

> State-mandated blood tests, interrogation of the most private aspects of our lives, the public humiliation of having to beg officials for food and medicine, and the loss of all right to privacy, teach us that our bodies are only useful as lesson, warnings, and signs of degradation that everyone loves to hate.[83]

In this sense, then, the film is acutely aware of white privilege and indeed exposes this as the brutal framework through which Precious is made legible and vulnerable.[84]

A further way in which the film is in active dialogue with the tyranny of idealised whiteness is through the hyperbolic fantasy sequences. Precious fantasises about being white, about having a light-skinned boyfriend, about marrying her white teacher, about being a famous celebrity, an object of desire. She also imagines her mother being kinder to her in the sequence which sees them on-screen inside their TV, suspended within Vittorio de Sica's *Two Women* (1960) – a film in which a woman tries desperately to protect her daughter from the terrors of World War II. This latter sequence appears to intertextually acknowledge the war-like context of Precious's environment (both domestically and in Harlem), as well as her mother's failure to protect her. The recurrent full-flight fantasy sequences, however, are deliberately drenched in whiteness. At a superficial level, one could argue that this, therefore, implies that whiteness is uncritically endorsed as the aspirational norm by the film. Indeed, in her reading of the second fantasy sequence, Debbie Olson argues Daniels frames Precious as bestial: 'She is physically depicted on the ground [when she has been knocked over] at the level of the dog, and therefore more deserving of kisses from an animal [than a light-skinned boy].'[85] She also reasons that the picture frames Precious as 'unfeminine: she is morbidly obese and is displayed as vulgar.'[86] In both instances, Olson arrests the discussion at an associative level: dog = bestial; fat = vulgar. However, if one interrogates the aesthetic qualities of the fantasy sequences and daydreams, they become palpable critiques of the tyranny of white neoliberal ideals. For example, the lurid photography of the scenes serves not only to underscore their unreal nature but, more pivotally, to remind an audience of the grotesque and hyperbolic violence of aspiration. The heightened visual register renders garish the ideological cruelty of inculcating the desire to be outside one's own skin.

FIGURE 5.4 'Illuminations', *Precious*

Quite literally bathed in dazzling white lights, Precious enacts and embodies desire (Figure 5.4). These scenes contain double exposures: what she is – black and heavy – and her fantasy to become what she is not – white and light. The film, then, far from celebrating whiteness, instead exposes the profoundly damaging psychological effects of growing up fat, black, and poor in a culture that pathologically privileges the opposite. In this sense, the white-authored conditions of degradation that have created the self-loathing and despair in Precious's consciousness are far from invisible within the film. Rather, at both an aesthetic and narrative level, whiteness is writ large as a determining context of black female 'pathologies'. Moreover, far from suggesting that one reads whiteness as the ultimate cipher for black pathology, I am proposing that it is the black body of Precious that makes the violent glare of white lights visible. In this way, rather than being simply illuminated *in* whiteness, her body is inscribed with agency by illuminating white privilege.

'I only ask to be free. The butterflies are free.'[87]

One of the central publicity images for the film release was of the actor, Sidibe, silhouetted by giant butterfly wings. The image was frequently accompanied by the strapline: 'You feel you've witnessed nothing less than the birth of a soul.'[88] The marketing of the film thus trades on tropes of overcoming, triumph, and spiritual rebirth. As A. O. Scott writes in the *New York Times*, 'it's partly a bootstrap drama of resilience and redemption ... it's also a nearly gothic story of a child tormented by the cruelty of adults.'[89] However, I would texture this reading further to argue that, in fact, the instances in which *Precious* rejects, resists, or problematises a tale of rising, butterfly-like, out of adversity come to form its most incisive political moments. On the one hand, Precious escapes the abuse of her domestic home. On the other hand, however, she remains firmly tethered to her social reality as well as her pathologised body. It is, curiously, this tethering that productively bypasses the false warmth of a narrative of individualised self-actualisation, promised in the butterfly imago. By remaining heavy, poor, and black the film partially disturbs a Hollywood narrative arc of transcending adversity via personal psychological resources. Indeed, by rejecting a narrative of blossoming, both in terms of appearance and opportunity, *Precious* turns an audience's attention to the interlocking, systemic, and cultural mechanisms of deprivation. This is not to deny the Mariah-Carey-lyric sentimentality that the film also expounds: 'So when you feel like hope is gone, look inside you and be strong. And you'll finally see the truth, that a hero lies in you.'[90] To be sure, Precious is a cinematic antihero. Nevertheless, she remains a complicated one.

Fat is a racialised discourse. In her discussion of discourses of evolution that were in circulation in the nineteenth and early twentieth century, Amy Erdman Farrell explains that 'much of the writing in this time period described in detail the fatness of "primitive" people and of all women, using that trait as evidence of inferior status.'[91] She traces the lineage of this thinking to the contemporary moment and proposes that bodily 'excess' (both in terms of weight and sexuality) remains a key visual-cultural marker of inferiority: 'the "welfare queen" is simply a more recent version of the Venus Hottentot, a fat woman whose appetites for sex and food know no bounds.'[92] It would be tempting, therefore, to reason that *Precious* ought to problematise this stereotyped image of the 'excessive' black body in some way. A predictable and marketable narrative in the context of this mainstream film would see Precious, then, in her journey to liberation, shedding pounds in an assumed act of radical self-love. It is key, therefore, that the film refuses to participate in this available and highly gendered story of fat girl thin. Indeed, here is an example of the limits of 'positive' imagery as political strategy. As Le'a Kent articulates, much dieting rhetoric (both visual and verbal) frames fatness as cage or shroud that the 'real' person is trapped within: 'In this scenario, the self, the person, is presumptively thin, and cruelly jailed in a fat body. The self is never fat. To put it bluntly, there is no such thing as a fat *person*.'[93] The film's overall disinterest in Precious's body and weight is thus crucial. While it is far from irrelevant (we hear her mother force-feeds her, for example) and makes important points about the selling of cheap food to poor populations (the key meals framed are pigs' feet and fried chicken), food and fat are sidelined in important ways. In this sense, Precious's personhood is not predicated precariously on her size. The film certainly exposes the discrimination she experiences as a consequence of her body shape (and the reviews expose a fat-hating culture). However, crucially, within the narrative there is no caterpillar to butterfly dynamic at play. Indeed, in both the book cover and poster image, the butterfly wings are greyed out ghosts – symbolically evident but unable to really fly. The 'real', thin Precious thus does not emerge in a consumable narrative of transition to (beautiful, thin) autonomy. This is a vital means by which the film decisively rejects fat as a symbol of shameful uncivility.

A final intervention *Precious* makes with respect to pathological bodies lies in its exploration of happiness. At the film's conclusion, Precious is not 'happy'. She has escaped her abusive childhood, has developed some friendships, and is improving her education, but the narrative is not triumphalist. Indeed, one could argue that the lack of transformation in terms of her circumstances offers a bleak and condemning image of the possibilities for poor, black girls in some politically problematic ways. Against such a charge of racial nihilism, however, I propose that the film also exposes and critiques the politics of happiness as an available narrative for young women like Precious. Sara Ahmed writes:

> Black feminists such as bell hooks teach us that some women — black and working-class women — are not even entitled to be proximate to the fantasy [of the good life] … We can consider not so much how happiness is distributed (this would forget what was important about the second-wave critique of the unhappiness concealed in the figure of the happy housewife) but the distribution of the *relative proximity of ideas of happiness*.[94]

Precious is a figure who is categorically not entitled to be proximate to happiness. Crucially, nor is her mother, Mary. Moreover, both women are reliant on the state for the modicums of happiness that each enjoys. Escape is thus unavailable in ways that point to the systemic violence that keeps women and girls in poverty, violence, and dependency. Perhaps one of the most challenging scenes of the film is Mary's monologue at Social Services that pleads for empathy regarding her failure to protect Precious from abuse. She lays claim to victimhood in ways that are both appalling and understandable. One is not invited to forgive Mary; rather, one is challenged to consider the conditions that produce and sustain endemic violence. The film here challenges the myth that women do *or can* simply leave situations of abuse and violence. The film does not create an equivalence between Precious and Mary here. However, these elements of conflicted generosity towards Mary signal important political thought about what sorts of stories and selfhoods are available for what 'sorts' of women. Women and girls in the kinds of situations an audience sees Mary and Precious in do not simply shrug off their cocoons and fly, buffeted by positive thinking and resilience. Moreover, sounding a related note in terms of addiction, Nancy D. Campbell and Elizabeth E. Horre explain:

> the politics of neuroscience and the biomedicalization of women's health are entangled with the politics that keep some women poor and enmeshed in circumstances where they and their children have little choice but to participate in the drug economies that overwhelm their cultural geographies.[95]

In this sense, by insisting on the quicksand of systemic violence and intersectional inequality, survival, hope, overcoming, and happiness are framed as precarious, daily wars: wars that are fought on and by pathologised women's bodies. In markedly different manners, then, *Precious* considers, like *Life Is Sweet*, what lives young women are permitted to linger within. It considers how far happiness is a graspable figure for Precious. While wrestling unevenly with the constraints and conventions of Hollywood, *Precious* thus manages to raise fundamental questions about the politics of race, weight, and class in relation to psychopathology and lived experiences of profound distress.

'I want to live vividly and make huge, spectacular, heroic mistakes'[96]

A striking similarity between Nicola, Precious, and the protagonist of *People, Places and Things* [hereafter, *PPT*], Emma, is the mood of invulnerability. All three women perform grit, tenaciously. The temptation here is to surmise that what is in operation in all three cases is a form of titanium self-defence that serves to keep their souls untouchable. While certainly thematically plausible, I wonder if there might also be a further dimension that speaks to the psychopathological framing of the three women. Bordo observes of anorexia that, curiously, the wasted body is commonly experienced powerfully – as strength not frailty: 'it is striking that although the anorectic may come very close to death (and 15 percent do indeed die), the dominate experience throughout the illness is of invulnerability.'[97] Describing her experiences of self-starvation in her play *Mess*, Caroline Horton writes: 'I think it's important you understand that like being drunk or getting high or winning something – it feels amazing – at times … Let's just be honest – certain moments make you feel invincible … nothing can stop you and you know you're winning and at this point everything looks amazing!'[98] In this sense, the life-giving, meaning-making audacity of self-destruction is central to a rounded understanding of the felt experiences of certain forms of mental distress. Emma, in *PPT*, is positively raging with life in her self-harming behaviours. Moreover, as Chris Bennion notes, the play 'does not pretend that there aren't some serious upsides to hedonism.'[99] Macmillan captures the siren lure of intoxication which, as Stuart Walton writes in his history of intoxication, 'reminds you gloriously that you exist.'[100] Alongside this honest appraisal of the pleasures of apparently uncontrolled and uncontrollable behaviour, however, is a question around what the pursuit of vividness might specifically reveal about women's relationships to their own bodies and minds. This enables us to shift beyond a Romantic notion of personal freedom unbound. It is perhaps not incidental that Nicola claims to be writing a novel, Precious fantasises about celebrity fame, and Emma is an actor who wants to not only live 'a hundred lives' on stage but also be the tragic hero of her own story to avoid the 'Shame and boredom and orange fucking squash' of ordinary life.[101] In all three cases a desire for cultural visibility is cast. In this way, a hyperawareness of meaningful life narratives in a neoliberal capitalist economy and the pursuit of exceptionality shimmers through. In what follows below, then, I will attend to the politics of excess and virtuosity, consider the normative values of recovery, and pause to contemplate the universalisability of wellness in the context of Duncan Macmillan's 2015 play, *PPT*.

PPT ran from 25 August to 4 November 2015 on the Dorfman stage at the National Theatre in collaboration with Headlong. It later transferred to the Wyndham's Theatre from 15 March to 4 June 2016. Directed by Jeremy Herrin with set design by Bunnie Christie and music composed by Matthew Herbert, it was synthesis of the vibrant and mundane. The play is both heavily located and familiar, suspended in familiar tropes of the clinic (white tiles, audience's gaze foregrounded, and so on), and a giddy evocation of distorted subjectivity (multiple

Emmas, moving and pixelated walls, and so forth). Moreover, it bears the neon, high-octane hallmarks of a Headlong production. In one sense, it is a play about a woman's addiction to drugs and drink. In another way, however, it is much more a meditation on the corrosive impact of capitalism on belonging, connection, and human worth. The press response was overwhelmingly positive with reviewers universal in their exalted praise of the actor who played Emma, Denise Gough. Gough is described as 'barnstorming', 'extraordinary', 'superlative', 'stunning', 'shattering' and giving a 'career-defining performance'.[102] In a curious and paradoxical parallel, Gough is acclaimed for her exceptional qualities in a play that spins on catastrophic normalcy. In this sense, Gough's virtuosity appears to run counter to Emma's ordinariness. Yet, it is precisely the collision of Gough's performance and Macmillan's text that serves to render the quotidian vivid. Ostensibly, the play charts Emma's addiction and recovery in a 12-step programme. A fiercely astute voice, Emma rails against both herself and the means by which she is offered an alternative:

> I'm not powerless. I'm not helpless. I don't believe addiction is a disease and I'm scared and angered by the suggestion that from now on its either eternal abstinence or binge to death. I can't surrender to a higher power because there isn't one. There just isn't.[103]

Similarly, another resident, Paul, explosively (and recurrently) articulates: 'They're going to ask for everything but you've got nothing to begin with. Nothing.'[104] Both, in markedly different ways, perceive the sham, of both addiction and abstinence, with seer-like perspicacity. What is particularly noteworthy for our purposes, however, is the modes in which both the play and the press response illuminate the politics of aspiration and the politics of just getting by.

The art of existence

The existential quality of Emma's despair is spliced with a diagnosis of contemporary culture:

> I find reality pretty difficult.
> I find the business of getting out of bed and
> getting on with the day really *hard*. I find
> picking up my phone to be a mammoth
> fucking struggle. The number on my inbox.
> The friends who won't see me anymore. The
> food pictures and porn videos, the bombings
> and beheadings, the moral ambivalence you
> have to have just to be able to carry on with
> your day. I find the knowledge that we're all
> just atoms and one day we'll stop and be dirt in
> the ground, I find that overwhelmingly
> disappointing.[105]

Later, more explicitly, she eloquently rages that:

> I'd like to believe that my problems are
> meaningful. But they're not. There are
> people dying of *thirst*. People living in
> war zones and here we are thinking about
> *ourselves*. As if we can solve everything
> by confronting our own defects. We're
> not defective. It's the world that's fucked.[106]

Like Nicola's invective, it is tempting to hear glib superficiality in the relativity of suffering. However, crucially she identifies both the life-seeking impulse at the heart of intense behaviours and also the flaw at the heart of much addiction treatment. Walton argues that part of the reason that no recorded human societies (apart from Inuits prior to European presence) have existed free from psychoactive substances is both 'the ache of existential angst' but also the 'unquenchable ambition in most of us to have more of whatever it is about life that makes it feel dynamic.'[107] Furthermore, as Campbell and Horre explain:

> The contradiction is clear: the governing mentalities that position addiction
> as a 'brain disease' also place responses to it within the purview of the moral
> obligations of citizenship, not unlike other such similar 'brain diseases' as obe-
> sity, alcoholism, and major and minor mental illnesses.[108]

While Emma's clinic is not biologically minded, the questions of her therapeutic citizenship and moral obligations to the 'group' resonate throughout the play. Moreover, Emma's distrust of, and resistance to, 'recovery' is studded with her desperation to find a life that matches the one neoliberalism promises, or at least envisions. It is here, in the articulation of the devastating gap between aspiration and normalcy, that the play's central theatrical analogy comes alive, politically speaking:

> With a play you get instructions … You get to live the most intense moments
> of a life over and over again … And you're *applauded* … I want to live a
> hundred lives and be everywhere and fight against infinitesimal time we have
> on this planet. Acting gives me the same thing I get from drugs and alcohol.
> Good parts are just harder to come by.[109]

This finds further echo in the 'Quixotic' speech Emma has learnt, reasoning that 'if I could make this bullshit marketing speak work … they'd see how good an actress I am.'[110] If she can make the vacuous rhetoric of neoliberal subjectivity sing, then, in a sense, she will have mastered the imitation of existence in a marketised culture of self-actualisation. In this way, *PPT* drains the colour from the grandiloquent promises of capitalism to expose the ravaged bodies beneath. As Phipps notes, 'Individualization is part of a lengthy process of depoliticising the postmodern and neoliberal subject: inner transformation has taken the place of social change.'[111]

Emma's pathologised body bears witness to the wretched gap between the positivist futurity of capitalist imagination – 'We look at the world with *joy* … looking towards the future' – and the airless difficulty of actually living in it – 'All the boring stuff left in. Waiting. Temping. Answering phones and serving canapés. Nothing permanent. Can't plan. Can't get a mortgage or pay for a car.'[112]

Consumer capitalism, as Émile Durkheim exposed more than a century before, produces cultures of suicidal disappointment.[113] The individualism, promise of boundless achievement, and elevation of choice and competition as core values dissolve social bonds and produce despair and self-alienation. Emma is thus at war with her own despicable ordinariness. Having been taught to desire without 'boundaries or limitations', she is perpetually caught in a vortex of her own inadequacy: 'staring into the blank void of my own personality.'[114] She has thus found connection in the only thing that ever loved her back: booze and drugs. Further, this is not simply a solipsistic gesture. Some may, like Quentin Letts, wish to dismiss Emma as a 'self-indulgent' 'middle class … spoilt youngster', as though pain is neatly cordoned off from privilege.[115] However, this view also fails to attend to the political import of a preoccupation with the self in this theatrical critique of individualism. Moreover, in a way, Emma is right. As her mother reminds her: 'If you want honesty, real, no bullshit, gloves-off truthfulness, sweetheart, drink and drugs were the only things that made you any fun.'[116] Further, at her audition that concludes the play, there '*is a queue of ACTRESSES, all the same age and demographic as EMMA*' who also played her other selves in the bedroom sequences.[117] In this way, in its exposure of the violence of aspirational capitalism, *PPT* strews Emma's (multiplied) 'pathologised' body across the stage in the form of repeated accusation. In attempting to press out a life in the cutter image of Quixotic, Emma is in violent dialogue with 'What a thing it is to be alive'.[118] Moreover, as the play's climactic scene between Emma and her mother reveals, there is no inner transformation; rather there are only moment-by-moment blistered decisions about how to live. And, more particularly, how to live amidst people, places, and things:

> *EMMA reaches under the bed and pulls out a large clear plastic box full of pills, bottles of alcohol and various drug paraphernalia.*
> EMMA: Holy shit.
> MUM: Look what you were doing to yourself.
> *EMMA pushes the box across the floor away from her. She stares at it.*
> […]
> MUM: You want rid of this stuff go ahead. If you want to use it then take it and go. But don't come back to us if you do. We've had too much Lucy.
> […]
> *She [EMMA] walks back to the box and takes the lid off it. She is breathing heavily.*
> *She takes her phone out and calls a number.*
> Hi yes hello
> I was given your number by Mark
> Yes hi, that's me

I was hoping there might be a meeting this
evening and maybe
Great, yes, I've got a pen.
*She finds a pen, a fluffy-ended child's pen, and writes an
address on her hand.*[119]

'I don't ever want to drink again, I just, oh, I just need a friend'[120]

In her study, *Epidemics of Will*, Eve Kosofsky-Sedgwick examines the discursive and cultural movement from 'opium-eaters' to 'addicts'. As Samantha Murray summarises:

> Sedgwick illustrates the ways in which the figure of the 'addict' is constituted, and how she operates within discourses that necessarily impel her into a spiral of disease, death, and destruction: the only escape from this inscription of addiction is to 'kick the habit', a 'technology' which is also always already marked with pathology.[121]

A further violence of this model of compulsion is how far it mutes the addict, who is 'reduced to an object that can be read and understood within a range of disciplinary technologies that insist they know the "truth" of the addict, a truth that is always already located in a logic of pathologisation.'[122] The clinic in *PPT* lays heavy emphasis on truth: 'You have to be completely truthful or the process won't work ... Denial is what kills you.'[123] Furthermore, the traumagenic origins of addiction are presumed: 'You've addressed the chemical hooks but not the central cause of your addiction ... trauma.'[124] However, I am less interested in whether or not trauma causes addiction in Emma's case (or more broadly); rather what matters for our discussion is the way in which the mechanism of 'truthfulness' operates as an authenticating discourse in recovery. This model validates an essentialised truth about personhood and, moreover, promises that therein lies the (self) cure. The capacity to heal thus pivots on confession and self-reckoning (and subsequent self-management). While there can be little doubt a degree of critical self-examination is important in all our lives, *PPT*, I propose, troubles the authenticating seal of truth in recovery and in so doing points to the normative values that cling to 'wellness'. The play investigates how far finding one's 'truth' necessarily relies on acquiescing to a shared sense of how to live. As Ahmed argues, 'Good subjects will not experience pleasure from the wrong objects (they will be hurt by them or indifferent to them) and will only experience a certain amount of pleasure from the right objects.'[125] Instead, Macmillan turns the character of Emma inside out, both thematically and dramaturgically, as a means to expose the absence of such singular happiness. Inner truth as both the site of recovery and the wellspring of private resolve is exposed as a dubious conceit.

Dramaturgically, we are positioned within Emma's purview. Our perception, in the original production, of the reality of the clinic shuddered in tandem with hers:

EMMA sits on the bed. Snow falls onto her ... EMMA approaches the THERAPIST but she's vanished. She watches her UNDERSTUDY, in costume, walk across the room holding a dead seagull, then climb out of the window.[126]

Furthermore, our sense of time and space ricochets in sync with Emma's:

The room is moving, warping, tilting with the thumping bass. The lights of the club flash red and blue, the emergency light from an ambulance. DRESSERS dress EMMA as Marie Antoinette. The sound of a truck approaching, sounding its horn ... EMMA is given a bouquet of flowers. A woman holds out a clipboard.[127]

In contradistinction to *Life Is Sweet*, in this sense, we are invited to look, at least partially, *with* not *at* her. There are innumerable moments in the play when an audience is positioned to either see or hear what Emma sees or hears. The visual exuberance of her hallucinations, for example, deliberately contrast with the naturalism of the group therapy scenes in order to achieve this alignment. However, crucially, our proximity to any sense of 'truth' about Emma, her addiction, or her life is fundamentally volatile. Indeed, the volatility of 'knowing' productively places an audience within the destabilisation Emma herself experiences: 'I never had a brother. And he didn't die in front of children. He died in his car. Or he was stillborn maybe. Or he grew up and died of old age ... It's not lying. It's admitting there's no truth to begin with.'[128] In the course of the second act, an audience is lulled into believing that the 'real' Emma has spoken. She has completed the programme. She is 'recovered'. I am not proposing that the play offers a damascene moment and thereby implies that recovery is stable – it doesn't. Nevertheless, there is a palpable shift – both in register and expectation – between the acts that appears to offer a more stripped back Emma: 'I don't want medication. I want to feel it. I need it to be *irrevocable*.'[129] Indeed, the theatrical coup of Emma's mum calling her 'Lucy' at the play's climax precisely rests on this sense of the 'real' Emma having been present in tandem with the conventions of addiction narratives – from chaos to recovery via relapse. However, *PPT*, echoing the uncertain endings of *Life Is Sweet* and *Precious*, dramaturgically upends such genre convention. In this structural swipe, Macmillan troubles the 'truths' of identity, meaning, and reality on which life, therapy, and theatre all rest. Instead, we are reminded: 'This is all bullshit. None of it's real.'[130] Emma's body is thus represented as an inconstant, accumulating tissue of narratives in manners that politically destabilise central tenets of essentialised personhood.

Truth and its revelation are, then, destabilised as the paths to 'wellness', both as an individual and collective pursuit. However, the coercive pressure for 'openness' within the group lest 'you jeopardise everyone's recovery' because 'we're only as sick as our secrets', exposes a curious dynamic of community at play in recovery.[131] Emma describes herself as a 'lone wolf':

THERAPIST: Who else here is a lone wolf?
             Everyone in the GROUP puts their hands up.
             Take a seat Emma.[132]

In this way, one can perceive a clear enactment of the highly individualised way we culturally tend to conceptualise addiction and recovery in the contemporary moment. As James Reynolds and Zoe Zontou suggest, 'addiction is now ubiquitous, offering a paradigm through which to understand compulsive consumption, and the place that holds in the crises of Western culture produced by late capitalism.'[133] Yet simultaneously, and somewhat paradoxically, this recovery model is predicated on a sense of community, belonging, and bonding. Moreover, as David Best has written, this model of lone wolves in a circle of mutual aid is one that is proliferating:

> A recent survey in the UK indicated that in 2011 there were approximately 4600 AA [Alcoholics Anonymous] meetings, 896 NA [Narcotics Anonymous] meetings, 90 Al-Anon [support group for friends and relatives of alcoholics] meetings, 242 CA [Cocaine Anonymous] meetings and 88 SMART Recovery [general addiction] meetings.[134]

Best understands this model as an antidote to the biomedical framing of addiction recovery: 'recovery is something characterised by personal experiences, embedded in families and communities – and so it is not at all obvious that something that looks diagnostic is helpful or within the spirit of a recovery definition.'[135] *PPT* certainly dramatises this sense of the value of connection as a means of survival: 'All I need you to do is sit with me and hold my hand without speaking okay?'[136] However, beyond a potentially vague sense of the vital nature of collectivity, Macmillan is careful to illuminate the norms that govern recovery. Recovery is not neutral nor are all recovery goals equal and valid. In this way, *PPT* opens up a dialogue around the ideology of recovery: 'Ninety meetings in ninety days … How do I go back to normal?'[137] However, perhaps more crucially, Macmillan's text reminds us that normalcy is a collective imaginary: 'It's the same with the programme. With everything, really. Language. Politics. Money. Religion. Law. At some level, we all know it's all bullshit. A magical group delusion.'[138] Emma goes on to describe this, just as Žižek did in relation to the financial collapse of 2008, in terms of Wile E. Coyote: 'It's only when he looks down and sees that he should be falling that gravity kicks in.'[139] Survival is thus predicated on one's participation in the multiple ways we collectively author the delusion of a meaningful, normal life: 'Don't look down.'[140] The final intervention, then, that *PPT* makes is to lay waste to the false universal of 'well'. There is no singular truth, then, only the stories we are telling ourselves and each other. In this way, as with *Life Is Sweet* and *Precious*, the gaze is redirected away from the pathologised female body and towards a mangled body politic.

Sight lines

Emma's final line in *PPT* is 'Thank you for seeing me.'[141] Elsewhere in the play we have heard characters similarly expressing gratitude for feeling seen or being heard: 'I used to go days without talking to anyone. But this. Here. Now. Listening and being listened to. Being *seen*. It's saving my life I think.'[142] As noted earlier, Precious describes how speaking in her class makes her feel present for the first time. Similarly, Nicola intimates that what she wants most of all is just to talk to her mum. This clarion desire to be heard speaks to the central thesis of this chapter and this book. These three art works, though strikingly distinct, expose the urgency of looking and listening beyond the surfaces of bodies and behaviours and instead situating them in time and space. Indeed, as Cvetkovich suggests: 'Epidemics of depression can be related (both as symptom and as obfuscation) to long-term histories of violence that have ongoing impacts at the level of everyday emotional experience.'[143] All three create room to consider how one might begin to listen to the tales such bodies might be attempting to relate. More specifically, through their respective engagements with form, these three pieces return an audience to their acts of spectatorship. This poses the vital question, following Arthur W. Frank, as to what *kind* of listener each story calls upon you, as an audience, to be. Their respective cinematic and dramaturgical strategies similarly attempt to tune in to what conditions produce, obscure, and amplify political audibility and agency for women like Nicola, Precious, and Emma. Likewise, they ask what conditions one's gaze upon these women's bodies. Indeed, all three invite and disturb ordinary ways of perceiving and reading pathological female bodies in manners that push back against a notion that perception is a spontaneous apprehending of simply what *is*.

The artists examined do not propose that bodies and behaviours are irrelevant. They do not create works that suggest distress is just relative and all socially constructed, in any case. Nor do they simply suggest that one ought to just listen *better*. Rather, what I have argued here is that these works attempt to explore how and why pathologised women's bodies speak or are made to speak. It is my contention that moving beyond a model that understands such bodies as simply confessional and readable (therefore knowable and treatable) is paramount. All three examples instead resist such certainty. The women's bodies are situated in time, space, families, and social environments and through this question the ideological terms of such structures and institutions. An audience is thus invited to explore the complex entanglements of the personal, social, and biological: and always in incomplete, contingent, partial manners. Furthermore, at the conclusion of all three pieces the female protagonists are not 'better', rising to become their 'true' selves that have been obscured by their previously excessive bodies. Instead all three remain alive. In this sense, the artists examined trouble the idea that one may simply travel from illness to wellness. Instead, the languages of distress and joy and just getting by are redistributed across these women's lives and experiences. This is a vital intervention in the field of mad studies insofar as it encourages a more hopeful appraisal of the ordinary difficulty of living. By shifting the discourse of survival and recovery on to more ambiguous terrain, the artists open up valuable spaces in which to dissect nothing less significant than the meaning and purpose of life. While it may appear glib or facile to suggest that this is what these works examine, it is critical to do so in the context of a crisis of distress and anxiety enacted under late Western capitalism. Instead, in their attention to different ways of telling, listening, and being,

Life Is Sweet, Precious, and *People, Places and Things* invite audiences to critique the normative values of wellness and happiness, and aspire instead to the complex messiness of just getting by together.

Notes

1 Sapphire, *Push* (London:Vintage, 1998), p. 31.The novel is written with a phonetic register and here 'tesses' can be understood as 'tests'.
2 There are, of course, body-based experiences that are particular to men, trans, and otherwise identifying peoples. However, this chapter is expressly concerned with female experience and attendant gendered pathologies.
3 Susie Orbach, *Hunger Strike: Starving Amidst Plenty* (London: Karnac, 2005), 2nd edn, p. 174.
4 Orbach, p. xvii.
5 Kim Chernin, *The Hungry Self: Women, Eating, and Identity* (London:Virago, 1986), p. ix.
6 See, Darian Leader, *What Is Madness?* (London: Hamish Hamilton, 2011).
7 Susan Bordo, *Unbearable Weight: Feminism, Western Culture, and the Body* (Berkeley, CA: University of California Press, 2008), p. 141.
8 Fiona, quoted in Rosemary Shelley (ed.), *Anorexics on Anorexia* (London: Jessica Kingsley, 1997), p. 3. I recognise that this source is dated. However, many contemporary accounts likewise complain of the short-term, weight-gain focus in approaches to responding to anorexia.
9 Devine, quoted in Rosemary Shelley (ed.), *Anorexics on Anorexia* (London: Jessica Kingsley, 1997), p. 98.
10 Sara Ahmed, *The Promise of Happiness* (Durham, NC and London: Duke University Press, 2010), p. 65.
11 Ibid., p. 68.
12 Becky Thompson, 'Food, Bodies, and Growing Up Female: Childhood Lessons about Culture, Race, and Class' in Patricia Fallon, Melanie A. Katzman, and Susan C.Wooley (eds), *Feminist Perspectives on Eating Disorders* (London: The Guilford Press, 1994), pp. 355–80, pp. 373–4.
13 The character 'Emma' uses several names in the play, but Emma is the one listed in the printed text so I will use this throughout to refer to this character.
14 Men were subject to procedures such as leucotomy too. However, there remains a gendered dimension to the distribution and rationale for somatic interventions that is notable.
15 Nikolas Rose and Joelle M.Abi-Rached, *Neuro:The New Brain Sciences and the Management of the Mind* (Princeton, NJ: Princeton University Press, 2013), p. 140.
16 Ann Cvetkovich, *Depression:A Public Feeling* (Durham, NC and London: Duke University Press, 2012), p. 159.
17 Bordo, pp. 49–50.
18 Ibid., p. 53.
19 Nurse, quoted in Julie Hepworth, *The Social Construction of Anorexia Nervosa* (London: Sage, 1999), p. 73.
20 Cvetkovich, p. 125.
21 Ibid., p. 2.
22 Richard Porton, 'Mike Leigh's Modernist Realism' in Ivone Margulies (ed.), *Rites of Realism: Essays on Corporeal Cinema* (Durham, NC and London: Duke University Press, 2003), pp. 164–84.
23 Dennis Potter, *The Sunday Times*, 6 November 1977.
24 See, for example, Ray Carney and Leonard Quart, *The Films of Mike Leigh* (Cambridge University Press, 2000), Amy Raphael, *Mike Leigh on Mike Leigh* (London: Faber and Faber, 2008), Tony Whitehead, *Mike Leigh* (Manchester University Press, 2007), Edward

Trostle Jones, *All or Nothing: The Cinema of Mike Leigh* (Oxford: Peter Lang, 2004), and Sean O'Sullivan, *Mike Leigh* (Urbana, IL: University of Illinois Press, 2011).
25 Mike Leigh, quoted in Raphael, p. 218.
26 Trostle Jones, p. 22.
27 Ibid., p. 95.
28 Alison Phipps, *The Politics of the Body* (Cambridge: Polity Press, 2014), p. 9.
29 Ibid., p. 11.
30 Elizabeth Grosz, *Space, Time & Perversion: The Politics of Bodies* (Sydney: Allen & Unwin, 1995), p. 35.
31 Mike Leigh (dir.). *Life Is Sweet.* Thin Man Films. 1990, 56:17, 1:01:35.
32 Bordo, p. 199.
33 Cecilia Hartley, 'Letting Ourselves Go: Making Room for the Fat Body in Feminist Scholarship' in Rose Weitz (ed.), *The Politics of Women's Bodies: Sexuality Appearance, and Behaviour*, 3rd edn (Oxford University Press, 2010), pp. 245–54, p. 247, emphasis original.
34 Colette Conroy, *Theatre & the Body* (London: Palgrave, 2010), p. 19.
35 Patrick Anderson, *So Much Wasted: Hunger, Performance, and the Morbidity of Resistance* (Durham, NC and London: Duke University Press, 2010), p. 139, emphasis original.
36 *Life Is Sweet*, 06:37.
37 Ibid., 05:18, 1:03:13, 1:02:29.
38 Ibid., 08:27.
39 Hal Hinson, *The Washington Post*, 27 December 1991 and Jay Boyar, *Orlando Sentinel*, 6 March 1992.
40 Vincent Canby, *NY Times*, 25 October 1991, emphasis added.
41 *Life Is Sweet*, 47:06.
42 Ibid., 1:22:05.
43 Ibid., 08:20.
44 O'Sullivan, p. 15.
45 Carney and Quart, p. 204.
46 Ibid., p. 6.
47 Ibid., p. 206.
48 Ibid., p. 212.
49 Michael Moon in Michael Moon and Eve Kosofsky-Sedgwick, 'Divinity: A Dossier, a Performance Piece, a Little-Understood Emotion' in Jana Evans and Kathleen Le Besco (eds), *Bodies Out of Bounds: Fatness and Transgression* (Berkeley, CA: University of California Press, 2001), pp. 292–328, pp. 305–6, emphasis original.
50 Peter Kay. *Live at Bolton Town Halls.* Universal Pictures UK. 2003.
51 Ibid.
52 Orbach, p. 41.
53 Gaye Poole, *Reel Meals, Set Meals: Food in Film and Theatre* (Sydney: Currency Press, 1999), p. 179.
54 Orbach, p. 23.
55 *Life Is Sweet*, 1:26:35.
56 Ibid., 1:26:55.
57 Ibid., 1:36:04, emphasis added.
58 Ibid., 1:36:08.
59 Ibid., 1:33:06.
60 Frantz Fanon, *Black Skin, White Masks*, trans. by Charles Lam Markmann (New York: Grove Press, 1967 [1952]).
61 Lee Daniels (dir.). *Precious.* Lionsgate. 2009, 01:10.
62 Sapphire, p. 6.
63 Bordo, p. 57, emphasis original.
64 Michael Bennett and Vanessa D. Dickerson (eds), *Recovering the Black Female Body: Self-Representations by African American Women* (New Brunswick, NJ: Rutgers University Press, 2001), p. 13.

65 Toni Morrison, *Playing in the Dark: Whiteness and the Literary Imagination* (London: Picador, 1992).
66 One key distinction is that in the film adaptation Precious reclaims her first child whereas in the novel 'Mongo' is made a ward of the state.
67 *Precious*, 1:21:53.
68 Ibid., 31:14.
69 Sukhdev Sandhu, *The Telegraph*, 28 January 2010.
70 See, Ed Gonzalez, *Slant Magazine*, 1 October 2009 and Ishmael Reed, *Counter Punch*, 5 December 2009.
71 Armond White, 'Pride and Precious', www.NYPress.com, 4 November 2009, np. (last accessed 1 July 2016).
72 Ralph Ellison, *The Invisible Man* (New York: Vintage Books, 1995), p. 58.
73 Patricia Hill Collins, '"Get Your Freak On": Sex, Babies, and Images of Black Femininity' in Weitz, p. 151.
74 Mia Mask, 'The Precarious Politics of *Precious*: A Close Reading of a Cinematic Text' in *Black Camera*, 4:1, Winter 2012, pp. 96–116, p. 102.
75 James Snead with Colin McCabe and Cornel West (eds), *White Screens, Black Images: Hollywood from the Dark Side* (London: Routledge, 1994), p. 139.
76 White, np.
77 Sandhu, np.
78 Ibid., np.
79 Bob Mondello, 'All Things Considered' on NPR. Aired 5 November 2009, np.
80 David Ikard, 'Who Speaks for *Precious*? A Black Feminist Analysis' in *African and Black Diaspora: An International Journal*, 6:1, pp. 17–29, p. 25.
81 *Precious*, 18:27.
82 Ibid., 47:57.
83 Vivyan C. Adair, 'Branded with Infamy: Inscriptions of Poverty and Class in the United States', in Weitz, pp. 232–44, p. 238.
84 Precious is also in some ways, of course, made less vulnerable by the state insofar as these mechanisms help move her out of her domestic situation. However, in state care she remains vulnerable to a different set of controlling and determining mechanisms of worth and value.
85 Debbie Olson, 'Monstrous Mammies in Lee Daniels' *Precious*' in Markus P. J. Bohlmann and Sean Moreland (eds), *Monstrous Children and Childish Monsters: Essays on Cinema's Holy Terrors* (Jefferson, NC: McFarland, 2015), pp. 188–205, p. 197.
86 Ibid., p. 196.
87 Charles Dickens, *Bleak House*, Patricia Ingham (ed.), (London: Broadview Books, 2011), p. 123.
88 Owen Gleiberman, *Entertainment Weekly*, 19 November 2009.
89 A. O. Scott, *New York Times*, 5 November 2009.
90 Mariah Carey, 'Hero' in *Music Box* (Los Angeles: Right Track Studio, 1993).
91 Amy Erdman Farrell, *Fat Shame: Stigma and the Fat Body in American Culture* (New York: New York University Press, 2011), p. 64.
92 Ibid., p. 135.
93 Le'a Kent, 'Fighting Abjection: Representing Fat Women' in Jana Evans Braziel and Kathleen Le Besco (eds), *Bodies Out of Bounds: Fatness and Transgression* (Berkeley, CA: University of California Press, 2001), pp. 130–50, p. 135.
94 Ahmed, p. 51, emphasis original.
95 Nancy D. Campbell and Elizabeth E. Horre, *Gendering Addiction: The Politics of Drug Treatment in a Neurochemical World* (London: Palgrave, 2011), p. 202.
96 Duncan Macmillan, *People, Places, & Things* (London: Oberon, 2015), I, p. 95, emphasis original.
97 Bordo, p. 153, emphasis original.
98 Caroline Horton, *Mess & You're Not Like Other Girls Chrissy* (London: Methuen, 2012), p. 11.
99 Chris Bennion, *The Telegraph*, 23 March 2016.

100 Stuart Walton, *Out of It: A Cultural History of Intoxication* (London: Hamish Hamilton, 2001), p. 271.

101 Macmillan, I, p. 95.

102 Stuart Boyland, *The Upcoming*, 25 March 2016, Susannah Clapp, *The Observer*, 6 September 2015, Michael Billington, *The Guardian*, 2 September 2015, Andrzej Lukowski, *Time Out*, 24 March 2016, Henry Hitchings, *Evening Standard*, 2 September 2015, Neil Normal, *The Daily Express*, 24 March 2016.

103 Macmillan, I, p. 53.

104 Ibid., I, p. 24.

105 Ibid., I, p. 57, emphasis original.

106 Ibid., I, p. 95, emphasis original.

107 Walton, p. 207.

108 Campbell and Horre, p. 185.

109 Macmillan, I, pp. 89–90, emphasis original.

110 Ibid., II, p. 107.

111 Phipps, p. 35.

112 Macmillan, II, p. 135 and I, p. 89.

113 Émile Durkheim, *On Suicide*, trans. by Robin Buss (London: Penguin, 2006 [1897]).

114 Macmillan, I, p. 92.

115 Quentin Letts, *The Daily Mail*, 26 March 2016.

116 Macmillan, II, p. 131.

117 Ibid., II, p. 137.

118 Ibid., II, p. 136.

119 Ibid., II, p. 134.

120 Amy Winehouse, 'Rehab' in *Back to Black* (London: Island Records, 2006).

121 Samantha Murray, *The 'Fat' Female Body* (London: Palgrave, 2008), p. 62.

122 Ibid., p. 62.

123 Macmillan, I, p. 49, p. 58.

124 Ibid., I, p. 51.

125 Ahmed, p. 37.

126 Macmillan, I, p. 46.

127 Ibid., I, p. 96.

128 Ibid., I, pp. 54–5.

129 Ibid., I, p. 101, emphasis original.

130 Ibid., II, p. 118.

131 Ibid., I, p. 71, p. 86

132 Ibid., I, p. 60.

133 James Reynolds and Zoe Zontou (eds), *Addiction and Performance* (Newcastle: Cambridge Scholars Press, 2014), p. 1.

134 David Best, *Addiction Recovery: A Movement for Social Change and Personal Growth* (Brighton: Pavillion, 2012), p. 19.

135 Ibid., p. 4.

136 Macmillan, II, p. 109.

137 Ibid., II, p. 121. I have spliced the Doctor's voice and Emma's here as their voices overlap. For clarity, the Doctor says 'Ninety meetings', the rest is Emma's voice.

138 Ibid., II, p. 119.

139 Ibid., II, p. 119. Žižek spoke of this cartoon trope in a speech to Occupy Wall Street on 16 September 2013.

140 Ibid., II, p. 119.

141 Ibid., II, p. 137.

142 Ibid., I, p. 85, emphasis original.

143 Cvetkovich, p. 7.

6

SOMETHING AND NOTHING
Moods of Madness

How are you feeling? Are you in a good mood? Where does your mood begin and end? When will it pass or shift? These questions frame the central concerns of this chapter. That is to say, I am concerned with the nature of mood as a prolonged feeling state; the social, moral, or other value systems attached to such feeling states as 'good', 'bad', 'pathological'; the material and immaterial boundaries of moods and their tethering to personhood; their time signatures and temporalities. This chapter is occupied with temporarily inhabiting artistic evocations of pathological mood states in order to better understand how moods think, feel, and communicate the state of things. In this regard, I wish to confer a certain agency to mood as an active constituent of political sense-making in the context of mad studies and mad politics. If one accepts that mood is a form of embodied, socialised communication that is both tangible and intangible, both something and apparently, nothing, then one can begin to ask a curious and important set of questions regarding the structures and systems of knowing, particularly with respect to grasping our 'inner' lives. Understanding moods, I shall argue, invites different ways of *knowing* in manners that are politically urgent in the fields of madness and psychiatry. If moods are subject to particular regimes of knowledge and interpretation, at individual, institutional, and social levels, then attending to what forms of knowledge become operative in these spheres is a valuable question. This is especially acute in the context of mental health both owing to the fact that they can initiate psychotropic and physical incarceration, and also that our moods, I propose, are ways of telling the world who we are, what we might need, and what we might want to question. To put it another way moods are ways of asking, with others, how (and sometimes why) to live. How we come to understand and respond to our moods and the moods of others, then, matters. As we shall see, however, mood is both absolute and smoky: often something we find ourselves *in*, without always being able to perceive its exact qualities or fathom quite how we got there. Yet it is perhaps precisely this ungraspable, disorientating characteristic that enables mood to continue to move and to move us. Mood, I will demonstrate, productively undoes some forms of orthodox sense-making, by being the intangible air that disturbs branches of more rooted, familiar thought. In short, by engaging more closely with how moods themselves think and speak, we may be able to begin to generate some alternative political structures and categories of legitimate feeling. I argue, then, that, far from aberrant, moods are politically and personally fecund acts of being.

Three artists will offer the materials with which to carve this discussion at its joints: Marsha Norman's 1982 play *'night, Mother*, Ellen Forney's 2012 graphic memoir *Marbles*, and Lodge Kerrigan's 1993 film *Clean, Shaven*. Broadly speaking, moods of melancholy, mania, and paranoia infuse these art works. I am, however, less concerned with the possible pathology of such mood states than lingering with how mood is made *with* audiences and readers and, moreover, what questions such feeling states invite us to ask of ourselves and each other through our encounters with these art objects. If mood is performative insofar as it necessarily requires an addressee for its conjuring, I am concerned with how the artists explore relationality both between bodies and things, but also between landscapes and the apparently immaterial (such as sound or time). What emotional labour and traffic is staged within these examples to evoke such feeling states, and to what end? Furthermore, instead of seeing such amplified moods in these works as symptoms or pathologies to be, at best, managed, or, at worst, banished, I am interested in how the pieces instead offer moods as creative, embodied, articulations of distress, resistance, and hope. In this way, I would like to reject a normative model of surplus and deficit with respect to understanding mood (and in particular mood hygiene) and instead advance and examine a more diffuse understanding of the making and meaning of mood. Through a critical interrogation of these three works, then, I will argue that recalibrating our understanding of mood as collective, uncertain, and incomplete acts of communication may go some way towards assuaging the tyranny of normal. In agitating the fixity of individualism, emotional constancy, and the false universal of 'wellness', these artists open up a more flexible space to get to grips, more hopefully, with the varying moods we find ourselves in. Moods, I propose, then, might usefully be understood as spaces of self and world discovery.

Atmospheres of living

A common narrative that cleaves to pathological mood is that it is exceptional and unreachable. It is, in this way, an undiscoverable landscape. For example, Lewis Wolpert narrates his own depression thus: 'Severe depression is a weird state – if you can describe your depression you almost certainly have not truly experienced it … Severe depression borders on being beyond description.'[1] There is a certain orthodoxy of thinking inherent in this statement. Yet the sheer volume of artistic work about melancholia alone testifies to an alternative possibility. Of course, the volubility of work may paradoxically underscore the unnarratability or unspeakabillity of extreme experiences. Indeed, work in both pain studies and trauma studies has paid much attention to the understanding that to render such experiences in language or image is to always and necessarily partially falsify the experience. Perhaps, however, if one dispenses with any totalised notion of 'understanding', a different attitude of empathic looking and listening is fostered. If I explain to you that falling in love feels like the whole of the night sky being poured into your chest, such a description does not require sameness in order for you to have a feeling encounter with the qualities of what I may be trying to communicate. You may not feel *exactly* as I do but that does not render a such feeling fundamentally unreachable. Instead feeling is hyphenated, furling between bodies in such moments of expression. Moreover, it is the contention of the chapter that an aspect of the desire to keep certain types of experience – like depression – beyond understanding in fact marks a desire for these experiences to be taken more seriously and to therefore become more legitimate.[2] I would like to argue, however, that legitimacy may thrive better by being presumed. Legitimacy, I propose, may sediment more securely in acts of trying, *however failingly,* to reach the apparently unreachable. It is to this endeavour that I think the three artists discussed in this chapter are collectively committed. They do so, however, all the while in a ready embrace with the inevitable incompleteness of such ventures. Discussing directorial practices, Tom Cornford reminds us that, for Michael Chekhov, 'This very objective thing we call atmosphere … in a person we call it a mood.'[3] I wonder, then, if one ought to consider how a conceptual reversal from mood to atmosphere may mark a decisive shift away from moods as sovereign and bounded. A slide to atmosphere may productively begin to fray the edges of an individualised, private notion of mood to something altogether more atomised and worldy. It is thus here that replacing mood with Tim Ingold's understanding of atmosphere becomes a helpful conceptual gesture.

Ingold's book, *The Life of Lines*, critiques a scholarly preoccupation with the material world of things at the expense of the apparently insubstantial: 'In all of this, however, no one has ever given a thought to the air. The reason for this omission, I believe, is simply that with the terms of accepted discourse, air is *unthinkable.*'[4] In paying attention to the atmospheres we think *in*, Ingold attends to the synergies of mood and weather, arguing that 'weather and mood are not just analogous but, more fundamentally, one and the same.'[5] We will return to this at length in the exploration of *Clean, Shaven*'s ecological framing of paranoia. However, what is of note at this juncture is how far he conceives of atmosphere as forging new critical furrows in and around the 'terms of accepted discourse'. Indeed, he writes: 'it is in the coming together of persons and things that atmospheres arise: they are not objective yet they inhere in the qualities of things; they are not subjective yet they belong to sensing beings.'[6] Ingold's offer is thus to conceive of atmosphere both itself as an alternative mood of perceiving but simultaneously as forming the conditions of understanding. Atmosphere is thus both an act of thought and, at the same time, the conditions for thinking *in*. It is my contention that *'night, Mother, Marbles,* and *Clean, Shaven* give shape to Ingold's understanding of atmosphere as a cosmic, relational, elusive encounter: as thought and environment; as something and nothing; as action and air. Conceptually, atmosphere creates a space for Ingold to consider how to think about, and with, air, which is in some senses 'unthinkable'. These three works, I propose, likewise create space to think about, and with, the apparently unthinkable atmospheres of madness. Here, in following Ingold, I hope to shuffle slightly closer to Eve Kosofsky Sedgwick's critical challenge to move beyond simply prodding dualisms. She remarks: 'But of course it's far easier to deprecate the confounding, tendentious effects of binary modes of thinking – and to expose their often stultifying preservation – than it is to articulate or model other structures of thought.'[7] In sitting in the atmospheres of these three art works, my aim is to throw light, however incompletely, on their attempts at remodelling structures of feeling and consider why this might matter for the tender politics of madness.

The mood of nations

In his brief biography of mania, David Healy observes the contemporaneity of mood as a discourse in global psychiatry. The first use of 'mood stabilizer' as a term in a title or an abstract for a psychiatric article appears in 1985. However:

> Then suddenly, in 1995, the use of the term mood stabilizer explodes exponentially. By 2001 more than 100 articles a year featured it in their titles and abstracts. Everyone was talking about mood-stabilizing drugs, even though reviews written by those most in favour of the concept make it clear that no one had worked out what mood stabilization meant.[8]

Darian Leader makes a more direct case: 'It was precisely when the patents began to run out on the biggest-selling mainstream antidepressants in the mid-90s that bipolar suddenly became the recipient of the vast marketing budgets of the pharmaceutical industry.'[9] Emily Martin similarly notes that 'Frank Ayd, co-editor of *Mood Disorders*, ran Merck's clinical trials for the antidepressant drug amitriptyline, marketed under the name Elavil. Merck bought fifty thousand copies of Ayd's book *Recognising Depression*, and distributed them worldwide.'[10] Indeed, it is notable that in the many disease biographies of both mania and melancholia, drugs form a core organising principle of the prose. The cultural rhetoric of moods is similarly ubiquitous from the end of World War II to the present, and is frequently tied to economic prosperity. As Laura D. Hirshbein notes in *American Melancholy: Constructions of Depression in the Twentieth Century*:

> In the magazine literature on the United States between the 1960s and the 1990s, depression appeared prevalent, responsible for a tremendous social and economic burden, and problematic in terms of American life … As commentators increasingly pointed out in the 1980s, bad feelings were costly to the nation.[11]

Moods are, thus, to be managed and mobilised. Likewise, developing the work of Arlie Hochschild and discussing emotional labour, intelligence, and its relationship to capitalism, Martin Welton reminds us that 'once affect is seen as having some use, it forms part of and becomes subject to an economy of that use.'[12] Welton goes on to propose that 'feelings', as a concept, pushes beyond the notion that 'emotion' embodies; that of singularity and interiority, and towards something altogether messier. Feelings, he suggests, are muddier, murkier, and altogether more 'world-directed'.[13] What then of moods? If moods are similarly wrinkled with associations of pathology, capitalism, and emotional hygiene – things to be monitored and managed with discipline – ought a more *feeling* term be employed to discuss artistic experiments in mood states? Might 'atmospheres', following Ingold, enable a different type of description of feeling states that more flexibly accounts for alterity and the generative potential of 'bad' moods?

One of the dominant modes of understanding and interpreting mood is via psychopathology, both in terms of formal psychiatric care provision and via informal psychological means such as online mood monitoring and self-diagnosis tests. Under such regimes of thinking, moods fall along a spectrum from normal to disordered. One is invited here to be like Goldilocks: to feel not too hot, nor too cold, but just right. There is no suggestion in such schemes of thought that to be 'well' is to be free from mood; rather the well person simply has enough mood (not too much, nor too little) and of the *right* sort in the *right* contexts. Moods, thus, only become visible or legible when they are somehow out-of-sync with the dominant order of feeling and, crucially, with the dominant thinking about feeling. *DSM V*, for example, suggests that to feel sad for two weeks is ordinary. Longer than two weeks and one's sadness sediments into the shape of tick on a diagnostic chart for clinical depression. Grief, likewise, has an ever-shrinking proscribed shelf-life.[14] Our moods, now, are, like our bodies, on the clock.

In one sense, such 'mood-care' ought not automatically pose a problem. Online self-diagnosis could simply be a form of curiosity for living. Yet, as Healy argues,

> The criteria involved are so vague that, in the absence of judgement, this exercise differs little from reading a horoscope. None of this might count for much more than reading a horoscope but for the fact that meeting criteria for a disease now brings with it a need for, and indeed expectation of, treatment.[15]

Likewise, Emily Martin suggests:

> Through the simple act of recording their moods in terms of these categories [on mood charts], people form the habit of thinking in terms of a standardised taxonomy of mood. As they become more and more aware of their mood at a detailed level, they are likely to feel greater personal responsibility for practising good mood hygiene.[16]

Furthermore, the readier we are, as a culture, to pathologise our moods, the more our feelings and experiences come to be things to be managed or even eradicated as one inevitably finds oneself in a spiral away from 'normal'. This leads to the over-diagnosis and over-treatment of adults with 'mood disorders', half of whom, as Wakefield *et al.* explain, 'do not perceive a need for treatment'.[17] Moreover, as Healy relates, 'Children as young as one and two years old … were put on antipsychotics and anticonvulsants, with their clinicians apparently unable to see the very visible weight gain, tardive dyskinesia, and diabetes that resulted.'[18] Perhaps most startlingly, however, the recent and vigorous attention to matters of disordered mood has not led to clinical success for patients:

> Rates of suicide for patients with schizophrenia have increased more than tenfold. Uniquely among major illness in the Western World, the life expectancy for patients with serious mental illness has declined. Patients with manic-depressive illness have a several-fold greater rate of admission than they had before the advent of mood stabilizers.[19]

It would appear, then, that while mood is a preoccupation of the contemporary, it is paramount that we reconsider the terms of our engagement with this concept. Artistic practice, I propose, may offer one such sprocket in a multi-dimensional dialogue with, and around, mood. Moreover, the three artists discussed in this chapter – Norman, Forney, and Kerrigan – pay particularly acute attention to mood as a *feeling dialogue* that, I suggest, shifts structures of understanding onto new, politicised terrain. A clinical lesson thus may be to examine how art understands the practices of how and why moods think, speak, and act and to consider how this may offer alternative ways to shape the nature of psychiatric encounters. In this regard, the chapter will also consider the political distinction between knowledge and understanding, between static and dynamic positions of thinking.

Origin of the species

It is perhaps unsurprising that much effort has been ploughed into trying to better understand the causes of challenging or complicated mood-experiences. The purpose of this chapter, as with all six collected in this book, is not to diminish the value of work taking place in other disciplines and, in particular, in the psy and neuro disciplines. Instead, this chapter, like the book, seeks robust critical dialogue with these fields of expertise in pursuit of alternative and expanded understandings and approaches to human experience. In this respect, I echo Martin who notes that her:

> primary goal is not to take sides in the debate over whether social causes of mood disorder are more important than biological ones. Rather I am interested in issues that are simply left out of that debate. I want to offer different kinds of descriptions of the experiences and actions of people said to have

manic depression, descriptions that allow such people to belong fully to the human condition rather than to an outer-sphere of "irrationality."[20]

In a related manner, I share Christopher Bollas' agnosticism towards causality: 'I have refrained from discussing the possible causes of schizophrenia. I do not know the answer to this. To me it is rather like asking what causes the being of human being.'[21] The chapter is less concerned, then, with *why* the moods in the three examples may be described as 'mad' or pathological than with what the artistic articulations of mood may invite their audiences to feel and consider. If mood is a performative, somewhat intangible, manifestation of feelings then how can we better read such acts for what they may be trying to tell us about the messy business of living? Indeed, in relation to his patients at the East Bay Activity Center, Bollas writes: 'Their reactions to the world were their way of telling us who they were.'[22] I propose that the three artists considered in this chapter are, in related manners, trying to grapple with what 'pathological' mood may be trying to tell us about being a feeling being in the world. A discursive shift from mood to atmosphere thus may enable a valuable political shift in several manners for our purposes.

Moods of death

In her volume, *Night Falls Fast: Understanding Suicide*, Kay Redfield Jamison describes the causes of suicide as 'the moods of death', by which she means mental illness.[23] Writing from a biomedical vantage point and, in part motivated by her own history of suicide attempts and ideation, Redfield Jamison elegantly describes suicide's desire to master time:

> Hannibal, for example, took poison rather than be captured or dishonoured, as did Demosthenes, Cassius, Brutus, Cato, and scores of others. Socrates, who refused to renounce his teachings and beliefs, drank hemlock. Gladiators thrust wooden sticks or spears down their throats or forced their heads in the spokes of moving carts in order that they might choose their own, rather than another's time and way of dying.[24]

Yet, despite drawing on this classical lineage, she underscores the fumbling nature of the Humanities' hands in the execution of suicide prevention:

> For those whose primary interests are in the arts and humanities, it will almost always be more intriguing to read about psychological conflicts or social determinants of suicide – and certainly, such matters are crucial to the understanding of suicide – but these factors alone may not be terribly helpful in predicting or preventing unnecessary early deaths in others.[25]

Elsewhere in the book, she draws distinction between existential, that is to say conceptual, death and suicide as a medical problem.[26] This bifurcation of despair from disease, of biology and society, is reductive. To be sure her arguments depart from an unwavering sense of the biological causes of mental illness and ergo suicide (and, therefore, their dual prevention). And under such a scheme of thinking the humanities' metaphorical, conceptual, or aesthetic approaches to suicide are, indeed, largely redundant. However, rather than argue as to the mutuality of the biological and the social or the medical and the literary, I would instead like simply to draw attention to three tacit questions that snake through her writing and pertain to the first example of this chapter, *'night, Mother*: how far is suicide an attempt to master time and if so does melancholia have a time signature? To what extent should suicide be understood as protest? Is prevention always the necessary start or end point in discourses of self-killing? I would like to argue that, in fact, by eschewing questions of cause (through the eradication of dramatic suspense), and engaging in a sustained manner with the atmosphere of melancholy, Norman's play opens up a more ambiguous but more hospitable space to carefully consider the feeling states of those who need, and choose, to leave early.

Clock watching

'night, Mother was first produced by the American Repertory Theatre in Cambridge, Massachusetts in 1982 and subsequently opened on Broadway in March 1983. The play ran for 11 months and was awarded the Pulitzer Prize. The critical reception was uneven. As Jill Dolan summarises: 'it provoked a media response polarized around gender differences.'[27] The academic response is also fractured. Much of the academic analysis of the play pays attention to the divergent responses of male and female critics, questions the status of Norman's work as canonical, and troubles the gender politics of the play by asking how far realism necessarily reinscribes the dominant order of patriarchy. A further recurrent note is sounded in the play's academic afterlife: there is a general consensus that the play is definitively *not about* suicide, nor is the act of self-killing pathological in Jessie's case. For example, Louis K. Greiff argues that it is vital to understand Jessie's suicide as a '"creative" act'.[28] Likewise, Jenny S. Spencer claims that: 'We do *not* leave the theatre asking why Jessie commits suicide.'[29] Christopher Bigsby concurs: 'The play is not, however, a pathological study ... It is most assuredly not a study of a suicide. It is the study of a life.'[30]

On the one hand, I share a sense that the play is certainly not preoccupied with suicide as an act of illness (as Redfield Jamison might have it). Indeed, though suicide forms the ticking clock of the drama, curiosity in it as an object or action rapidly falls away. Indeed, suicide is lost within the air of melancholy that pervades the stage. In this way, it seems accurate to argue that it is a play about living. On the other hand, however, I wonder what else is set adrift in the jettisoning of a pathological imagination altogether. Is to abandon pathology to simultaneously abandon any sense of protest or rage? Does it rob the suicide of its resistive dynamic? If melancholia is, in ways, a refusal of ordinary categories of living then does overlooking questions of pathology entirely neuter its political force as an action? It may be perhaps more useful to suggest that though the play is not thematically *about* suicide, dramaturgically it very much is. Indeed, the dramaturgy depends upon the suicide for the rest of the action to have feeling consequence. Rather than re-imposing a diagnostic gaze upon Jessie as a character, I am concerned to consider what a pathological reading might illuminate about the politics of the play's form. If we accept that *'night, Mother* is cast within a melancholic atmosphere, what does this enable us to read about the nature of melancholia as a feeling state? I argue that an attempt to understand the atmosphere of the play (which transcends individualised pathology) yields an alternative way of understanding how to think *with* melancholy as a pathologised state. It creates room to think about the generative capacity of distress. The following analysis, therefore, considers how *'night, Mother*, creates space to reimagine our understanding of melancholy beyond individualised psychopathology. Through a discussion of realism, objects, and time I will argue that Norman's play employs a melancholic atmosphere that invites a different, more expansive, mode of understanding the feelings of sustained despair.

'night, Mother is a one act, realist play conducted in real time. It stages an evening at home between a mother, Thelma, and her daughter, Jessie. There is little dramatic action. The women talk, eat, and perform acts of domestic organisation. Jessie very quickly tells her mother that at the end of the evening, she will kill herself and that she has made multiple, necessary practical arrangements to help sustain the current structure of her mother's life: 'The account at the grocery is in Dawson's name when you call. The number's on a whole list of numbers on the back cover of the phone book.'[31] Indeed, the dramaturgy of the play in some ways explicitly rests on a warren of organisational mundanity. Thelma's life is exposed as a succession of exercises in pointless distraction – from fudge to manicures to perfunctory family engagements. The forensic quality of Jessie's anticipatory posthumous administration hereby exposes the ordinary mechanisms by which we fictionalise meaning and purpose in our lives. Jessie's perspicuous gaze, however, penetrates through such charades and instead she opts for death:

> I'm just not having a very good time and I don't have any reason to think it'll get anything but worse. I'm tired. I'm hurt. I'm sad. I feel used ... I would wonder, sometimes, what might keep me here, what might be worth staying for, and you know what it was? It was maybe if there was something I really liked, like maybe, if I really liked rice pudding or cornflakes for breakfast or something, that might be enough.[32]

Critics such as Jill Dolan and Elin Diamond have critiqued this sense of gendered defeat in the play and taken issue with the fact that Norman's entrance to the canon was predicated on female suicide. While I appreciate the limitations of Norman's project and the ideological constraints of the context into which her work was inserted via the Pulitzer Prize, I propose that by paying closer attention to the value of her suicide set against a different context of pathology, a less static and more ideologically complex reading of the play emerges. If neoliberal individualism promises self-actualisation and agency, Jessie's suicide explodes the myth of universal exceptionality. As Alain Ehrenberg argues, depression and melancholia are both 'the unhappiness of self-consciousness heightened to the extreme, the awareness of being only *oneself*. If melancholia was the domain of the exceptional human being, then depression is the manifestation of the *democratization of the exceptional*.'[33] Becoming one's 'true' self, without limits, as we saw with *People, Places, and Things* is an ideological narrative that sustains capitalism and corrodes humans. Jessie's suicide then may be less defeat and more revolt. Life in this sense is a disgusting ritual, claggy and cheap, like the milky cocoa that coats the women's throats: 'I should've known not to make it. I knew you wouldn't like it. You never did like it.'[34]

Multiple critics have mounted the case for understanding *'night, Mother* as bolder in terms of its feminist politics than might have previously been granted. Varun Begley, for example, maintains that 'this extreme realism masks a covert hostility toward reality, resulting in a quasi-feminist aesthetic that can only be described as contradictory.'[35] It is not new, therefore, for me to suggest that the hyperrealism of the play (particularly when performed today) contains within it an absurd quality that is political in intent. However, if we turn to notions of pathology and gender, it becomes possible to further texture this critique. Charting the exponential rise of both 'depression' and discourses of self-help in America in the 1970s and 1980s, Hirshbein draws our attention to the politically neutralising impact of 'pathology' in women's lives:

> The context of women's discontent that had been defined by Betty Friedan – woman's isolation with a few intimate relationships – became the locus for treatment. Instead of the collective action urged by Friedan, American women by the 1970s and 1980s, expressed their distress by increasingly getting help for depression.[36]

Norman's decision, then, to resist a framing of Jessie as depressed is critical in the climate in which the play emerges. However, crucially, Norman turns an audience's attention from body to environment and matter. In so doing, she evokes an atmosphere of melancholy that exists beyond the silhouettes of her female characters.[37]

Melancholy, to return to Ingold, is the atmosphere Jessie thinks in, as opposed to being an externalisation of her psyche:

> I read the paper. I don't like how things are. And they're not any better out there than they are in here … And I can't do anything either, about my life, to change it, make it better, make me feel better about it. Like it better, make it work. But I can stop it.[38]

It is thus possible to understand the play as engaged with melancholia without locating the 'fault' or origin within the individual women themselves. Melancholia in this way becomes a public feeling. *'night, Mother* may not be a radical feminist play. Nonetheless, in its evocation of melancholy realism, it valuably prompts an audience to consider how profound sadness is made, sustained, and distributed in ways that remain politically urgent. As Matthew Bell narrates, melancholia has always possessed a dual identity as both 'disease' and 'temperament'.[39] I am arguing, therefore, that if one considers melancholia as a complicated feeling state that is public, relational, and performative then one is able to ask what it *wants* in manners that transcend reductive individual illness models. Starting from here, I wish to turn our attention to gaze and objects in a bid to articulate what the melancholic atmosphere of *'night, Mother* may want.

'Then glut thy sorrow on a morning rose'[40]

A central claim that melancholia has historically staked is one of 'truth'. This claim is often refracted through the prism of art. As Bell argues, in relation to Keats:

> Whereas the sublime confronts us with a universe that exceeds our capacity to comprehend it, the melancholy sublime contains a sudden realisation that the world is not far greater than we can comprehend but far sadder or more terrifying than we can cope with ... To see things differently is to risk alienation from common modes of thought and being.[41]

More recently there have been numerous psychological studies that have attempted to assess the veracity of melancholic perception. Participants are tested on the accuracy of their predictions for the likely outcomes of varied scenarios. This has generated the 'depressive realism hypothesis' that argues that the melancholic actually sees things more clearly than the non-melancholic. Bell argues that, if correct, this accounts for the particular quality of melancholic art works:

> If the depressive realism hypothesis is correct, melancholy cognition may have the power to cut through conventional illusions, to replace optimistic healthy illusions with a more compelling truth. If we transfer this idea to the cultural sphere, we might be able to argue that melancholy art has a special force, a capacity to move us from our conventional assumptions to a different and more compelling vision of reality.[42]

The question emerges, then, as to the precise relationship between depressive realism and theatrical realism. If, as noted above, the realism of *'night, Mother* has proved an obstacle for feminist critics, might depressive realism, in its hyper-amplification of reality, serve to actually unmask and undo the taken-for-granted qualities of the quotidian? It is my contention that in the acute attention to domesticity, stuff, and objects that Norman renders realism sticky. The play's melancholy is thus infused with a cloying perfume that catches in an audience's throat. Moreover, if objects in realist theatre tend to have legible, causal logics for an audience to read, then *'night, Mother* repeatedly fractures such visual scores. In disturbing normative dramaturgies in this way, Norman invites less linear acts of interpretation. At root, by lingering too long within the fatal realism of Jessie's gaze, the objects, routines, and worlds are made newly heavy, absurd, and futile. Here again Norman renders melancholy a public atmosphere, and one that is made with an audience through form.

'I found out the hard way one can't possess another'[43]

Stuff and time compass *'night, Mother.* Alongside the domestic rituals and planning noted above, there is a marked attention to objects. The burdened naturalism of the set in the original (and subsequent) productions is weighted further by the character's interactions with things: towels, jars, foodstuffs, pans, calculators, bullets, notepads, shoeboxes, and so on. Indeed, the original play script features a property list that runs to seven pages. While this is, in part, a reflection of the conventions of stage practice at the time in mainstream theatre, the accumulation of stuff and the discursive engagement with objects in the text are nonetheless acute. Thelma reminds Jessie that, despite the volume of possessions: 'We don't have anything anybody'd want. I mean, I don't even want what we've got, Jessie.'[44] Jessie describes herself as the physical leftovers of her marriage, as the detritus her husband left behind: 'Mama, you don't pack your garbage when you move.'[45] To reassure Jessie of the value of staying alive, Thelma suggests 'buying us all new dishes … let's rearrange the furniture.'[46] And Jessie feels exposed through objects, as if they can betray who she is to others without her consent: 'They know things about you, and they learned it before you had a chance to say whether you wanted them to know it or not … Like my mail order bra got delivered to their house.'[47] Moreover, it is through objects that Jessie attempts to leave a trace more permanent then herself for her mother to live alongside:

> Those are just little presents. For whenever you need one. They're not bought presents, just things I thought you might like to look at, or things you think you've lost. Things you didn't know you had, even. You'll see … They're just things, like a free tube of toothpaste I found hanging on the door one day.[48]

Here, in her attempt to transform ordinary objects into company for her mother, Jessie underscores the refraction of self through things that are at play within *'night, Mother.* Indeed, the play concludes with Thelma's lament that one cannot possess another, cannot press them into object-hood: 'Jessie, Jessie, my child … Forgive me. (*A pause.*) I thought you were mine.'[49] There is a conceptual porosity, then, between flesh and stuff.

The women are suspended and animated (even in moments of transformation such as here) by the empty stuff that engulfs them. There is a striking dialogue in the play, therefore, between bodies and objects that raises curious questions about identity, capitalism, and meaning. Do the objects give material form to existential despair? Or, rather, do the objects effect an invasion of ennui that makes us ill? Or perhaps it is to the dialogic space between objects and people that such melancholy clings. By making theatrical realism almost hyperventilate under the weight of its own traffic, Norman, I propose, troubles and denaturalises our relationship to the things that, performatively, appear to make us who we are. If the stuff of realism ordinarily serves a semiotic function, then Norman tightens this string to its breaking point. In the resulting snap one can hear the unsaid. That is to say, in the building cacophony of stage realism affected by objects, what is allowed to become felt and audible is the existential silence that hangs beneath all these words and all these things. As Jessie expounds from the opening: 'I'm through talking' and thus an audience is invited to occupy the atmosphere between what is said and what is taking place, between characters and the object signs that apparently decipher them. This, I propose, is a stark, melancholic space. In this way, the play uses theatrical form to turn against its own realist logic as a means to underscore the invidious, grounded position of the melancholic feeling state.

Time's up

If the ordinary logic of realist stage objects is distended in *'night, Mother*, one likewise witnesses a smudging of time signatures. Melancholia is marked by loss and retrospective gaze. Likewise, depression is often described in terms of slowed or suspended time. Ehrenberg remarks that 'Frozen action sculpts the depressive universe' and argues that 'Depression is a pathology of time (the depressed person has no future) and a pathology of motivation (the depressed person has no energy, his movement is slowed, his words slurred).'[50] While Michael Middeke and Christina Wald argue that:

> From a psychological or psychoanalytical perspective, a melancholic experience of time and temporality unveils itself as a pathological sadness, a paralysing anxiety and, particularly, as an agonizing (if sometimes comforting) insistence on the past ... The insistence on the past entails the loss of the future; it creates the impression, as it were, of a standstill of time.[51]

Elsewhere Ehrenberg critiques the pathological consequences of individualism: 'the aspiration to be oneself leads to depression, depression leads to dependency, to the nostalgia for the lost self.'[52] *'night, Mother* is preoccupied by lagging time and irrecoverable loss. Indeed, in the play's final moments Jessie finds herself erased in time:

> That's what this is about. It's somebody I lost, all right, it's my own self. Who I never was. Or who I tried to be and never got there. Somebody I waited for who never came. And never will. So, see, it doesn't much matter what else happened in this world or in this house, even. I'm what was worth waiting for and I didn't make it. Me ... who might have made a difference to me ... I'm not going to show up, so there's no reason to stay, expect to keep you company, and that's ... not reason enough because I'm not ... very good company.[53]

Furthermore, there is sustained attention to time in both the play's form and content: Norman specifies that clocks running in real time must be present and 'visible by the audience'; clocks are wound in the course of the action; time is given as a gift in the form of a watch by Jessie to her son, Ricky; time and memory are abolished in Jessie's epileptic fits; thematically, the play finds metaphors of time in burning houses and bus journeys; pastimes of crochet and television are discussed; objects such as eternity rings are inherited.[54] Much has been written about the time signature of the play in relation to issues of gender or its relationship to Southern history and landscape.[55] However, little has been said with respect to understanding the time signature as pathologically marked.

The hyperrealism of real time underscores the dragged temporality of the play. Indeed, it is telling that the play's most dramatic action is deliberately ransacked of momentum through the discarding of suspense. Time, in this way, is rendered purposefully airless. The play text describes this quality as the 'inexorability of genuine tragedy' and there is a keen sense of catastrophic inevitability to which this claim presumably refers. Indeed, Norman has claimed that the play has a 'sonata' form thus further scoring a sense of inescapability owing to the sonata's structure of concluding with recapitulation. Bigsby also argues that 'though there are, necessarily, no act divisions, no intervals to relieve the building tension, there are three clear movements.'[56] *'night, Mother* occupies a hinterland of temporal warping. However, this sense of the piece as possessing a musical architecture also betrays the dual nature of time at work. The emotional movements that Bigsby identifies serve as rip tides against the quotidian clock time of the play's content. Time moves forward in relation to the stage business of *doing* in the very same moment it swerves into vertiginous stasis with respect to its stage business of *feeling*. Moreover, it is in the mutual reinforcement of these dynamics that the melancholic atmosphere is permitted to take possession of the stage. Discursively and thematically the women articulate their sense (both tacit and explicit) of the banal cruelty of the everyday time signatures they find themselves suspended within. Notably, these signatures are marked by gender, geography, age, class, health, and so forth. For example, Thelma quietly resents waiting for the washing machine to finish turning: 'The waiting's the worst part of it.'[57] More overtly, Jessie repeatedly articulates a desire to control time:

> I can get off right now if I want to, because even if I ride 50 more years and get off then, it's the same place when I step down to it. Whenever I feel like it, I can get off. As soon as I've had enough, it's my stop. I've had enough.[58]

Yet it is through an existential mode of time, witnessed perhaps most obviously in the door to Jessie's death, that one *feels* time occurring: 'It [the door] should be, in fact, the focal point of the entire set and the lighting should make it disappear completely at times and draw the entire set into it at others.'[59] This black hole quality of melancholic time described here in the stage direction evokes the doubled nature of time in *'night, Mother*: time that is at once ordinary and discursive (that of birthdays and lists) and extraordinary and felt (that of existential despair). There is a scenographic doubling at play here too insofar as the central door (recalling countervailing aesthetic logics of classical theatres) functions as both realist structure and symbolic image. However, most crucially here, as with the object-bodies relations, it is in the imprecise dialogue between practical and emotional time signatures that Norman creates the atmosphere of melancholy with, and through, her audience. In exposing the inhospitality of ordinary time when set against feeling time, she offers a new description and affective way of understanding the atmosphere of unendurable living.

Losing your …

Marbles is Ellen Forney's graphic memoir recounting her bipolarity. First published in 2012, it joins a burgeoning body of comic book work centred on mental distress and therapy including examples such as Katie Green's *Lighter than My Shadow*, Justin Green's *Binky Brown Meets the Holy Virgin Mary*, Nate Powell's *Swallow Me Whole*, Philippa Perry's *Couch Fiction*, and Daryl Cunningham's *Psychiatric Tales* (to say nothing of illustrated companion works such as Richard Appignanesi's *Graphic Freud* series or Bobby Baker's *Diary Drawings*). Moreover, there are websites such as www.graphicmedicine.org and a growing interest in the interactions between visual gaming cultures, madness, and psychotherapy. This is not to equate games and comics; rather it is to acknowledge that their shared commitment to the synthesis of pictographic and textual yields particular aesthetic insights with regard to the articulation of non-normative states. For example, the commix form's simultaneity, perceptual dynamism, and plural foci for attention combine to create an animated mode of reading that is affective.[60] Further, as Hilary Chute and Marianne Dekoven explain, commix have a notable capacity to give complex form to the habitually unspoken:

> There are many reasons comics is such an apt form for serious non-fiction. There is the iconic nature of the traumatic image – the fact that the intensity of trauma produces fragmented, imagistic memories … And comics may be particularly suited to express traumatic histories because its basic narrative form works with a counterpoint between presence and absence, from frame to gutter to frame to gutter.[61]

Several of the press reviews for the memoir are keen to underscore the emotionally dynamic encounter *Marbles* engenders in a reader. Frank Barrows, for example, describes how 'The illustrations move your eyes around in an exhausting manner.'[62] Likewise David L. Ulin proposes that 'the book reads less like a comic than a scrapbook, in which traditional strip-style layouts alternate with lists, sketchbook pages, re-created photos – all to reproduce the swirling chaos of her inner life.'[63] It is the visual qualities of the form in general, and of this example in particular, that I wish to draw attention to. I am concerned with how the collision between text and image creates a performative feeling encounter with mania. I propose that *Marbles*, in its atomisation of manic atmospheres, creates a space in which to understand literature as aesthetic companionship. This, in turn, yields valuable insights with regard to the values of keeping distress company. Nevertheless, I will also argue that in its adherence to biomedical models, mood hygiene, and normative narrative arcs of 'overcoming', *Marbles*, at times, forecloses more expansive meanings of manic-depression in too rigid frames.[64]

Clement Hawes' study of mania and literary style argues that the manic tendency in British prose can be traced to the English Civil War:

> The pathologising of enthusiasm [such as Richard Burton's characterisation of Puritans in *The Anatomy of Melancholy*] thus became part of a broader elite hegemony. It is obvious enough that the pathologising of manic rhetoric served to denigrate it and eventually to justify "shutting up", in all possible senses, its users.[65]

Hawes characterises the hallmark of manic rhetoric as a 'rebellious stance towards traditional hierarchies of socio-economic privilege' and identifies common tropes of the writing, including lists, wordplay, blends of genres, transgression, and imagery of self-fortification.[66] In a different discipline, reflecting on both autobiography and the experiences of his patients, Leader characterises the manic temperament thus:

> the sense of connectedness with other people and with the world; the spending of money which the person usually does not have; the large appetite, be it for food, sex, or words; the reinvention of oneself, the creation of a new persona as if one were someone else; the verbal dexterity and sudden penchant for wit and punning; the movement toward paranoid thoughts, so apparently absent at the beginning of the manic curve.[67]

In both examples a clear sense of breaching, boundlessness, and a constellation of thoughts and feelings is expressed. This sense of radical hyper-connectivity and iridescent beauty as a common feature of mania in part explains the paradox that Leader also observes: 'ask a manic-depressive subject if they could push a button and make their bipolarity disappear and many will say No.'[68] Speaking of her own experiences, Forney relates that 'colours felt vivid and vibrant; the world felt fascinating and interconnected – and I felt powerful, sexy, and full of love and curiosity.'[69] *Marbles*' pages are, likewise, fretted with the animate, sensate energy of manic feeling. As Courtney Donovan suggests: 'The manifestation of mania is a frenzy of lines and action, coupled with a concoction of energetic, large, and bold text. Forney communicates visually and graphically how she is feeling.'[70] For example, exuberance finds visual register in the multiple passages in which Forney's body and ideas exceed the comic strip panels, stretching and grasping across pages, gutters, and frames. Forney appears a kaleidoscope in such pages. To read here is to engage with the scattering energy of pluralising thought.

Marbles gives visual form to the exquisiteness of mania along with the violence of its careering crashes and blistered depressions. In its textured images, it goes some way towards offering a sensate encounter with a manic atmosphere. However, the memoir also remains tethered, weighted down like the anchored balloon Forney fears she will become under a pharmacological regime.[71] And worn questions of madness and genius, madness and creativity, madness and identity scratch its pages. In its adherence to normative codes of personhood, tolerance, and recovery *Marbles* reifies an ordered narrative of overcoming in ways that diminish its radicalism for those who come after. Indeed, one can find quiet evidence of this in the reviews of the memoir, which persistently and uncritically echo an ideology of disease, treatment, and moral hygiene. For example, Myla Goldberg writes of *Marbles*: 'Bipolar disorder defies easy treatment; each individual patient must become their own guinea pig to discover the balance of medication and lifestyle therapies that will allow him or her to achieve long-term stability.'[72] If the greatest intervention that *Marbles* makes is to shape literature as aesthetic company for those who, for whatever reason, seek out a memoir of mania, then the conservatism of some of the framing serves to shrink the room in which such aesthetic hospitality towards another can take place. There is, of course, no 'right' way to write mania and thus Forney has not got it 'wrong'. As Arthur W. Frank argues: 'Stories analyse us by allowing us to notice what attracts us to them, and what we resist about them. They show us what we want, and ask us what we need.'[73] There is room then for infinite acts of telling. Instead, I simply wish to draw attention to the limitations of *Marbles'* politics in its absorption of a neoliberal, biomedical landscape of cause, cure, and self-management. I will argue that a degree of the memoir's political power as a literary act of mood-full company is diminished by the conservative axioms on which the narrative arc turns.

Getting inked

Marbles is a tale of diagnosis, therapy, and survival. It begins with sensation (Figure 6.1). Narratively, the memoir sketches Forney's life from diagnosis, through treatment, and to a place of recovery. The tale is not totalised or triumphant, but, nonetheless, culminates in a reflective chapter about finding 'balance' and concludes with a final panel of Forney holding our gaze, brushing her teeth (presumably ready to face or conclude a day) along with the text 'I'm okay!'[74] The story charts birthdays, art projects, family trips, therapy sessions, and so forth. However, the drive of the text is, at heart, a quest narrative. Forney is desperately seeking Forney, and more particularly, the *real* Forney. Indeed, the very act of creating a memoir, especially in graphic form, itself comprises an act of self-dialogue and self-deciphering. Moreover, the memoir concludes with Forney talking to her younger self to reassure her that, despite it all, she still remains *her* (Figure 6.2). There is an essentialising dynamic here that threads throughout the book. Forney – like many of us in her position – is caught within the pharmacological quandary as to whether drugs will fog her 'essential' self or, instead, provide her with a gasmask to wear against the miasma of disease in order to recover her 'true' self. While I would suggest that such questions are ideologically driven red herrings, the book is certainly consumed with a dialogue between authentic selves and pharmacology.[75]

FIGURE 6.1 'Needlework', *Marbles*

FIGURE 6.2 'Self-talk', *Marbles*

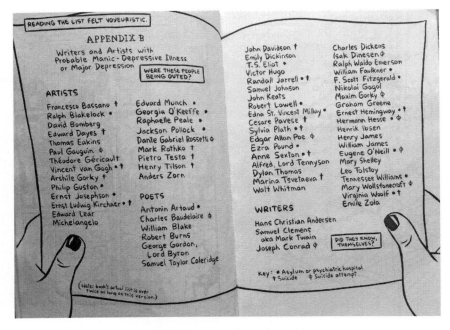

FIGURE 6.3 'Family tree', *Marbles*

Elsewhere, we see numerous panels of Forney cast within scattered coordinates of novels, artists, research texts that are bent on telling her who she is. This dynamic is perhaps most keenly felt in the artistic lineage that she repeatedly tries to find her position within over the course of the memoir (Figure 6.3). Heavily influenced by Kay Redfield Jamison's *Touched with Fire: Manic-Depressive Illness and the Artistic Temperament*, Forney's primary project in *Marbles*, then, is an act of sense-making: Is bipolar something I have or who I am? If I medicate will I still be an artist? Does my art require suffering? What role did my genes play? Have I always been ill? Who am I?

The memoir seeks explanations to these riddles of selfhood in life (via relationships, work, exercise, and so forth) but also turns repeatedly and, at times, conflictually, to two dominant languages of knowledge: psychiatry and art. Indeed, early in the memoir, we witness a *DSM* 'mugshot' of Forney. In this full-page panel, one encounters an abolition of personhood via her recasting in a diagnostic identity (Figure 6.4). Yet, elsewhere, there are acts of self-knowing via (less narratively minded) art that offer a counterpart to the biological identity that increasingly forms the rubric of personhood in *Marbles*. I propose that such acts are less acute in the moments in which she situates herself alongside Van Gogh *et al.*, and perhaps more keenly felt in the passages that attempt to give form to defiant landscapes of feeling (Figure 6.5).

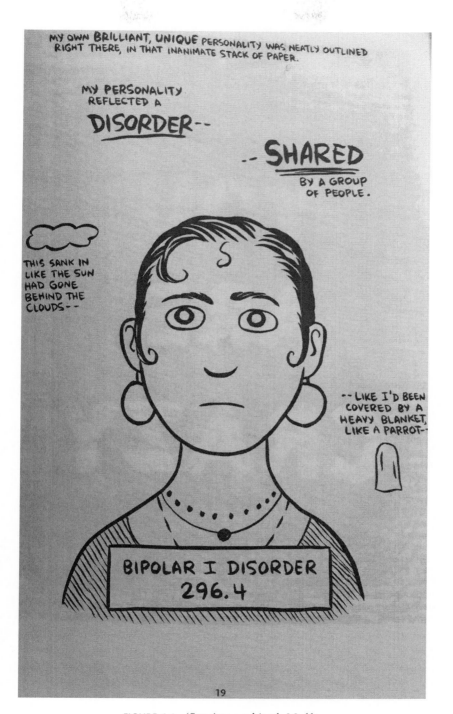

FIGURE 6.4 'Specimen subject', *Marbles*

FIGURE 6.5 'Smushed', *Marbles*

In this sense, there are twin epistemologies at work in *Marbles*. On the one hand, it swims, pictographically, with manic-depression and thereby evokes atmospheres with its reader. On the other, it tries to locate such atmospheres within the established tramlines of bipolarity and psychiatry (and lineages of mad artists). In these latter gestures, Forney, I argue, becomes roped on neoliberal tracks of 'empowerment' that are politically stultifying. In the former, however, when it exceeds its own frames of reference and moves away from an explanatory register, *Marbles* offers affective visual companionship for readers within atmospheres of alterity. Such pages do not tell a reader what they need to know about bipolar but instead (falteringly) attempt to understand its feelings and contours. Indeed, speaking of her sketchbook self-portraits, Forney says:

> I often knew what I was aiming to draw – some mental image that I needed to get outside of me. Sometimes I would have to draw it several times before I was satisfied I had caught it. Other times I didn't know what I would draw & just let the images pour out of my pen.[76]

It is here, I propose, that Forney offers new, creative, formations of understanding around profound feeling states.

I recognise your pain

As *Marbles* progresses, there is an increasing accommodation of orthodox psychiatry. The initial resistance Forney expresses to her psychiatrist around prescription medication, limiting her use of recreational drugs, or doing yoga indicates a clash of world views: I am an artist not a patient and yoga is a 'Wishy-washy noncompetitive new age stretching fad.'[77] The memoir begins, however, to increasingly enfold a biomedical sense of self into the frame. Drug charts, mood trackers, aerial views of brains, CBT exercises, and *DSM* checklists populate the pages and culminate in a view that 'The "crazy artist" is a *scientifically-based* phenomenon.'[78] Notably, all of the therapeutic dialogues with her psychiatrist take place within ordered panels that progress logically against the more 'disordered' backdrop of the rest of the memoir. In this sense, they exist in normative time and space and thought. An aspect of this trajectory towards biomedicine in the memoir is perhaps related to the understandable desire, particularly acute for the oft-maligned mental illnesses, to be witnessed as authentically ill. As Leader and David Corfield explain: 'it is perfectly possible that the patient is both ill and in need of being authenticated as ill.'[79] Biological psychiatry, thus, forms an authenticating seal on Forney's experiences (while still maintaining, indeed legitimating, her blood line to her 'mad' artistic heritage). However, I wish to pick a little at the corners of this seal. As a reader, we witness Forney become an increasingly 'good' patient. I am concerned as to what the unintended consequences of such an uncritical acquiescence to 'science' and hygiene may be.

Wendy Brown problematises an individualised concept of freedom and rights arguing that these are embodied, relational, contextual practices as opposed to ideas one can simply materialise. In her critique of 'empowerment', she questions how far, in:

> its almost exclusive focus on subjects' emotional bearing and self-regard, empowerment is a formulation that converges with a regime's own legitimacy needs in masking the power of the regime … Indeed the possibility that one can 'feel empowered' without being so forms an important element of legitimacy for the antidemocratic dimension of liberalism.[80]

Elsewhere in this volume, as we saw in the introduction, she critiques pain as a foundational political claim and pays attention to the limitations of 'identity' as opposed to 'wanting', to the limitations of I *am* as opposed to I *want*. This shift from being to wanting, she argues, moves one, politically speaking, from an arrested, unliveable present to a dynamic, alternative future.[81] In a sense, she argues from a static place of known identity to a dynamic space of self-understanding. I raise Brown here as I am arguing that there is a connection between her interrogation of the politics of 'tolerance' and the political effects of *Marbles*. More specifically, I would like to claim that the sanitising of manic-depression that cumulatively takes place in Forney's memoir speaks to a politics of tolerating difference as opposed a more radical politics of equality. Brown argues that discourses around 'difference' too often mask the reality that 'differences' are direct effects of social power.[82]

Two panels, towards the memoir's conclusion, perhaps best illustrate this concern. One takes the form of a pictorial treatment plan. The second is the economic cost of this plan (Figures 6.6 and 6.7). Perhaps the most obvious issue here is that the pharmaceutical companies who author the research that props up the science of *Marbles* also reap the profits of such treatment plans. As Healy reminds us: 'by 2000, 75 percent of the RCTs [Random Controlled Trials] appearing in major journals like *JAMA*, *NEJM*, and the *Lancet* were sponsored by pharmaceutical companies.'[83] However, I instead wish to draw our attention to the tacit values that undergird the graphic panels. Bipolarity is framed as a permanent, individualised problem that must be managed with vigilance in order to remain a balanced and productive subject: 'Stability is good for my creativity.'[84] Psychological constancy is thus a sovereign state to be guarded through obedience to discourses of health hygiene. There is no engagement with 'health' (and for that matter 'mood') as encultured, socialised, ecological, relational (beyond needing support). This is particularly challenging in the field of mad politics. The consciousness-raising, counter-stigma claims attached to works such as *Marbles* reinscribes this as *the* narrative of 'positive' madness – of positive overcoming through self-management. However, when scrutinised, the dominant, orthodox ideologies of mental illness and psychiatry remain intact at the memoir's conclusion. Moreover, a tacit sense that 'overcoming' is a question of individual self-discipline (and esteem) overlooks the interlocking, intersectional social inequities that might impair one's path to 'wellness' in a neoliberal context. It likewise looks askance at the notion that such discourses of 'wellness' parasitically beget 'illness'. In this way, I propose, *Marbles* becomes a politically impotent text of liberal tolerance. To return to Healy, here: animals are given drugs to make their slaughter less stressful. The question that remains, then, he argues, is whether 'the point of [pharmaceutical] branding is not to do the same to us?'[85] While this may sound an inflammatory note for some, I am concerned to consider the social consequences of an uncritical acceptance, if not reification, of 'science' and medication as *the* response to manic-depressive feeling states. Furthermore, Healy reminds us there is a global question of responsibility here in manners akin to driving and carbon emissions. What are the global, emotional consequences of pharmaceutically managed mood hygiene?

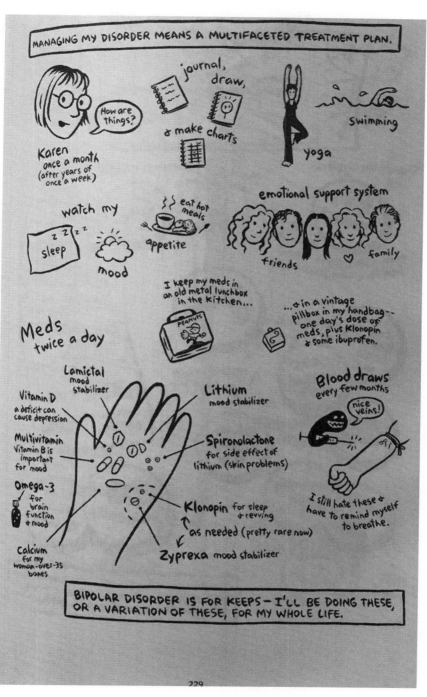

FIGURE 6.6 'Forward planning', *Marbles*

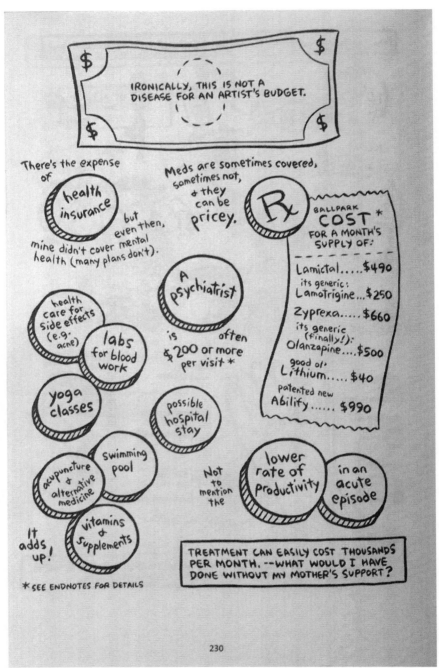

FIGURE 6.7 'The cost of living', *Marbles*

How do orthodox narratives (both medical and cultural) of overcoming delimit not only the range of 'good' mood but also the acceptable 'types' of response to them? In what ways might the pursuit of 'balance' render 'instability', paradoxically, endemic and intolerable? In this adherence to both psychiatric and narrative orthodoxy, then, *Marbles* remainders alternative structures for feeling and thinking in the gutter of its frames.

The company you keep

Arthur W. Frank writes, 'when ill persons try to talk in medicalese they deny themselves the drama of their personal experience.'[86] Therein lies the tension noted above. Yet this is not the whole story of *Marbles*. In the same volume, *At the Will of the Body: Reflections on Illness*, Frank argues for illness-writing as an act of tactile intimacy:

> I want what I have written to be touched as one touches letters, folding and refolding them, responding to them. I hope ill persons will talk back to what I have written. Talking back is how we find our own experiences in a story someone else has written.[87]

Alongside Forney's own pursuit of 'company' for her overwhelming feeling states, witnessed in the search for a people with whom she can walk, is a creation of just such companionship for her readership. Note, for example, the sketched hands captured in Figure 6.3 above that simultaneously foreground Forney's hand-held hunt for companionship in the same instance as it mirrors our own holding of her tale. Further, Forney describes figures such as William Styron as 'company' and children's books as a refuge during periods of profound distress: 'I got completely lost in them.'[88] More specifically her canon of 'mad' artists offers her 'connection, context, perspective, inspiration, company'.[89] However, in contradistinction to the biomedical, organised framing of the narrative and panels, there is simultaneously a different, altogether more atmospheric, messy mode of communication at play. Indeed, I argue that it is precisely in the moments that Forney breaks the form, exceeds the frame, defies narration, or disturbs commix conventions that *Marbles* evokes striking feeling dialogues (Figure 6.8). Furthermore, she finds company in stars, snowflakes, and trees in manners that return a reader to the ecological qualities of being and 'mood'. She sketches her sense of connectedness as though her body were a system of rivers, her expansive thoughts as if popping like corn, and her terror as if a nest of caged rats.[90] It is here, in utilising the performative qualities of commix – the dynamic collisions of text and image to create unstable motion – that *Marbles* startles and arrests a reader in a feeling dialogue. In this way, she creates what Hawes describes as 'a kind of specialized aesthetic haven or ghetto for alternative and marginalized elements that otherwise resist ready incorporation.'[91] Indeed, in eschewing normative explanation Forney here creates enough room for a reader to 'talk back' to her manic atmosphere and find complicated feeling within it (a possibility inhibited in the rigid panels of science).

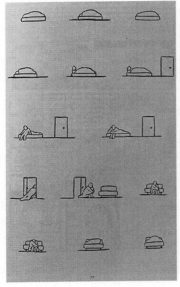

FIGURE 6.8 'Feel your way', *Marbles*

It is precisely when moving away from mood (as individual pathology) and towards atmosphere (as a relational feeling state), that is effected in her graphic moves away from ordinary telling, that *Marbles* makes understanding a different, expanded possibility. Indeed, in these ambiguous moments of graphic articulation, which have no need of emotional sameness, one is invited to both find, and be, company.

… Presumed lost

Lodge Kerrigan's 1993 debut *Clean, Shaven*, is a low-budget feature, filmed over the course of two years. It follows the protagonist, Peter, on his journey to find his daughter, Nicole (now living with her adopted mother). The film does not disclose the full contents of Peter's past but a clear evocation of his psychosis is offered as a partial account of their current estrangement. Moreover, while the film's content does not overtly diagnose Peter as schizophrenic, the film's marketing does: 'A compelling headfirst dive into the mindscape of a schizophrenic.'[92] Moreover, the psychotic atmosphere of the film encourages many reviewers to frame it as an immersive encounter with schizophrenia: '*Clean, Shaven* is an attempt to enter completely into the schizophrenic mind of a young man who is desperately trying to live in the world.'[93] Other critics tend to quantify the intensity of the cinematic experience as offering a quasi-disturbing encounter: 'harrowing, exhausting, painful'; 'unbearably intense … exceedingly concentrated … agonizingly close.'[94] Kerrigan himself explained the impetus to make the film was to:

> put the audience in that position to experience how I imagined the symptoms to be: auditory hallucinations, heightened paranoia, disassociative [sic] feelings, anxiety … I also wanted to attack the notion that people who suffer mental illness are more violent than other people.[95]

Wryly, Kerrigan established the production company DSM III to create the film. It is a film, then, that is self-avowedly engaged with the politics of mental health. Notably, the reviewers also often do comment on the 'outsiderness' of Peter – regularly casting him as a symbolic marginalised subject: 'a character one would like to get as far away from as possible.'[96] Furthermore, Dennis Lim comments that Kerrigan's cinematic output more generally 'insists on showing people we'd rather not think about, in places we'd rather not see, the forgotten backwaters and industrialised gray zones of present-day, minimum-wage America.'[97] *Clean, Shaven* is, then, a film that turns the inside out and moves the margin to centre. The central argument I wish to advance in this regard is that, through its filmic versioning of psychosis, *Clean, Shaven* offers an expanded understanding of the thresholds of self and world. In its hyper attention to subjective experience, it denudes ordinary poses and customs of how one comes to know an other's experience – both cinematically and in a day-to-day sense. More specifically, in the use of its audio track, its visual framing of matter and weather, and in its atomisation of Peter's subjectivity, the film both invites a contract with empathic understanding and simultaneously points to the limitations of such relational treaties. In framing psychosis as an expansion rather than a breach, I propose it offers up new coordinates for understanding feeling, being, and reality.

'Like gold to airy thinness beat'[98]

A common cultural narrative that attends on serious mental illness is one of absence and disappearance: by force of the illness, people become presumed lost unto themselves. However, Bollas offers a different proposition:

> Most people I know who have talked with schizophrenics have noticed that these feel like conversations not with someone whose ailment is derived from the fog of symptomatic preoccupation, or the dulling repetition of character patterns, but with a person who seems to be existing on the edge of human perception.[99]

In this sense, the schizophrenic subject operates within an expanded rather than a contracted perceptual field. *Clean, Shaven* challenges the misperception of schizophrenia that Martin observes:

> Psychiatrists have often assumed that schizophrenia is characterized by an absence of emotion … Contrary to this common perception, accounts of patients attest that "flat affect" does not entail lack of feeling. Instead of emotion, their interior landscape is often filled with free-floating tension, fear, and vague anxiety.[100]

Peter appears to be just such a character and *Clean, Shaven* stretches filmic convention to this effect. In particular, there appears to be multiple ruptures between the boundaries of the human and the non-human throughout his experience of himself and the world around him.

There is a persistent visual preoccupation with things and environments. As a viewer one encounters multiple extreme close ups of cracks in walls, cups of tea, fish heads, blades, library books, and so on, amidst tracking shots of houses, overhead cables, walls, grass, dirt. Moreover, there are numerous shots of weather and landscape. These shots do not all *mean* the same thing; nevertheless, their cumulative visual framing turns a viewer's attention to the structure of perception as much as to what is seen. The film thus shapes a coextension of self and environment in its visual frames. Most importantly, however, these things talk back to Peter. The audio track, by Hanh Rowe, hereby amplifies the near-constant traffic between bodies and things.[101] Notably, there is a rare moment of quiet on the audio track as Peter adds sugar to three cups of tea that is rendered deafeningly loud, owing to its juxtaposition with the cacophony of the rest of the film. Importantly, however, the intrusive audio is not mere sound and fury. In the library, for example, as Peter consults the picture books of Edward Steichen's infamous *The Family of Man* exhibition, the images communicate with Peter: they laugh, cry, chatter.[102] Notably, in his description of the exhibition Steichen suggested that:

We are concerned with man in relation to his environment, to the beauty and richness of the earth he has inherited and what he has done with his inheritance, the good and the great things, the destructive and the stupid things.[103]

The exhibition, therefore, aimed at accessing and celebrating a sense of common humanity after WW II via photographic evidence. It is striking, then, that far from closing Peter off from human interconnectivity because of his psychological experiences, Kerrigan employs the library sequence as a means to underscore how far he is a hyper-sonic character who hears all the feelings in all the things.

Bollas argues that the schizophrenic subject 'loses the function of historicity'.[104] This inability to transfigure the past into narrative, he proposes, goes some way to account for the tendency in psychosis of individuals to forge important bonds with inert objects: 'As the schizophrenic loses (or rejects) history in favour of mythology, he quietly goes about creating his own collective universe. He does so by framing relationships, not to people, but to things. He seeks the thingness of things.'[105] The mind, in some ways, then, is cast outwards and dispersed in things and elements. And by inviting us to look *through*, as opposed to *at*, Peter's feeling atmospheres in *Clean, Shaven*, Kerrigan exposes the functional fictions of ordinary gaze and ordinary listening. He exposes the artifice of the finite boundaries that contain quotidian perception. Kerrigan, like Ingold and Bollas, is thus concerned to expose the operative thinking that conditions and prescribes ordinary ways of seeing and hearing. All three are interested in pushing sense-making, perception, and modes of being-in-the-world onto new conceptual and felt territory. Indeed, if we accept that in *Clean, Shaven* profound feeling states are communicated less as narrative and more as atmosphere (via the audio track, the disturbances of time signature, the unusual cinematography, the preoccupation with subjectivity, and so on), then it becomes possible to unite the film with Ingold's arguments for a more cosmic world-sense:

> That a whole suite of etymologically cognate words should refer interchangeably both to the characteristics of the weather and to human moods and motivations amply demonstrates that weather and mood are not just analogous but, more fundamentally, one and the same. This unison of the affective and the cosmic ... is crucial to our understanding of the atmosphere.[106]

There is a clear geo-ecological argument for reinterpreting our world-making practices here. However, there is also a related argument that can be extracted from this position that relates to mad politics.

The imperative to expand our collective fields of perception is vital in order to create more peaceable atmospheres for those of us who find ourselves feeling inside out. If, as recent research suggests, psychotic symptoms appear to lie on a continuum with milder psychotic experiences that are common across the general population, then experiences like Peter's are different in degree not kind: 'Our findings suggest there may be shared psychological mechanisms in clinical and non-clinical paranoia and, therefore, that studies with high-scoring non-patients may be informative about targets for intervention.'[107] This marks an opportunity to reframe psychotic phenomena not as aberrant signs of malfunction but ordinary, if densely complicated, expressions of emotional living. *Clean, Shaven*'s engagement with expanded perception is thus an attempt to understand *with* psychosis. It is an attempt to communicate how far feeling states are neither in us or *out there*, but rather move like air – within, beyond, around. In this sense, feelings are inhaled and exhaled casting self and world in dynamic, reciprocal, and perpetual motion. Moreover, far from relegating Peter's experience as beyond comprehension, the film renders it felt and present. Here Kerrigan echoes Bollas' intervention against the assumption that psychotic phenomena have no meaning beyond mere symptomatology: 'What I came to realise was that almost all psychotic behaviour was comprehensible if one could discover the underlying logic of thought.'[108] This is not to glorify Peter's experience. Again, as Bollas argues, the schizophrenic subject often longs for the 'bliss of the ordinary'; nevertheless, 'their own radical visions pose a greater, and more generative challenge to our norms that anyone else.'[109] I argue, therefore, that Kerrigan's phenomenological framing of Peter calls into question what is remaindered by quotidian sense-making practices. In so doing, he tilts our gaze, politically, towards the generative capacity of psychotic experience.

What are you looking for?

It is evident that in its shot composition *Clean, Shaven* is keen to exploit cinematic gaze as a means to reconsider the politics of perception in psychopathology and everyday life. There is another dynamic of gaze, however, that further underscores the film's commitment to critique cultural attitudes towards madness. The film's acute attention to looking, evidence, and clues cumulatively problematise the politics of expectation. Throughout *Clean, Shaven* there are multiple shot of Peter being watched (Figures 6.9 and 6.10).

FIGURE 6.9 'Who's that girl?', *Clean, Shaven*

FIGURE 6.10 'I'm being watched', *Clean, Shaven*

Narratively, Peter is being followed and, therefore, surveyed. Indeed, the detective's storyline runs concurrent with Peter's search for Nicole throughout the film. Moreover, thematically speaking, *Clean, Shaven* makes multiple references to missing children and, as discussed above, contains an extended sequence exploring the documentary photographs of *The Family of Man*. Peter has also recently left an institution and the images of his incarceration are shot from above evoking a stark sense of observation. He also is at pains to avoid his own self-image throughout the film. For example, he turns the mirror over in his motel and papers over the rear-view, side-mirrors, and windows in his car. It is, then, a film that is persistently occupied with the act of looking and the experience of (not) being seen.

On the one hand, one could understand this as an attempt to allow the cinematography to visually create a sense of paranoia. Moreover, Peter's anxiety around his own acts of looking may reflect the depersonalised experience of gaze that can take place in psychotic experience. As Giovanni Stanghelli explains:

> This is the paradox: if the purpose of watching one's own gaze is evaluating its reliability (is it me? Or are things *really* this way?), this evaluation takes place at the expense of the myness of the gaze itself. Every observation involves an objectification.[110]

On the other hand, however, it is possible to also understand these tessellated motifs, themes, and shots as a political interrogation of objectivity, evidence, and expectation. Crucially, this interrogation is effected less by narrative and more through form and visual framing. Indeed, narrative is exposed as not only unstable but, in fact, itself something of a red herring. It also serves (as we saw in Chapter 4) to upset the assumed value of 'true' perception. In this way, I suggest, Kerrigan creates a film which blots the lines between fact and interpretation and, in so doing, productively bankrupts ordinary practices of knowing. This is particularly acute in the context of psychosis if we accept Stanghelli's argument that 'Images (and signs) are facts to schizophrenic persons as real as objects themselves.'[111] The challenge here, then, is to try to better understand the insights such expanded perception might yield for 'ordinary' vision. What are the consequences for taken-for-granted ideas around shared languages of perception that are catalysed in the psychotic subjects' decentring of such certainties? Stanghelli argues:

> meanings, that is words, escape the situation to which they are referred and the meaning they take on according to the context in which they are used. They too become disembodied and de-situated and acquire an existence of their own. They themselves become objects, that is entities undistinguishable from 'real' objects (these too disembodied and thus more similar to concepts and representations than to material objects).[112]

What might be politically generative about such a radical re-visioning of the established coordinates of seeing and knowing? What tyrannies and orthodoxies might be undone in thinking with psychotic unbindings of perceptual and conceptual certainties?

Kerrigan fractures the relationship between image and expectation in plural, interlocking manners. There are quiet examples of this such as when Peter's mother shows the detective photographs of her son. Mrs Winter narrates the photographs as a story of sudden undoing and subsequent misrecognition: 'When he was growing up he was a quiet boy but he was happy. And then all of a sudden, he changed.'[113] In the same sequence, she twice comments that 'he doesn't look like himself'.[114] In this scene, notably intercut with shots of Peter listening to *The Family of Man* photos of children, Mrs Winter articulates the gap between what the images of her son promised and meant, and their current actuality. There is a tacit sense of betrayal in this moment that highlights the precarious bond between image and story. Strikingly, the relationship between image, meaning, and text is more stable in Peter's multisensory perception of the photos. The images of children in distress and isolated are accompanied by sounds of weeping and text titles in the book including 'You look so all alone' and 'Did someone you love go away.'[115] In another sequence between Peter and his mother, what is said and what is seen are once again at odds. Peter remarks that he is not hungry. The next shot is of his mother placing food in front of him. The following morning when she offers him tea and he agrees, she only makes herself a cup. In these moments, the verbal and the visual are on alternate tracks. This schism between theses modes of telling further produce the film's atmosphere of unease but also serve to unbind what appears to be happening and what is actually happening.

More emphatically than these moments, the film also performs a dramatic reversal of narrative expectation and thereby more fundamentally explodes the oft-presumed-stable connection between visual evidence, truth, and narrative expectation. Throughout the film, we see the detective acquiring clues and accumulating evidence against Peter in order to prove he is the murderer of young girls: fag butts, splinters, flecks of paint, chunks of blood-stained mattress are stashed. Moreover, the film leaves a trail of circumstantial evidence readily in its viewer's grasp that connects Peter to the violence, as well as offering several ambiguous moments that further imply Peter's culpability (such as the early screams of the girl who stares in to his car). Elsewhere the audio track further scores this continual sense of dread and menace. However, the film posthumously exonerates Peter – or at least profoundly unseats any sense of certainty regarding his guilt. The 'body bag' in Peter's boot is a narrative hoax: where one expects to find a dead girl, one encounters a bundle of rubbish. Furthermore, the subsequent sequence of shots depict the detective visually reencountering his 'proof'. In its twice-appearance the evidence is thus rendered flimsy – and, moreover, unmasked as bonded to a 'horror' fantasy of bad mad men. In this strategy, Kerrigan not only exploits and exposes genre expectation, but crucially swivels the accusation back towards his audience. In this reversal of narrative expectation, he confronts an audience with the biases, stereotypes, and expectations that help produce such cinematic narratives of 'mad' murderers. One's familiarity, if not complicity, in this regard reminds an audience of the ideological work that is always at play between image and meaning, between 'fact' and interpretation, between evidence and knowledge. Moreover, the film's infusion of paranoiac atmosphere is retrospectively offered a further political texture: Peter is right to feel hunted. In this way, Kerrigan's exploration of evidence, truth, and expectation demands that an audience rethink how one comes to *know* what is really going on, and on what (and whose) terms. Our role, as co-creators of a stigmatising atmosphere of paranoia, thus invites a retroactive reassessment of the subjective and cultural values at play in acts of regarding and reading others. In exploding what we *know* about Peter, Kerrigan excavates a new space in which to *understand* him a little better.

Common people

The most often-remarked upon scenes in *Clean, Shaven* are the two moments of self-mutilation. Peter removes a radio receiver and a transmitter from his scalp and fingernail respectively, which he believes have been planted there while he was in hospital. It may be tempting to overlook these scenes as simply graphic illustrations of paranoid thinking. However, an alternative reading lies in reading these scenes in dialogue with the film's broader engagement with expanded understandings of the relationship between personhood, things, and environments. At the film's conclusion, *things* are left behind in space. In a long tracking shot of sky and trees from the window of the detective's car a viewer hears the distorted, 'paranoid' audio track that has heretofore been exclusively connected to Peter's subjectivity. The final shots we have of Mrs Winter are of her weeping in a windy breeze, clutching a man's shirt. *Clean, Shaven* concludes with Nicole on a boat repeatedly calling out into a radio 'Hello, Hello Daddy are you there?'[116] In this sense, Peter remains with the trio in objects and feelings and landscapes. However, what is crucial to observe in these moments, I propose, is less the thematic neatness of such lingerings but rather their curious evocation of both the importance and ambiguity of human (and non-human) communication.

In all three examples, the character's relationship with the things – the distorted police radio, the shirt, the boat radio – act as conduits for telling themselves and the world who they are, what they want, and what they might need. These moments, semiotically speaking, are easy to read. Indeed, feelings of paranoia, grief, and loss permeate the screen in each of the scenes. Such feeling states are more in-sync with accepted parameters of feeling and are thus more-readily graspable: a cop is *supposed* to feel paranoid and suspicious; mums are *supposed* to grieve their dead sons; daughters are *supposed* to long for their absent fathers. However, all three require objects to give form and meaning to pain. The *things* help make sense of the atmospheres the characters find themselves in. There is then a dialogue between human and non-human in these scenes that serves as an act of communication. This operates both internally within the logic of the film for these characters (Mrs Winter, for example, encounters her own grief *with* the shirt) and also externally at the level of viewing (the film communicates a visual gesture of mourning). While in one way, I am simply explaining the nature of cinematic interpretation, I am doing so in order to consider what implications this may have for clinical gaze towards psychosis.

While it may be tempting to pathologise Peter's self-mutilation as simply evidence of illness, it may in fact be more productive to extend the same generosity towards *proper* feelings (witnessed in the three examples above) as towards apparently *improper* ones (witnessed in the scenes of self-mutilation). If one attempts to understand Peter's paranoid feeling of being bugged as an attempt to communicate and give form to his overwhelming feeling state, then a different kind of dialogue between phenomenon and interpretation becomes legible. It differs in intensity but perhaps not in kind from Nicole's attempt to speak to her dead father with a boat radio. Understanding seemingly unthinkable feelings and behaviours is thereby made easier. Further, by foregrounding the commonality of human feelings between the four characters in these final sequences, Kerrigan invites one to consider what happens if one shifts away from identifying symptoms, measured against a system of pathological knowledge, and towards attempting to understand behaviour and experience as feeling communication. This is paramount given the erasure of subjectivity that can take place under the guise of treatment: 'That the symptom and the person are in many respects one and the same, and that medication can threaten to eradicate the human dimension, is too often disregarded.'[117] In placing an audience, then, temporarily in the 'unthinkable' space of psychosis, Kerrigan does not imply one now *knows* schizophrenia. Instead, he simply makes room to affectively consider the practices whereby one attempts to *understand* another's experience. The incompleteness of this gesture in *Clean, Shaven* signals his desire to de-situate the relationship between knowledge and empathy. And here an audience thinks *with* not *about* the atmosphere of profound paranoia.

'Birds flying high, you know how I feel'[118]

Darian Leader and David Corfield report that: 'In the US, the average time a patient is allowed to speak in a first consultation before being interrupted by their physician is twenty-three seconds.'[119] The average consultation time in London is six to eight minutes.[120] Later, they go on to argue for the centrality of a more human-centred practice of medicine:

> Study after study has claimed that the fewer social relationships, the shorter one's life expectancy and the more devastating the impact of infectious diseases … The implication here is radical: that physical health will be related to *the way the community is run*. And this, of course, is a political question. Wouldn't it become the *duty* of medicine, then, to debate the best ways to run the polis?[121]

While they are discussing physical illness here, there is no reason to suppose that the same ought to not apply to psychological experiences equally if not more. If creative literature (very broadly conceived) is anything, it is a slow dialogue around how to live and thus it is here that the basic clinical lessons of art perhaps lie. Indeed, there is increasing consensus that art and literature offer a vital (in the root sense) contribution to psychiatric care practices. As Bradley Lewis argues:

> they [clinicians] must come to understand the value of biography, autobiography, literature, and narrative theory for developing a narrative repertoire. Clinical competency for depression means a tremendous familiarity with the many possible stories of sadness … In addition, the more stories clinicians know, the easier it is for clinicians to appreciate that the person who should decide is the person whose life is at stake.[122]

Bollas concurs:

> The poets may have more to teach us about schizophrenia than do psychiatry and psychopharmacology. After all, they have learnt how to descend through the layers of our past, to mesh the sensorial, imaginary, and symbolic, in such a way as to convey our unconscious knowledge. Perhaps poets come close to the mental intersections experienced by the schizophrenic.[123]

This embrace of a slow descent through experience departs sharply from more pharmacologically minded thinkers whose focus lies on fixing: 'It seems unlikely that a treatment [talking therapies] that can take years could be shown to be better than other treatments for acute depression, which often remits without treatment in a shorter period.'[124] However, as Frank suggests, such thinking may be departing from a flawed premise and instead one ought to ask:

> Is society willing to recognize the suffering of the ill as a common condition of humanity, and can we find value in illness? I believe that when society learns to value the ill, the other questions of rights – the complicated question of payments and technologies and treatments – will fall into place with remarkable ease.[125]

'night, Mother, Marbles, and *Clean, Shaven,* I argue, may be seen to be taking steps towards reshaping pathological feeling states as politically generative.

The central shift that this chapter has proposed is a move from thinking *about mood* to thinking *with atmosphere.* If mood implies sovereignty, constancy, and privacy, atmosphere is altogether more diffuse. I would like to argue that atmosphere rejects the surplus/deficit model of mood hygiene and management in favour of understanding feeling states as simply complex acts of communication. I would like to argue that atmosphere moves away from a sovereign model of individual feeling and towards a more relational and cosmic space of intersubjective experience. I would like to argue that atmosphere troubles the ties between mood and notions of constancy, singularity, and fixity. Atmospheres are uncertain, incomplete, and impossible to fully grasp but are available as shared experience. All three of the works examined in this chapter use aesthetic means to shape new understandings of 'pathological' moods as feeling atmospheres. Indeed, in their acute attention to sound, time, and stuff they invite plural and unstable ways of being *with* profound feeling states. Moreover, all three in their respective amplifications of viewership (via formal experiment) redistribute the authority for understanding in the hinterlands between spectator and page/stage/screen. In one sense, there is nothing unique about this insofar as all acts of interpretation exist in the interval between art and reader. Nevertheless, there remains particular political import in these three artists' specific foregrounding of the reciprocal, uncertain, and incomplete nature of acts of interpretation. As William Davies reminds us, the historical tendency to frame pain as beyond description 'opens the way for experts to grasp or describe that reality'.[126] The three works analysed in this chapter, in their attempts to carve atmospheres that apparently defy description, disrupt such monologues of knowing expertise. Moreover, in their place, Norman, Forney, and Kerrigan offer feeling dialogues of tender understanding. Their framing of atmosphere as a shared practice between individuals, communities, and environments poses a profound challenge for how we, as a culture, create room for, and respond to, such feeling states. In plural vital manners, then, they open up a different set of political and affective possibilities for communicating with the question, how do you feel?

Notes

1 Lewis Wolpert, *Malignant Sadness: The Anatomy of Depression,* rev'd edn (London: Faber & Faber, [1999] 2006), p. 1.
2 Anecdotally, it is striking the frequency with which qualifiers are attached to descriptions of mental illness. People commonly describe theirs or others' depression/psychosis/bipolar, and so on as 'severe', 'extreme', 'really bad'. It is my suspicion that such qualifiers are likewise seeking legitimacy in the vale of seriousness.
3 Michael Chekhov, quoted in Tom Cornford 'Michael Chekhov: Directing and Actor's Theatre' in Amy Skinner (ed.), *Great Russian Theatre Directors,* forthcoming (London: Bloomsbury: 2018).
4 Tim Ingold, *The Life of Lines* (London: Routledge, 2015), p. 69, emphasis original.
5 Ibid., p. 72.
6 Ibid., p. 77.

7 Eve Kosofsky Sedgwick, *Touching Feeling: Affect, Pedagogy, Performativity* (Durham, NC and London: Duke University Press, 2003), p. 2.

8 David Healy, *Mania: A Short History of Bi-Polar Disorder* (Baltimore, MD: The Johns Hopkins University Press, 2008), p. 161.

9 Darian Leader, *Strictly Bipolar* (London: Penguin, 2013), p. 4.

10 Emily Martin, 'Imagining Moods as a Public Health Crisis' in David Serlin (ed.), *Imagining Illness: Public Health and Visual Culture* (Minneapolis, MN: University of Minnesota Press, 2010), pp. 245–63,

11 Laura D. Hirshbein, *American Melancholy: Constructions of Depression in the Twentieth Century* (New Brunswick, NJ: Rutgers University Press, 2014), p. 71.

12 Martin Welton, *Feeling Theatre* (London: Palgrave, 2012), p. 24. See also, Arlie Hochschild, *The Managed Heart: Commercialisation of Human Feeling* (Berkeley, CA: University of California Press, 1983).

13 Welton, p. 50.

14 In *DSM III*, there was a notional understanding of grief as commonly enduring for up to a year. In 1994, this was reduced to a two-month threshold before grief could be considered pathological. Under *DSM V*, this was reduced to two weeks, owing to the removal of the bereavement exclusion for depression. See Jerome C. Wakefield, Allan V. Horwitz, and Lorenzo Lorenzo-Luaces, 'Uncomplicated Depression and Normal Sadness: Rethinking the Boundary Between Normal and Disordered Depression' in Robert J. DeRubeis and Daniel R. Strunk (eds), *The Oxford Handbook of Mood Disorders* (Oxford University Press, 2017), pp. 83–94.

15 Healy, p. 202.

16 Emily Martin, 'Imagining Moods', p. 254.

17 Wakefield, Horwitz, and Lorenzo-Luaces, p. 91.

18 Healy, p. 204.

19 Ibid., p. 243.

20 Emily Martin, *Bipolar Expeditions: Mania and Depressions in American Culture* (Princeton, NJ and Oxford: Princeton University Press, 2007), p. 29.

21 Christopher Bollas, *When the Sun Bursts: The Enigma of Schizophrenia* (New Haven, CT: Yale University Press, 2015), p. 4.

22 Ibid., p. 10.

23 Kay Redfield Jamison, *Night Falls Fast: Understanding Suicide* (New York: Vintage, 1999), p. 7.

24 Ibid., p. 13.

25 Ibid., pp. 20–1.

26 Ibid., p. 21.

27 Jill Dolan, *The Feminist Spectator as Critic* (Ann Arbor, MI: University of Michigan Press, 1988), p. 19.

28 Louis K. Greiff, 'Fathers, Daughters, and Spiritual Sisters: Marsha Norman's *'night, Mother* and Tennessee Williams's *The Glass Menagerie*' in *Text and Performance Quarterly*, 9:3, 1989, pp. 224–8, p. 226.

29 Jenny S. Spencer, 'Norman's *'night, Mother*: Psycho-Drama of Female Identity' in *Modern Drama*, 30:3, Fall 1987, pp. 364–75, p. 367, emphasis original.

30 Christopher Bigsby, *Contemporary American Playwrights* (Cambridge University Press, 1999), p. 230, p. 233.

31 Marsha Norman, *'night, Mother* (New York: Dramatists Play Service, 1983), I, p. 20.

32 Norman, I, p. 22, p. 50.

33 Alain Ehrenberg, *The Weariness of the Self: Diagnosing the History of Depression in the Contemporary Age* (Montreal: McGill Queen's University Press, 2010), p. 218, emphasis original.

34 Norman, I, p. 31.

35 Varun Begley, 'Objects of Realism: Bertolt Brecht, Roland Barthes, and Marsha Norman' in *Theatre Journal*, 64:3, October 2012, pp. 337–53, p. 346.

36 Hirshbein, p. 118.
37 Melancholia has a long history of being understood as much more than psychopathology in its creative, artistic, and philosophical lineages. However, what I wish to draw attention to here is how this history is textured in the 1980s in particular in relation to Norman's play.
38 Norman, I, p. 23, p. 26.
39 Matthew Bell, *Melancholia: The Western Malady* (Cambridge University Press, 2014), p. ix.
40 Keats, 'Ode on Melancholy' in *Bright Star: The Complete Poems and Selected Letters* (London: Vintage, 2010), p. 250.
41 Bell, pp. 175–6.
42 Ibid., p. 160.
43 Tracy Chapman, 'All That You Have is Your Soul'. *Crossroads*. Warner Music Group. 1989.
44 Norman, I, p. 12.
45 Ibid., I, p. 41.
46 Ibid., I, p. 25.
47 Ibid., I, p. 19.
48 Ibid., I, p. 56.
49 Ibid., I, p. 58.
50 Ehrenberg, p. 188, p. 233.
51 Michael Middeke and Christina Wald (eds), 'Introduction' in *The Literature of Melancholia* (London: Palgrave, 2011), p. 4.
52 Ehrenberg, p. 20.
53 Norman, I, p. 50.
54 Ibid., Author's Note, p. 6.
55 See, for example, Linda Rohrer Paige, '"Off the Porch and into the Scene" Southern Women Playwrights Beth Henley, Marsha Norman, Rebecca Gilman, and Jane Martin' in David Krasner (ed.), *A Companion to Twentieth Century American Drama* (Oxford: Blackwell, 2005), pp. 388–405 and David Radavich, 'Marsha Norman's Bi-Regional Vision in 'night, Mother' in *Mississippi Quarterly*, 64, 2011, pp. 115–28.
56 Bigsby, p. 238.
57 Norman, I, p. 18.
58 Ibid., I, p. 24.
59 Ibid., Author's Note, p. 6.
60 I am here employing Art Spiegelman's term 'commix' that signals the hybrid nature of the comic book form.
61 Hilary Chute and Marianne Dekoven, 'Comic Books and Graphic Novels' in David Glover and Scott McCracken (eds), *The Cambridge Companion to Popular Fiction* (Cambridge University Press, 2012), pp. 175–95, p. 193.
62 Frank Burrows, www.graphicmedicine.org, no date (last accessed 28 March 2017).
63 David L. Ulin, *LA Times*, 23 November 2012.
64 I use the term manic-depression as opposed to bipolar in keeping with Emily Martin who argues that 'it bares open the question whether the condition is to be understood only as an illness or also as a psychological style', Martin, p. 28. I employ bipolar only when reflecting Forney's own sense of her experiences.
65 Clement Hawes, *Mania and Literary Style: The Rhetoric of Enthusiasm from the Ranters to Christopher Short* (Cambridge: Cambridge University Press, 1996), p. 5.
66 Hawes, p. 2, p. 9.
67 Leader, *Strictly Bipolar*, p. 15.
68 Ibid., p. 3.
69 Ellen Forney, Interview with John Crace, *The Guardian*, 1 September 2013.
70 Courtney Donovan, 'Representations of Health, Embodiment, and Experience in Graphic Memoir' in *Configurations*, 22:2, Spring 2014, pp. 237–53, p. 248.
71 Forney, p. 23.
72 Myla Goldberg, www.npr.org, 8 November 2012, no page (last accessed 26 March 2017).

73 Arthur W. Frank, *The Renewal of Generosity: Illness, Medicine, and How to Live* (Chicago: University of Chicago Press, 2004), pp. 6–7.
74 Ellen Forney, *Marbles* (London: Robinson, 2013), p. 237.
75 I am not suggesting that drugs have no impact on personhood or personality (quite the contrary). What I am troubling here is the reductive idea of a true self and diseased self in the case of madness.
76 Forney, p. 99.
77 Ibid., p. 26.
78 Ibid., p. 210, emphasis original.
79 Darian Leader and David Corfield, *Why Do People Get Ill?* (London: Hamish Hamilton, 2007), p. 318.
80 Wendy Brown, *States of Injury: Power and Freedom in Late Modernity* (Princeton, NJ: Princeton University Press, 1995), p. 80.
81 Brown, p. 75.
82 Ibid., p. 66.
83 Healy, p. 235.
84 Forney, p. 218.
85 Healy, p. 248.
86 Arthur W. Frank, *At the Will of the Body: Reflections on Illness*, rev'd edn (Boston, MA: Mariner Books, 2002), p. 4. Medicalese is a term Frank employs to characterise medical jargon and theory.
87 Ibid., p. 4.
88 Forney, p. 90, p. 89.
89 Ibid., p. 222.
90 Ibid., see pp. 52–3, pp. 6–7, p. 69 respectively.
91 Hawes, p. 234.
92 Lodge Kerrigan. *Clean, Shaven*. DSM III and Warner Bros. 1993. This description appears on the back of the DVD and the criterion collection website.
93 Roger Ebert, www.rogerebert.com, np (last accessed 6 April 2017).
94 Ebert and McCarthy, np.
95 Lodge Kerrigan, Interview, www.filmfreakcentral.com, 27 November 2005, np (last accessed 5 April 2017).
96 Todd McCarthy, *Variety*, 27 September 1993.
97 Dennis Lim, '*Clean, Shaven*: Inside Man', on www.criterion.com, np (last accessed 5 April 2017).
98 John Donne, 'A Valediction Forbidding Mourning' in *Selected Poems* (New York: Dover Press, 1993), p. 22.
99 Bollas, p. 3.
100 Martin, *Bipolar Expeditions*, p. 51.
101 A related audio strategy is employed by the artist Dolly Sen in her short film *Outside* (2013).
102 *The Family of Man* exhibition ran at MOMA from 24 January to 8 May 1955 and comprised 503 pictures by 273 photographers from 68 countries. It was organised around thematic groupings from 'childbirth' to 'famine' to 'learning'. It toured the world for 8 years and attracted over 9 million visitors. It has, however, been subject to extensive criticism for the tacit racial, gender, and other stereotyping and biases in the framing and selection of the images.
103 Edward Steichen, 'Press Release', 31 January 1954, www.moma.org (last accessed 5 April 2017).
104 Bollas, p. 88.
105 Ibid., p. 90.
106 Ingold, p. 72.
107 A. Elhai, G. Perez Algorta, F. Varese, J. C. McIntyre, and R. P. Bentall, 'Do Paranoid Delusions Exist on a Continuum with Subclinical Paranoia? A Multi-Method Taxometric Study' in *Schizophrenia Research*, forthcoming.

108 Bollas, p. 20.
109 Ibid., p. 10.
110 Giovanni Stanghelli, *Disembodied Spirits and Deanimated Bodies: The Psychopathology of Common Sense* (Oxford University Press, 2004), p. 4, emphasis original.
111 Stanghelli, p. 21.
112 Ibid., p. 22.
113 *Clean, Shaven*, 43:54.
114 Ibid., 43:24.
115 Ibid., 36:34.
116 Ibid., 1:14:17.
117 Bollas, p. 8.
118 Nina Simone. 'Feelin' Good'. *I Put a Spell on You*. Philips. 1965.
119 Leader and Corfield, p. 33.
120 Ibid., p. 33.
121 Ibid., p. 155, p. 158, emphasis original.
122 Bradley Lewis, *Depression: Integrating Science, Culture, and Humanities* (London: Routledge, 2012), p. 108.
123 Bollas, p. 197.
124 Steven L. Dubovsky and Amelia Dubovsky, *Mood Disorders* (Washington, DC: American Psychiatric Publishing, 2002), p. 209.
125 Frank, *At the Will of the Body*, p. 115.
126 William Davies, *The Happiness Industry: How Government and Big Business Sold Us Well-Being* (London: Verso, 2015), p. 20.

APPENDIX

Selection of further primary works

Below is a, far from exhaustive, list of some relevant creative works that are engaged with the depiction of madness on stage, screen, and in print. I have omitted both the examples discussed in the chapters and also the more canonical or well-known works such as those by Tennessee Williams, William Shakespeare, Woody Allen, Alfred Hitchcock, Sylvia Plath, and so forth. The list is offered as a tangle of threads for students and researchers to pick up, explore further, and braid with new connections. The examples are not offered as exemplars of any kind; rather they are a deliberately diverse selection (aesthetically, in terms of prestige and so on) in order to offer plural points of critical engagement. There is a bias in the theatre and performance section towards British theatre owing to my location in the UK. I have included a selection of novels (with a particular emphasis on autobiography), even though this book does not discuss prose works, as I hope these examples will provide a further fertile resource for further work. I hope that this may be of some use to students and academics engaged in the field of creative arts and madness.

Theatre and performance

Aston, Elaine, and Griffin, Gabrielle (eds), 'Lear's Daughters' in *Herstory Volume One: Plays by Women for Women* (Sheffield, Sheffield Academic Press, 1991)
Auburn, David, *Proof* (London: Faber and Faber, 2001)
Ayckbourn, Alan, *Woman in Mind* (New York: Samuel French, 1987)
Barnes, Peter, *The Ruling Class* (London: Methuen, 1972)
Benett, Alan, *The Madness of King George* (London: Faber & Faber, 1995)
—— *The Complete Talking Heads* (London: BBC Worldwide Ltd, 1998)
—— *The Lady in the Van* (London: Forelake Ltd, 2000)

Birch, Alice, *Anatomy of a Suicide* (London: Oberon, 2017)

Brook, Peter, and Estienne, Marie-Hélène, *The Man Who* (London: Methuen, 2002)

Buchanan, Wayne, *Under Their Influence* (London: Aurora Metro Press, 2001)

Büchner, Georg, *Woyzeck*, trans. by John MacKendrick (London: Eyre Methuen, 1979)

Brogan, Linda, and Polly Teale, *Speechless* (London: Nick Hern Books, 2010)

Brown, William F., *The Girl in the Freudian Slip* (New York: Samuel French, 1959)

Cartwright, Jane, *St Anne's* (unpublished play script produced in association with Vita Nova, first performed at Boscombe Fringe Festival, 2013)

— *KERB* (unpublished play script produced in association with Vita Nova, first performed at Boscombe Fringe Festival, 2014)

Churchill, Caryl, *The Skriker* (London: Nick Hern Books, 1994)

— *Blue Heart* (London: Nick Hern Books, 1997)

— 'A Mouthful of Birds', *Plays: Three* (London: Nick Hern Books, 1998)

— 'The Hospital at The Time of the Revolution', *Churchill: Shorts* (London: Nick Hern Books, 1990)

— 'Lovesick', *Churchill: Shorts* (London: Nick Hern Books, 1990)

— 'Softcops', *Plays: Two* (London: Methuen, 1990)

Cresswell, Janet, *The One-Sided Wall* (London: Methuen, 1990)

Craze, Tony, *Shona* (London: Methuen, 1983)

Crimp, Martin, *The Treatment* (London: Nick Hern, 1993)

Crouch, Tim, 'I, Malvolio', *I, Shakespeare* (London: Oberon, 2011)

Cullen, Mike, *Anna Weiss* (London: Nick Hern Books, 1997)

Daniels, Sarah, 'Masterpieces', *Plays: One* (London: Methuen, 1991)

— 'Beside Herself', *Plays: Two* (London: Methuen, 1994)

— 'Head Rot Holiday', *Plays: Two* (London: Methuen, 1994)

— 'The Madness of Esme and Shaz', *Plays: Two* (London: Methuen, 1994)

Dean, Laura Jane *Head, Hand, Head* (unpublished, first performed at Marlow Theatre, Kent, 2013. See www.laurajanedean.com for details)

Dowie, Claire, 'Adult Child / Dead Child', *Why Is John Lennon Wearing a Skirt* (London: Methuen, 1996)

Durrenmatt, Friedrich, *The Physicists* (London: Samuel French, 1963)

Eldridge, David, 'Incomplete and Random Acts of Kindness', *Plays: One* (London: Methuen, 2012)

— 'The Knot of the Heart', *Plays: One* (London: Methuen, 2012)

Eno, Will, *The Flu Season* (London: Oberon, 2003)

Franceschild, Donna, *Taking over the Asylum* (London: Methuen, 2013)

Franzeman, Vivienne, *Pests* (London: Nick Hern Books, 2014)

Furse, Anna, *Augustine (Big Hysteria)* (London: Routledge, 1997)

Gecko, *The Institution* (unpublished, www.geckotheatre.com)

Giraudoux, Jean, *The Madwoman of Chaillot*, adapted by Maurice Valency (New York: Dramatists Play Service, 1950)

Glaspell, Susan, 'The Verge', *Four Plays* (Fairford: Echo Library, 2007)

Goode, Chris, *Mad Man* (unpublished, first performed Plymouth Drum 2014)

Grace, Fraser, *Breakfast with Mugabe* (London: Oberon, 2005)

Gray, Spalding, *Rumstick Road* (unpublished, www.thewoostergroup.org)

Greig, David, *San Diego* (London: Faber & Faber, 2003)

Haddon, Mark, *Polar Bears* (London: Methuen, 2010)

Hall, Lee, 'Spoonface Steinberg' in *Plays: One* (London: Methuen, 2002)

Hampton, Christopher, *The Talking Cure* (London: Faber & Faber, 2002)

Haynes Jon, and David Woods, *The Eradication of Schizophrenia in Western Lapland* (London: Oberon, 2014)

—— *Give Me Your Love* (London: Oberon, 2016)

Hennessy, Steve, *The Lullabies of Broadmoor* (London: Oberon, 2011)

Hutchinson, Ron, *Head/Case* (London: Oberon, 2005)

Jarvis, Liam et al., *Beachy Head* (London: Oberon, 2010)

Johnson, Terry, 'Hysteria', in *The Methuen Book of Modern Drama: Plays of the '80s and '90s* (London: Methuen, 2001)

Jones, Judith and Campbell Beatrix, *And All the Children Cried* (Oberon: London, 2002)

Kane, Sarah, *Complete Plays* (London: Methuen, 2001)

Kelly, Dennis, 'After the End' in *Plays: One* (London: Oberon, 2007)

Kennedy, Fin, *How to Disappear Completely and Never Be Found* (London: Nick Hern, 2007)

Kimmings, Bryony, *Fake It Til You Make It* (London: Oberon, 2015)

Kostick, Gavin, *The Asylum Ball* (unpublished, first performed SFX City Theatre, Dublin 2000)

Lavery, Bryony, 'A Wedding Story' in *Plays: One* (London: Faber & Faber, 2007)

Leyshon, Nell, *Bedlam* (London: Oberon, 2010)

McCartney, Nicola, *Home* (unpublished, first performed Traverse Theatre, 2000)

McDonagh, Martin, *The Beauty Queen of Leenane* (London: Methuen, 1996)

Macmillan, Duncan, *Every Brilliant Thing* (London: Oberon, 2015)

MacLeod, Iain F., *I Was a Beautiful Day* (London: Nick Hern Books, 2005)

McNamara, Julie, *The Knitting Circle* (unpublished, first performed Soho Theatre 2011, www.juliemc.com)

McPherson, Conor, *Shining City* (New York: Theater Communications Group, 2005)

Maran, Mike, *Did You Used to Be R. D. Laing?* (unpublished play script, first performed at the Edinburgh Fringe Festival in 2000 and subsequently toured. See www.mikemaran.com for production details)

Neilson, Anthony, 'Normal' in *Plays: One* (London: Methuen, 1998)

—— *The Wonderful World of Dissocia* (London: Methuen, 2007)

Nichols, Peter, *A Day in the Death of Joe Egg* (London: Faber & Faber, 1967)

Parkin, David, *Good Friday: The Clinical Depression Concept Album Show* (™) (unpublished, first performed at Battersea Arts Centre in 2013)

Pinter, 'A Kind of Alaska' in *Plays: Four* (London: Faber & Faber, 1996)

—— *The Hot House* (London: Faber & Faber, 2013)

Plowman, Gillian, *Me and My Friend* (London: Samuel French, 1991)

Prebble, Lucy, *The Effect* (London: Methuen, 2012)

Shaffer, Peter, *Equus* (London: Penguin, 1977)

Sharma, Haresh, *Off Centre* (London: Ethos, 2000)

Simms, Willard, *Bye Bye Blackbird* (unpublished, first performed New End Theatre Hampstead, 1998)

Stephens, Shelagh, *The Memory of Water and Five Kinds of Silence* (London: Methuen, 1997)

Stephens, Simon, *Motor Town* (London: Methuen, 2006)

—— *Punk Rock* (London: Methuen, 2009)

Strindberg, August, 'The Father' in *Three Plays*, trans. by Peter Watts (London: Penguin, 1958)

Summerskill, Claire, *Hearing Voices* (London: Tollington Press, 2010)

St Germain, Mark, *Freud's Last Session* (New York: Dramatists Play Service, 2011)

Stan's Cafe, *The Anatomy of Melancholy* (toured UK 2014, script available to buy at www.stanscafe.co.uk)

Tighe, Dylan, *RECORD* (unpublished script, first performed in Dublin in 2012. Album available at www.dylantighe.bandcamp.com/album/record)

tucker green, debbie, *Born Bad* (London: Nick Hern Books, 2003)

Vincent, Byron, *Talk about Something You Like* (unpublished, first performed at Edinburgh Fringe Festival 2014)

Walsh, Enda, *Misterman* (London: Nick Hern Books, 2012)

Wesker, Arnold, *Denial*, unpublished manuscript. DVD of performance: *Denial*. Kultur International Films, 2000 (filmed at Bristol Old Vic)

Whittaker, Paul, *The Minotaur in Me* (unpublished, first performed Sherman Theatre, Cardiff, 2006)

Windsor, Valerie, *Effie's Burning* (London: Samuel French, 1995)

Wilson, Snoo, 'Sabina' *Plays: Two* (London: Methuen, 2000)

Woods, Sarah, *Nervous Women* (London: Oberon, 1992)

Woolf, Dennis, *Beyond Belief: Scenes from the Shipman Inquiry* (unpublished, first performed Woolf Library Theatre, Manchester, 2004)

Worton, Jenny, *Through a Glass Darkly* (London: Nick Hern, 2010)

Wymark, Olwen, *Find Me* (New York: Samuel French, 1980)

Film

A Beautiful Mind (dir. Ron Howard, prod. Universal Pictures, 2001)

A Dangerous Method (dir. David Cronenberg, prod. Lions Gate, 2012)

A Fine Madness (dir. Irvin Kershner, prod. Pan Arts, 1966)

A Nightmare on Elm Street 3: Dreamer Warriors (dir. Chuck Russell, prod. New Line Cinema, 1987)

Altered States (dir. Ken Russell, prod, Warner Bros, 1980)

An Angel at My Table (dir. Jane Campion, prod. Hibsicus Films, 1990)

Article 99 (dir. Howard Deutch, prod. Orion Pictures, 1992)

Asylum (dir. Roy Ward Baker, prod. Amicus Productions, 1972)

Asylum (dir. Peter Robinson, prod. Peter Robinson Associates, 1972)

Bedlam (dir. Mark Robson, prod. RKO Radio Pictures, 1946)

Benny and Joon (dir. Jeremiah S. Chechik, prod. Metro-Goldwyn-Mayer, 1993)

Beyond Therapy (dir. Robert Altman, prod. New World Pictures, 1987)

Bird (dir. Clint Eastwood, prod. The Malpaso Company, 1988)

Blind Alley (dir. Charles Vidor, prod. Columbia Pictures, 1939)

Bob and Carol and Ted and Alice (dir. Paul Mazursky, prod. Columbia Pictures, 1969)

Bronson (dir. Nicolas Winding Refn, prod. Vertigo Films, 2008)

Captain Newman MD (dir. David Miller, prod. Universal pictures, 1963)

Chattahoochee (dir. Mick Jackson, prod. Cineplex Odeon, 1989)

Crazy People (dir. Tony Bill and Barry L. Young, prod. Paramount Pictures, 1990)

Crimes of Passion (dir. Ken Russell, prod. New World Pictures, 1984)

David and Lisa (dir. Frank Perry, prod. Lisa and David Company, 1962)

Dialogues with Mad Women (dir. Allie Light, prod. Allie Light, Irving Saraf, Nancy Evans, 1994)

Diary of a Mad Housewife (dir. Frank Perry, prod. Frank Perry Films Inc., 1970)

Dr Dippy's Sanatorium (dir. G. W. Bitzer, prod. American Mutoscope and Biograph Co., 1906)

Equus (dir. Sidney Lumet, prod. Perksy Bright Productions, 1977)

Escape From Broadmoor (dir. John Gilling, prod. Harry Reynolds Productions, 1948)

Fight Club (dir. David Fincher, prod. Fox 2000 Pictures, 1999)

Filth (dir. Jon S. Baird, prod. Steel Mill Pictures, 2013)

Frances (dir. Graham Clifford, prod. Brooksfilms, 1982)

Girl, Interrupted (dir. James Mangold, prod. Columbia Pictures, 1999)

Glen or Glenda (dir. Edward D. Wood Jr., prod. Screen Classics II, 1953)

Happiness (dir. Todd Solodnz, prod. Good Machine, 1998)

Harvey (dir. Henry Koster, prod. Universal International Pictures, 1950)

Hide and Seek (dir. John Polson, prod. Twentieth Century Fox, 2005)

I Never Promised You a Rose Garden (dir. Anthony Page, prod. Edgar J. Sherick Associates, 1977)

Inside Out (dir. Pete Docter and Ronnie Del Carmen, prod. Pixar Animation Studios, 2015)

Instinct (dir. Jon Turteltaub, prod. Spyglass Entertainment, 1999)

Invasion of the Body Snatchers (dir. Philip Kaufman, prod. Solofilm, 1978)

Lady in the Dark (dir. Mitchell Leisen, prod. Paramount Pictures, 1944)

Let There Be Light (dir. John Huston, prod. US Army Pictorial Services, 1946)

Lillith (dir. Robert Rossen, prod. Centaur, 1966)

Manic (dir. Jordan Melamed, prod. Manic LLC, 2011)

Mary and Max (dir. Adam Elliot, prod. Melodrama Pictures, 2009)

Melancholia (dir. Lars Von Trier, prod. Zentropa Entertainments, 2011)

Network (dir. Sidney Lumet, prod. Metro-Goldwyn-Mayer, 1976)

Nightmare Alley (dir. Edmund Goulding, prod. Twentieth Century Fox, 1947)

Ordinary People (dir. Robert Redford, prod. Paramount Pictures, 1980)

Persona (dir. Ingmar Bergman, prod. Svensk Filmindustri, 1966)

Phoebe in Wonderland (dir. Daniel Barnz, prod. Silverwood Films, 2008)

Pressure Point (dir. Hubert Cornfield and Stanley Kramer, prod. Stanley Kramer Productions, 1962)

Proof (dir. John Madden, prod. Miramax, 2005)

Repulsion (dir. Roman Polanski, prod. Compton Films, 1965)
Rosemary's Baby (dir. Roman Polanksi, prod. William Castle Productions, 1968)
Safe (dir. Todd Haynes, prod. American Playhouse Theatrical Films, 1995)
Schizo (dir. Peter Walker, prod. Peter Walker (Heritage) Ltd, 1976)
Secrets of a Soul (dir. Georg Wilhelm Pabst, prod. Neumann-Filmproduktion, 1926)
Shine (dir. Scott Hicks, prod. Australian Film Finance Corporation, 1996)
Shock Corridor (dir. Samuel Fuller, prod. Allied Artists Pictures, 1963)
Shock Treatment (dir. Dennie Sanders, prod. Twentieth Century Fox Film Corporation, 1964)
Side Effects (dir. Steven Soderbergh, prod. Endgame Entertainment, 2013)
Silver Linings Playbook (dir. David O. Russell, prod. Weinstein Company, 2012)
Sling Blade (dir. Billy Bob Thornton, prod. Miramax, 1996)
Solaris (dir. Andrei Tarkovsky, prod. Creative Unit of Writers and Cinema Workers, 1972)
Splendour in the Grass (dir. Elia Kazan, prod. Warner Bros, 1961)
Strange Voices (dir. Arthur Allan Seidelman, prod. Forest Hills Production, 1987)
Sybil [TV miniseries] (dir. Daniel Petrie, prod. Lorimar Productions, 1976)
Tarnation (dir. Jonathan Caouette, prod. Film Museum Distributie, 2003)
The Babadook (dir. Jennifer Kent, prod. Screen Australia, 2014)
The Bridge (dir. Eric Steele, prod. Easy There Tiger Productions, 2006)
The Caretakers (dir. Hall Bartlett, prod. United Artists, 1963)
The Snake Pit (dir. Anatole Litvak, prod. Twentieth Century Fox Film Corporation, 1948)
The Cobweb (dir. Vincente Minnelli, prod. Metro-Goldwyn-Mayer, 1955)
The Dream Team (dir. Howard Zieff, prod. Universal Pictures, 1989)
The Idiots (dir. Lars Von Trier, prod. Zentropa Entertainments, 1998)
The Three Faces of Eve (dir. Nunnally Johnson, prod. Twentieth Century Fox Film Corporation, 1957)
The Virgin Suicides (dir. Sofia Coppola, prod. American Zoetrope, 1999)
There Might Be Giants (dir. Anthony Harvey, prod. Universal Pictures, 1971)
Through a Glass Darkly (dir. Ingmar Bergman, prod. Svensk Filmindustri, 1961)
The Tenant (dir. Roman Polanski, prod. Paramount Pictures, 1976)
The Fisher King (dir. Terry Gilliam, prod. TriStar Pictures, 1991)
Twelve Monkeys (dir. Terry Gillam, prod. Universal Pictures, 1995)
Whose Life Is It Anyway? (dir. John Badham, prod. Metro-Goldwyn-Mayer, 1981)
We Don't Live under Normal Conditions (dir. Rhonda Collins, prod. Aperio Films, 2000)
Warrendale (dir. Allan King, prod., Columbia Pictures, 1967)

Fiction and graphic fiction

Adam, David, *The Man Who Couldn't Stop: OCD and the True Story of a Life Lost in Thought* (New York: Sarah Chricton Books, 2015)
Allan, Clare, *Poppy Shakespeare* (London: Bloomsbury, 2006)
Baker, Bobby, *Diary Drawings: Mental Illness and Me* (London: Profile Books, 2010)

Bechdel, Alison, *Fun Home* (New York: Houghton, Mifflin, Harcourt, 2007)
— *Are You My Mother?* (New York: Houghton, Mifflin, Harcourt, 2012)
Bloch, Robert, *Psycho* (London: BBC Books, 1998)
Bowman, Grace, *Thin* (London: Penguin, 2007)
Bronson, Charles, *Insanity: My Mad Life* (London: Blake Publishing, 2003)
Brosh, Allie, *Hyperbole and a Half* (New York: Simon & Schuster, 2013)
Cockburn, Patrick and Henry, *Henry's Demons: Living with Schizophrenia, a Father and Son's Story* (Kansas, Missouri: Andrews McMeel, 2011)
Colas, Emily, *Just Checking: Scenes from the Life of an Obsessive-Compulsive* (New York: Pocket Books, 1998)
Collins Brown, Henry, *A Mind Mislaid* (New York: E. P. Dutton & Co, 1937)
Crawford, Paul, *Nothing Purple Nothing Black* (Leicester: Book Guild, 2002)
Cresswell, Janet, *Ox-Bow* (London: Chipmunka Publishing, 2005)
Crewe, Candida, *Eating Myself* (London: Bloomsbury, 2006)
Cunningham, Daryl, *Psychiatric Tales: Eleven Graphic Stories about Mental Illness* (New York: Bloomsbury, 2001)
De Hert, Marc, Geert Madgiels, and Erik Thys, *The Secret of the Brain Chip: A Self-Help Guide for People Experiencing Psychosis* (Antwerp: Janssen-Craig, 2000)
Dexter, Pete, *Paris Trout* (London: Harper Collins, 1988)
Dully, Howard, *My Lobotomy: A Memoir* (London: Crown, 2007)
Earl, Rae, *My Fat Mad Teenage Diary* (London: Hodder & Stoughton, 2007)
Eugenides, Jeffrey, *The Virgin Suicides* (New York: Farrar, Straus, and Giroux, 1993)
Field, Ellen, *The White Shirts* (Los Angeles: Self-published, 1964)
Filer, Nathan, *The Shock of the Fall* (London: Harper Collins, 2013)
Foster Wallace, David, *Infinite Jest* (Boston, MA: Back Bay Books, 2006)
Frame, Janet, *Faces in the Water* (New York: Braziller, 1962)
Galloway, Janice, *The Trick Is to Keep Breathing* (Normal, IL: Dalkey Archive Press, 1994)
Grass, Gunter, *The Tin Drum* (London: Martin Secker & Warburg Ltd, 1962)
Green, Katie, *Lighter Than My Shadow* (New York: Random House, 2013)
Greenberg, Joanne, *I Never Promised You a Rose Garden*, rev'd edn (New York: Henry Holt & Company, 2009 [1964])
Greenberg, Michael, *Hurry Down Sunshine* (New York: Other Press, 2008)
Heiney, Nicholas, *The Silence at the Song's End* (London: Songsend, 2007)
Hornbacher, Marya, *Wasted: Coming Back from an Addiction to Starvation* (London: Flamingo, 1998)
Johnstone, Matthew, *I Had a Black Dog* (London: Little Brown Books, 2005)
Kaplan, Bert, *The Inner World of Mental Illness* (New York: Harper & Row, 1964)
Kaysen, Susannah, *Girl, Interrupted* (New York: Turtle Bay Books, 1993)
Lathrop, Clarissa Caldwell, *A Secret Institution* (New York: Bryant Publishing Co., 1890)
LaValle, Victor D., *Ecstatic* (London: Crown, 2002)
Lessing, Doris, *The Golden Notebook* (New York: Simon & Schuster, 1962)
— *Briefing for a Descent in to Hell* (London: Jonathan Cape Ltd, 1971)
— *The Four Gated City* (New York: Plume, 1976)

McEwan, Ian, *Saturday* (London: Jonathan Cape Ltd, 2005)

McGrath, Patrick, *Spider* (London: Viking London, 1991)

— Asylum (London: Random House, 1997)

— Trauma (London: Bloomsbury, 2008)

Maine, Harold, *If Man Be Mad* (New York: Double Day, 1947)

Maupassant, Guy De, *The Diary of a Madman and Other Tales of Horror* (London: Pan Books, 1976)

Millet, Kate, *The Loony Bin Trip* (New York: Simon & Schuster, 1990)

O'Donaghue, John, *Sectioned: A Life Interrupted* (London: John Murray, 2009)

O'Farrell, Maggie, *The Vanishing Act of Esme Lennox* (San Diego, CA: Harcourt, 2007)

Perelman, S. J., *The Road to Miltown* (New York: Grove Press, 1962)

Perry, Philippa, and Junko Graat, *Couch Fiction: A Graphic Tale of Psychotherapy* (London: Palgrave, 2010)

Poe, Edgar Allan, *The System of Dr Tarr and Professor Feather* (Philadelphia, PA: George R. Graham, 1845)

Powell, Nate, *Swallow Me Whole* (Marietta, GA: Top Shelf Productions, 2008)

Reed, David, *Anna* (London: Secker & Warburg, 1976)

Reeve, Alan, *Notes from a Waiting Room* (London: Heretic, 1983)

Saks, Elyn, *The Centre Cannot Hold* (London: Virago, 2007)

Sechehaye, Marguerite, *Autobiography of a Schizophrenic Girl* (New York: Grune & Stratton, 1951)

Schiller, Lori, *The Quiet Room* (New York: Warner Books, 1994)

Schreber, Paul, *Memoirs of My Nervous Illness* (London: William Dawson, 1955)

Shrigley, David, *How Are You Feeling? At the Centre of the Inside of the Human Brain's Mind* (London: Canongate, 2012)

Smith, Lee, *Black Mountain Breakdown* (New York: Putnam, 1980)

Steele, Ken, *The Day the Voices Stopped: A Memoir of Madness and Hope* (New York: Basic Books, 2001)

Styron, William, *Darkness Visible* (New York: Pantheon, 1960)

Swados, Elizabeth, *My Depression: A Picture Book* (New York: Seven Stories Press, 2005)

Taylor, Barbara, *The Last Asylum* (London: Hamish Hamilton, 2014)

Torrey, E. Fuller, *Surviving Schizophrenia: A Family Manual* (London: Harper Collins, 1984)

Vincent, Norah, *Voluntary Madness: My Year Lost and Found in the Looney Bin* (New York: Viking, 2008)

Ward, Mary Jane, *The Snake Pit* (New York: Random House, 1946)

Warmark (pseud.), *Guilty but Insane: A Broadmoor Autobiography* (London: Chapman & Hall, 1931)

White, Curtis, *Memories of My Father Watching TV* (Normal, IL: Dalkey Archive Press, 1998)

Will, Elaine, *Look Straight Ahead* (Saskatchewan: Cuckoo's Nest Press, 2013)

Woolf, Emma, *An Apple a Day: A Memoir of Love and Recovery from Anorexia* (Berkeley, CA: Soft Skull Press, 2012)

INDEX